Google for Seniors

Studio Visual Steps

Google
for Seniors

Get Acquainted with Free Google Applications

www.visualsteps.com

This book has been written using the Visual Steps™ method.
Cover design by Studio Willemien Haagsma bNO

© 2010 Visual Steps
Edited by Jolanda Ligthart, Mara Kok and Rilana Groot
Translated by Chris Hollingsworth, *1st Resources* and Irene Venditti, *i-write* translation services.
Editor in chief: Ria Beentjes

First printing: February 2010
ISBN 978 90 5905 236 9

Do you have questions or suggestions?
E-mail: info@visualsteps.com

Would you like more information?
www.visualsteps.com

Website for this book:
www.visualsteps.com/google
Here you can register your book.

Register your book
We will keep you aware of any important changes that are necessary to you as a user of the book. You can also take advantage of our periodic newsletter informing you of our product releases, company news, tips & tricks, special offers, free guides, etcetera.

Table of Contents

Appendices

Foreword

Dear readers,

For most people what comes to mind when they hear the word *Google* is that it is something they use to search the web. In recent years, the *Google* company has produced many other useful applications besides its popular search engine. These applications are all free to download and install. This book guides you through some of the most popular *Google* products. *Google Search* not only makes it easy to find something on the Internet, but you can also use it to search your own computer as well. With *Google Earth* you can check out your vacation destination in advance from a bird's eye view and with *Google Maps* you can plan your route to it.

Other topics covered in this book include learning how to create a calendar that can be managed and consulted online. Learn about *Google Groups* where you can participate in a discussion on just about any topic you can imagine. Or chat and make phone calls free of charge with *Google Talk*. Publish an online diary or a travel journal with *Blogger* and create a simple website with *Google Sites*.

Google Docs offers a simple word processor that allows you to view, create, edit and save documents from any computer that has access to the Internet. For translating text you can get a good start with *Google Translate*. And last but not least this book will acquaint you with the popular photo editing program *Picasa*, a tool that allows you to manage your photos, create web albums and share them with other people.

Have lots of fun with this book!

Henk Mol

P.S.
Feel free to send us your questions and suggestions.
The e-mail address is: info@visualsteps.com

Visual Steps Newsletter

All Visual Steps books follow the same methodology: clear and concise step-by-step instructions with screen shots to demonstrate each task.
A complete list of all our books can be found on our website **www.visualsteps.com**
You can also sign up to receive our **free Visual Steps Newsletter**.

In this Newsletter you will receive periodic information by e-mail regarding:
- the latest titles and previously released books;
- special offers, supplemental chapters, tips and free informative booklets.

Also, our Newsletter subscribers may download any of the documents listed on the web pages **www.visualsteps.com/info_downloads** and **www.visualsteps.com/tips**

When you subscribe to our Newsletter you can be assured that we will never use your e-mail address for any purpose other than sending you the information as previously described. We will not share this address with any third-party. Each Newsletter also contains a one-click link to unsubscribe.

Introduction to Visual Steps™

The Visual Steps handbooks and manuals are the best instructional materials available for learning how to work with computers and computer programs. Nowhere else will you find better support for getting to know the computer, the Internet, *Windows* or related software.

Properties of the Visual Steps books:
- **Comprehensible contents**
  Addresses the needs of the beginner or intermediate computer user for a manual written in simple, straight-forward English.
- **Clear structure**
  Precise, easy to follow instructions. The material is broken down into small enough segments to allow for easy absorption.
- **Screen shots of every step**
  Quickly compare what you see on your own computer screen with the screen shots in the book. Pointers and tips guide you when new windows are opened so you always know what to do next.
- **Get started right away**
  All you have to do is switch on your computer, place the book next to your keyboard, and begin at once.

In short, I believe these manuals will be excellent guides for you.

dr. H. van der Meij
Faculty of Applied Education, Department of Instruction Technology, University of Twente, the Netherlands

What You Will Need

In order to work through this book, you will need a number of things on your computer:

Your computer should run the English version of **Windows 7**, **Windows Vista** or **Windows XP**.

The screen shots in this book have been made on a *Windows 7* computer. For using the exercises in this book it does not make any difference whether your computer runs *Windows 7*, *Windows Vista* or *Windows XP*. Any possible differences between the *Windows* editions will be clearly indicated in the text.

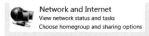

In order to download and use the programs you will need an active Internet connection.

How to Use This Book

This book has been written using the Visual Steps™ method. You can work through this book independently at your own pace.

In this Visual Steps™ book, you will see various icons. This is what they mean:

Techniques
These icons indicate an action to be carried out:

 The mouse icon means you should do something with the mouse.

 The keyboard icon means you should type something on the keyboard.

 The hand icon means you should do something else, for example insert a CD-ROM in the computer. It is also used to remind you of something you have learned before.

In addition to these icons, in some areas of this book *extra assistance* is provided to help you successfully work through each chapter.

Help
These icons indicate that extra help is available:

 The arrow icon warns you about something.

 The bandage icon will help you if something has gone wrong.

 Have you forgotten how to do something? The number next to the footsteps tells you where to look it up at the end of the book in the appendix *How Do I Do That Again?*

In separate boxes you will find tips or additional, background information.

Extra information
Information boxes are denoted by these icons:

 The book icon gives you extra background information that you can read at your convenience. This extra information is not necessary for working through the book.

 The light bulb icon indicates an extra tip for using the program.

Prior Computer Experience

If you want to use this book, you will need some basic computer skills. If you do not have these skills, it is a good idea to read one of the following books first:

 **Windows 7 for SENIORS**
Studio Visual Steps
ISBN 978 90 5905 126 3

 **Windows Vista for SENIORS**
Studio Visual Steps
ISBN 978 90 5905 274 1

 **Windows XP for SENIORS**
Addo Stuur
ISBN 978 90 5905 044 0

Website

On the website that accompanies this book, **www.visualsteps.com/google**, you will find practice files and more information about the book. This website will also keep you informed of any errata, recent updates or other changes you need to be aware of, as a user of the book.
Please, also take a look at our website **www.visualsteps.com** from time to time to read about new books and other handy information such as informative tips and booklets.

The Screen Shots

The screen shots in this book were made on a computer running *Windows 7 Ultimate*. The screen shots used in this book indicate which button, folder, file or hyperlink you need to click on your computer screen. In the instruction text (in **bold** letters) you will see a small image of the item you need to click. The black line will point you to the right place on your screen.
The small screen shots that are printed in this book are not meant to be completely legible all the time. This is not necessary, as you will see these images on your own computer screen in real size and fully legible.

Here you see an example of an instruction text and a screen shot. The black line indicates where to find this item on your own computer screen:

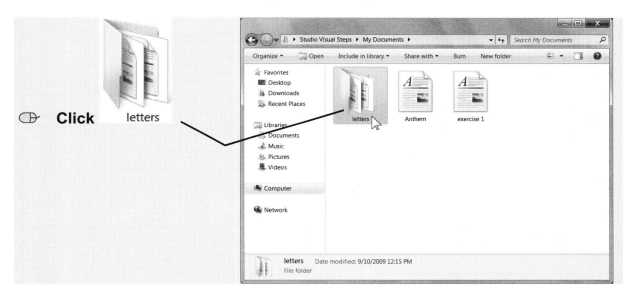

Sometimes the screen shot shows only a portion of a window. Here is an example:

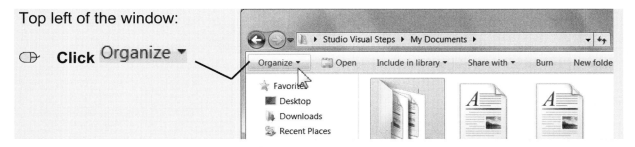

It really will **not be necessary** for you to read all the information in the screen shots in this book. Always use the screen shots in combination with the image you see on your own computer screen.

Test Your Knowledge

Have you finished reading this book? Then test your knowledge with the *Google* test. Visit the website: **www.ccforseniors.com**

This multiple-choice test will tell you how good your knowledge is of the *Google* applications covered in this book. If you pass the test, you will receive your free *Computer Certificate* by e-mail.

For Teachers

This book is designed as a self-study guide. It is also well suited for use in a group or a classroom setting. For this purpose, we offer a free teacher's manual containing information about how to prepare for the course (including didactic teaching methods) and testing materials. You can download this teacher's manual (PDF file) from the website which accompanies this book: **www.visualsteps.com/google**

Register Your Book

You can register your book. We will keep you informed of any important changes that you need to know of, as a user of the book. You can also take advantage of our periodic Newsletter informing you of our product releases, company news, tips & tricks, special offers, etcetera.

1. Searching the Internet and Your Computer

Most computer users think of *Google* only as a means of searching the Internet. In the meantime, *Google* has developed a wide variety of other handy tools and programs, besides its famous search engine. There is something for nearly everyone's interests. You can install or download these programs for free and give them a try.

This chapter will show you a number of tips to help you search the Internet more effectively. You will also learn how to install the *Toolbar* to quickly find your favorite web pages. And finally, you will see that the search box can be used for lots of other things, besides searching the Internet.

By installing *Google Desktop*, you will be able to use the *Google* search options on your own computer. Furthermore, you can create your own home page with *iGoogle* so that when you open *Internet Explorer* you will immediately see the contents of your favorite websites.

In this chapter you will learn how to:

- search more effectively;
- select your search settings;
- use *Google* for calculations and conversions;
- install the *Google Toolbar*;
- use the *Google Toolbar*;
- personalize your home page with *iGoogle*;
- install *Google Desktop*;
- search your own computer.

 Please note:

In this chapter you will see several screen shots of Internet pages. Since many web pages are updated frequently, the screen shots may look different from what you see on your own computer screen. This makes no difference, however, for the operations and programs you will be using.

 Please note:

The screen shots have been made in *Internet Explorer 8*. If you are using a different version of *Internet Explorer*, the images on your screen may look a little different.

1.1 Advanced Search Options

Above all, *Google* is known for being the most popular search engine on the Internet. In most cases you can find what you are looking for by using *Google*. If you cannot find what you are looking for, or if the search results are too extensive, you can always try using *Google's* advanced search options. This is how you do that:

☞ **Open *Internet Explorer*** ¹

☞ **Browse to www.google.com** ²

You are looking for information on *Visual Steps*. Normally, you would do that like this:

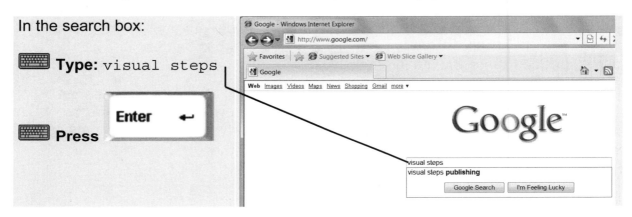

In the search box:

Type: visual steps

Press Enter ↵

Tip

Using a default search engine
If you have defined *Google* as your default search engine, you can also type your search terms directly in the search box at the top of the *Internet Explorer* window.

In the search box you will see the 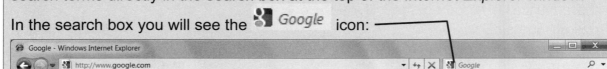 icon:

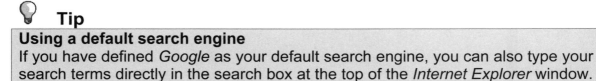

HELP! The Google home page looks different.

Now and then, the *Google* logo that is displayed on your home page will look a little different. *Google* does this to draw attention to a particular subject or activity (such as a famous person's birth date). If you want to know more about the subject, just click the logo. The search engine, however, will still work the same as usual.

In this example 19,400,000 pages have been found.

The most important website is usually at the top of the list. You can open this site straightaway:

☞ **Click**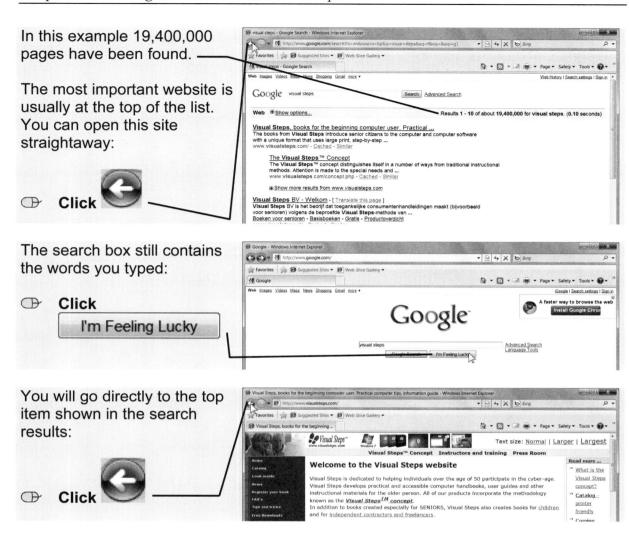

The search box still contains the words you typed:

☞ **Click**

I'm Feeling Lucky

You will go directly to the top item shown in the search results:

☞ **Click**

💡 **Tip**

Searching for images or videos
If you specifically want to search for images or videos, this is what you need to do:

☞ **Click** Images **or** Videos

☞ **Click**

Search Images **or**

Search Videos

Now you will exclusively see links to pages containing images or videos.

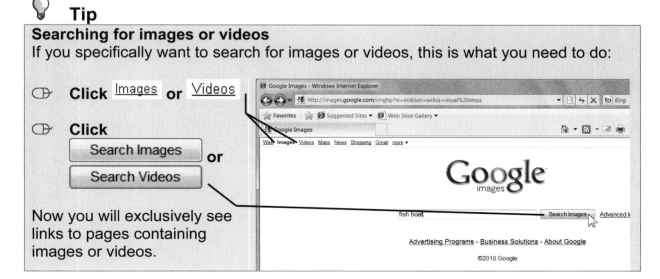

If this is not the website you were looking for, or if the search results show an overabundance of hits, you can use the *Advanced Search* options. By using the keywords 'visual' and 'steps' *Google* will search all websites and pages which contain one or both words. This search resulted in 19,400,000 pages. If you just want to search for the combination 'visual steps' in English websites:

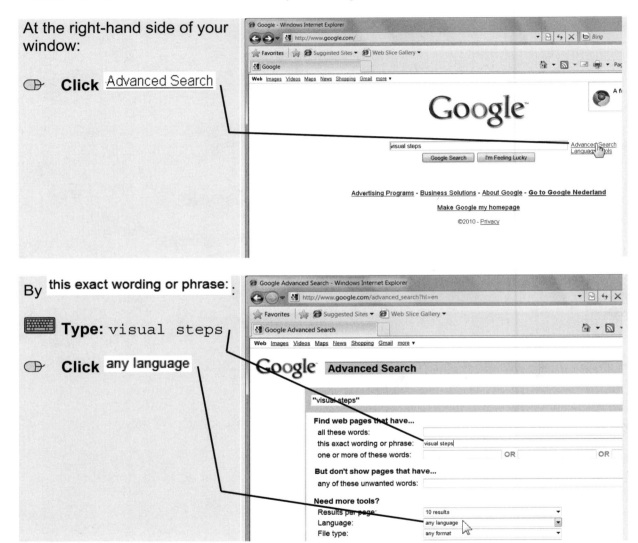

At the right-hand side of your window:

☞ **Click** Advanced Search

By **this exact wording or phrase:**

⌨ **Type:** visual steps

☞ **Click** any language

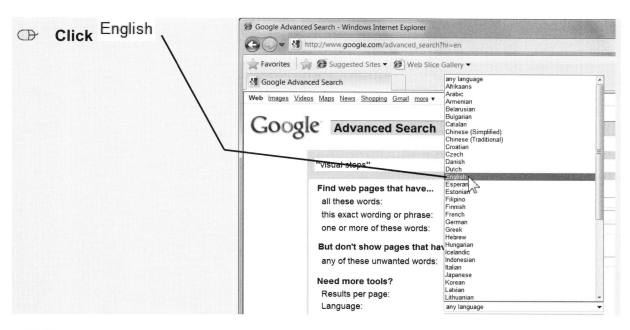

⊕ **Click** English

Various search methods

If you enter multiple keywords, you will be able to search in different ways. If you select:

all these words:	The website will contain all these words, but not necessarily in the same sentence or paragraph. For example, 'Visual' will appear at the top of the page, but 'steps' might appear somewhere else in the text.
this exact wording or phrase:	The keywords need to be positioned in the exact same order as you have typed them. You can use this method for searching first names and surnames.
one or more of these words:	The website does not need to contain all of the keywords. If one of the words is found, the link to the website will be displayed. You can use this method to search for alternative notations or descriptions of your keywords. For instance, 'Peking' or 'Beijing'.
any of these unwanted words:	The website will not contain a certain keyword. This only makes sense if you have previously started a search for the keywords you do want to find.

If necessary, you can activate *SafeSearch*, which will prevent any pornographic websites from being displayed.

At
Date, usage rights, numeric range, and

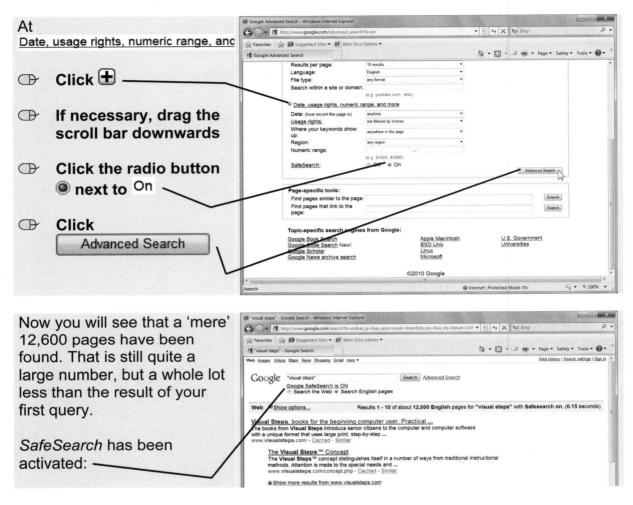

👉 **Click ➕**

👉 **If necessary, drag the scroll bar downwards**

👉 **Click the radio button ⦿ next to** On

👉 **Click** Advanced Search

Now you will see that a 'mere' 12,600 pages have been found. That is still quite a large number, but a whole lot less than the result of your first query.

SafeSearch has been activated:

The more you enter specific information by the advanced search options, the greater the chance you will quickly find the website you are looking for. However, if you enter too many specific search conditions, the website may not be found.

1.2 Setting Preferences

If you always want to search in a different language, or use *SafeSearch* by default, you can set these preferences:

At the top right of the window:

☞ **Click** <u>Search settings</u>

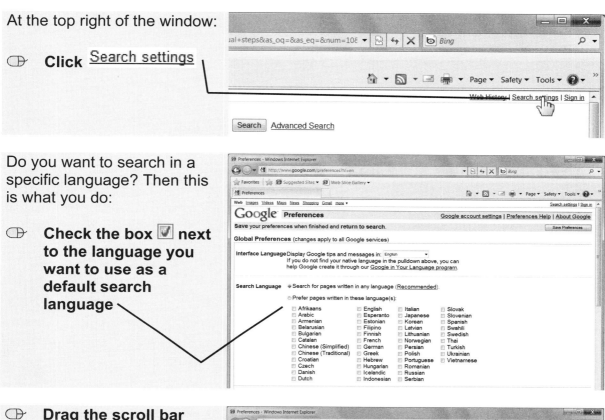

Do you want to search in a specific language? Then this is what you do:

☞ **Check the box ☑ next to the language you want to use as a default search language**

☞ **Drag the scroll bar downwards**

Here you will see the other preferences:

At **SafeSearch Filtering** :

☞ **Click the radio button ◉ next to** Use strict filtering

☞ **Click** Save Preferences

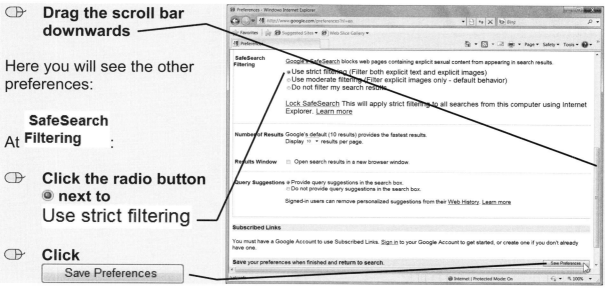

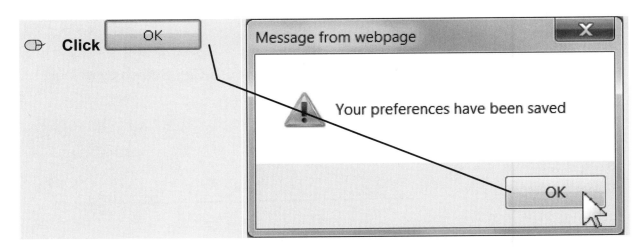

 Click OK

 HELP! I receive a warning message.

If you see a message that warns you that your cookies are disabled, you will not be able to change your preferences. The security settings for your computer are preventing the use of cookies. Depending on your web browser, you may be able to change these security settings and allow cookies to be stored.

💡 **Tip**

Not enough search results
Have you changed your preferences and you still do not see the web pages you were expecting to find? It is possible that these pages are blocked by *SafeSearch*, or by some other settings. Sometimes, a website is incorrectly marked as 'pornographic'. This can occur when using a very strict filter.

Also, the language settings may not function correctly if the website contains multiple languages, or if the language code of the website is not correct.

If this is the case, you need to restore the default settings, and try again.

1.3 Google Provides Answers

Google is not just a search engine. It can also answer simple, everyday questions. You can even use *Google* as a calculator:

In the search box:

Press ← Backspace
until the search box is empty

Type: 9+5

Press Enter ←

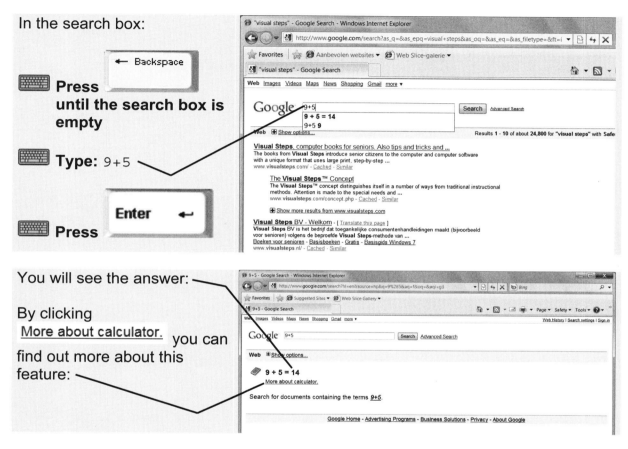

You will see the answer:

By clicking
More about calculator. you can
find out more about this
feature:

To convert US Dollars to Euros:

Press ← Backspace
until the search box is empty

Type: 500 usd in eur

Press Enter ←

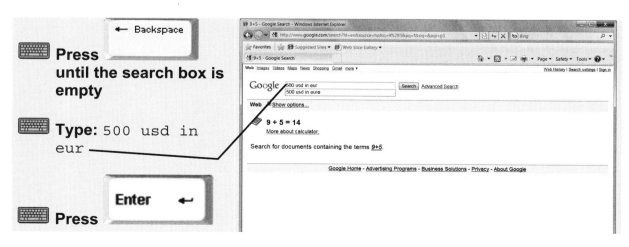

Now you will see the current rate:

To get the correct currency, you will need to use the standard financial currency codes. You can find these codes in the quotation lists of various banks. The amounts may differ accordingly.

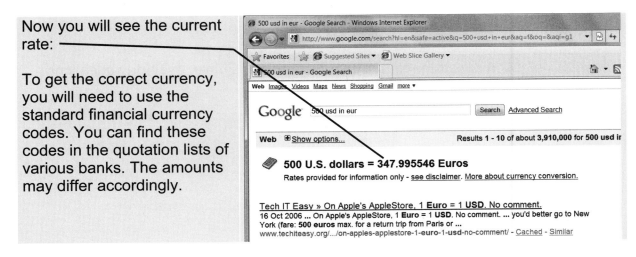

You can also use *Google* to convert dimensions:

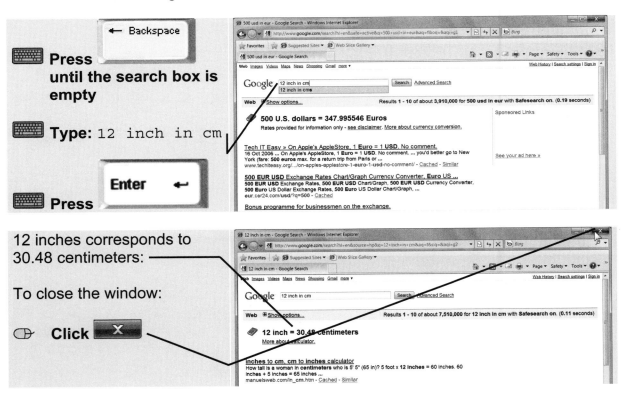

Press until the search box is empty

Type: 12 inch in cm

Press Enter

12 inches corresponds to 30.48 centimeters:

To close the window:

Click X

1.4 Install the Google Toolbar

The *Google Toolbar* lets you add a number of specific *Google* search functions to a separate *Internet Explorer* toolbar (or to the toolbar of one of the other web browsers). This means you will be able to access these functions much quicker. This is how to install the *Google Toolbar*:

☞ **Open *Internet Explorer*** 👣¹

☞ **Browse to www.google.com/toolbar** 👣²

🖰 **Click**

Install Google Toolbar

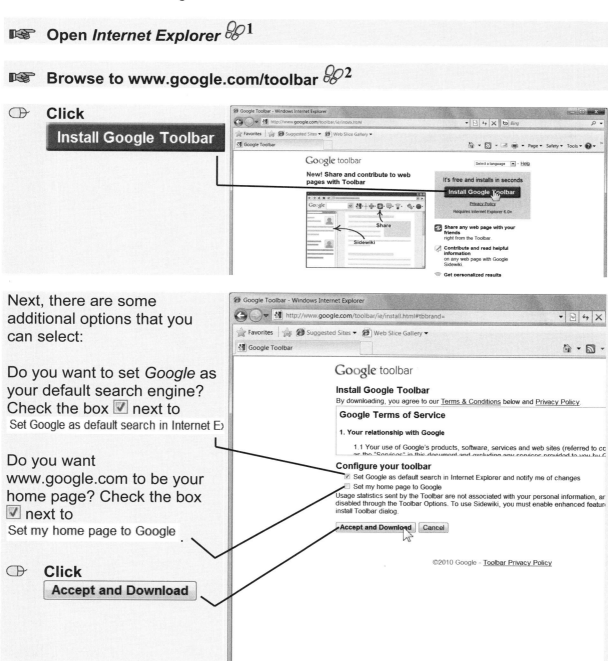

Next, there are some additional options that you can select:

Do you want to set *Google* as your default search engine? Check the box ☑ next to

Set Google as default search in Internet E⟩

Do you want www.google.com to be your home page? Check the box ☑ next to

Set my home page to Google

🖰 **Click**

Accept and Download

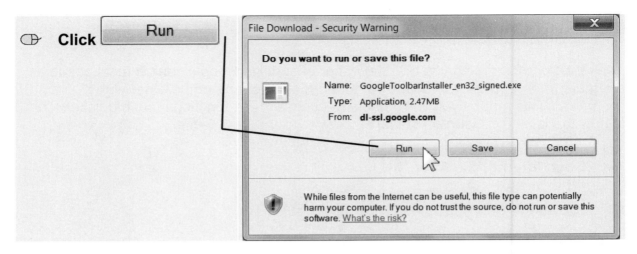

Click **Run**

Now the installation files will be downloaded:

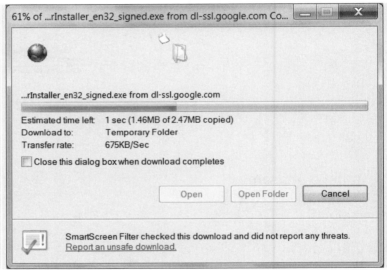

After the downloading process has finished you will see a warning message:

Click **Run**

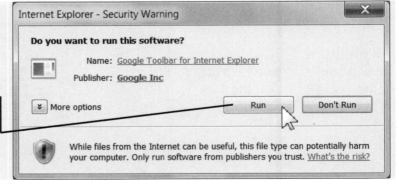

You may also see an additional security warning:

Click **Run**

In *Windows Vista* and *Windows 7* your screen will now turn dark, and you will need to give permission to continue:

If necessary, click Continue **or** Yes

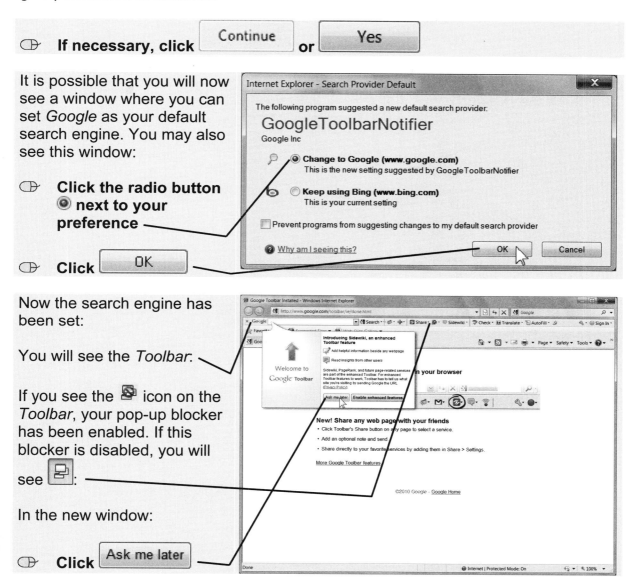

It is possible that you will now see a window where you can set *Google* as your default search engine. You may also see this window:

Click the radio button ⦿ next to your preference

Click OK

Now the search engine has been set:

You will see the *Toolbar*.

If you see the 🖼 icon on the *Toolbar*, your pop-up blocker has been enabled. If this blocker is disabled, you will see 🖼:

In the new window:

Click Ask me later

On the *Toolbar* you will see a search box and a number of different buttons. You can use these buttons to surf directly to certain website categories, or to a specific website. To add a button for a specific website:

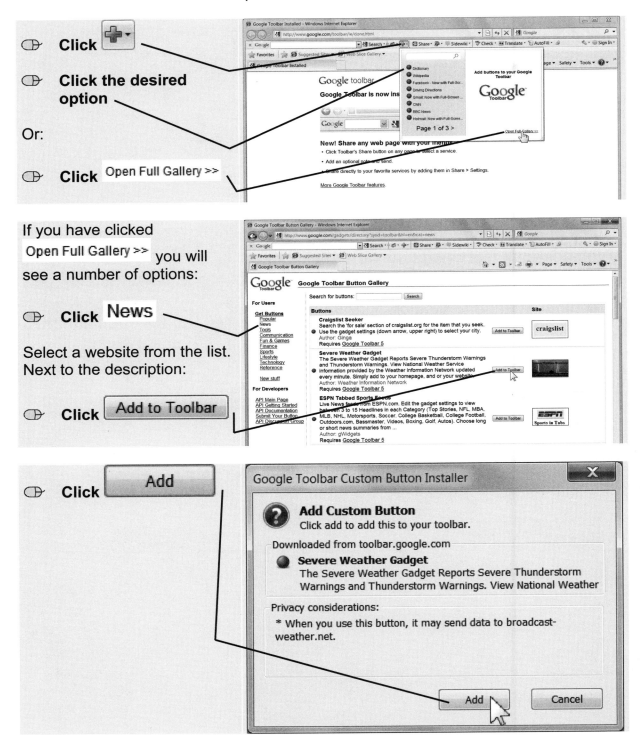

☞ **Click**

☞ **Click the desired option**

Or:

☞ **Click** Open Full Gallery >>

If you have clicked Open Full Gallery >> you will see a number of options:

☞ **Click** News

Select a website from the list. Next to the description:

☞ **Click** Add to Toolbar

☞ **Click** Add

Now you will see a new button on the *Toolbar*:

☞ **Click**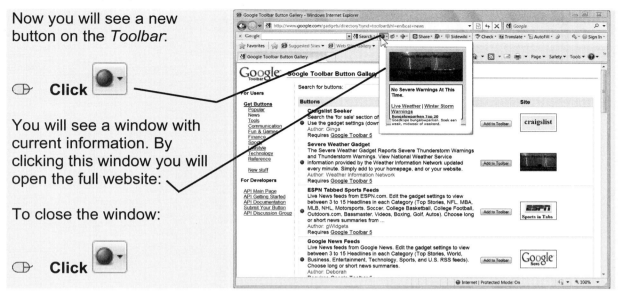

You will see a window with current information. By clicking this window you will open the full website:

To close the window:

☞ **Click**

To hide the button:

☞ **Right-click**

☞ **Click**
   Hide Severe Weather Gadget button

Other Toolbar buttons

This will open a window with news items from various newspapers and other media.

By clicking the button on the left you can block pop-ups. The button will turn into . If you click , the blocker will be disabled and you will again see the button.

This allows you to change the *Toolbar* preference settings.

⚫ Sign In   Here you can sign in to your *Google* account.

Depending on your window's settings, other buttons may be displayed. You may need to click ➤➤ first to see them. These are the buttons you use when typing or editing text, for instance when typing an e-mail message. You will learn more about this later on.

If you do not want to use the *Toolbar* any longer, you can hide it:

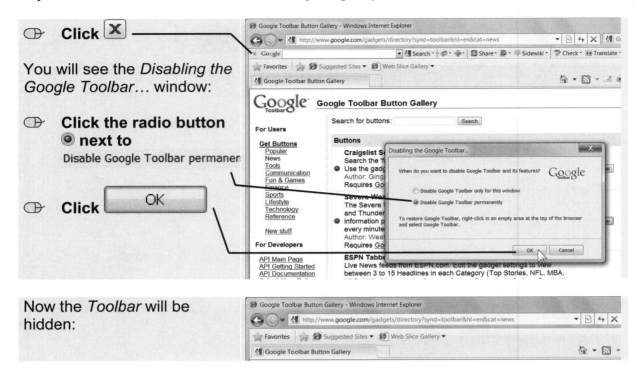

☞ **Click** ✕

You will see the *Disabling the Google Toolbar...* window:

☞ **Click the radio button** ⦿ **next to**
    Disable Google Toolbar permanen

☞ **Click** OK

Now the *Toolbar* will be hidden:

 Please note:

The *Toolbar* has been hidden and is disabled, but it has not been deleted. If you want to completely delete the *Toolbar* you need to use *Windows Control Panel*.

☞ **Close all windows** 👣³

1.5 iGoogle

iGoogle lets you create and customize your own page. You can add information blocks about the subjects that interest you. Afterwards you can set this page as your browser's home page. This is how you start *iGoogle*:

☞ **Open** *Internet Explorer* 🐾 **1**

☞ **Browse to www.google.com/ig** 🐾 **2**

You will see a welcome message:

☞ **Click** Cancel

Now you are going to add an item yourself:

☞ **Click** Add stuff »

Now you can select a category. On the left side of the window:

☞ **Click a category**

Under the item you want:

☞ **Click** Add it now

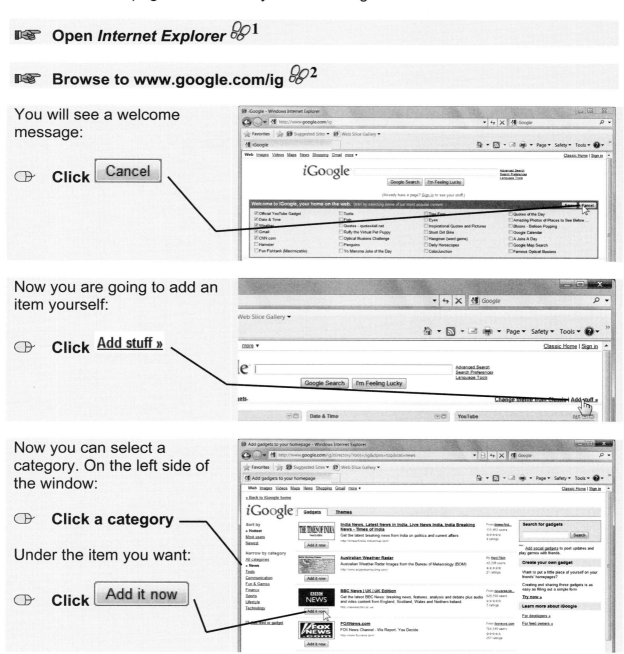

Now the item has been added:

⊕ **Click**

« Back to iGoogle home

Here you will see the new item. To maximize the item:

⊕ **Click**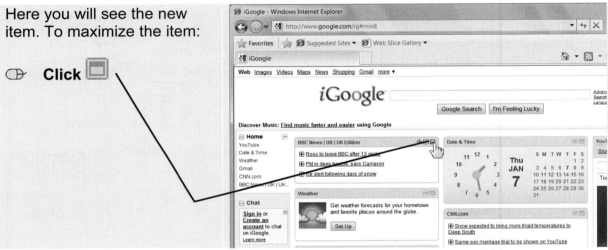

To minimize the item:

⊕ **Click**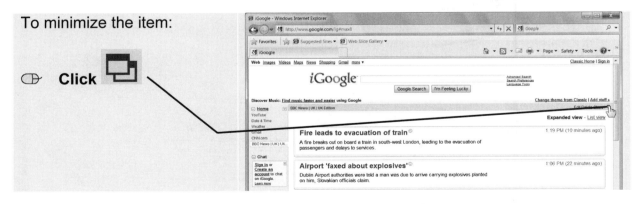

You can move an item by positioning the mouse pointer on the title bar of the item and dragging it to a different location:

☞ **Place the mouse pointer on the title bar**

The mouse pointer will turn into 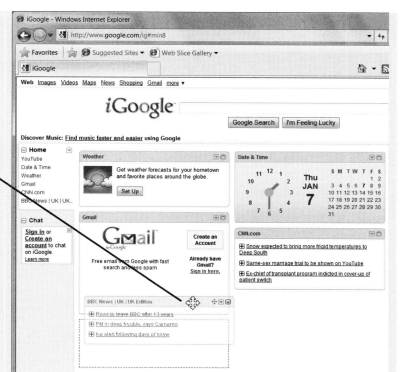 :

☞ **Drag the item to the desired location**

The item will be placed in the desired spot.

Now the item has been moved. To delete an item:

☞ **Click**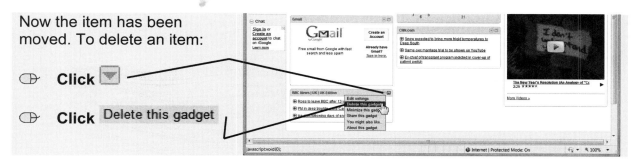

☞ **Click** Delete this gadget

☞ **Click** OK

If you select a different theme, the appearance of the page will change:

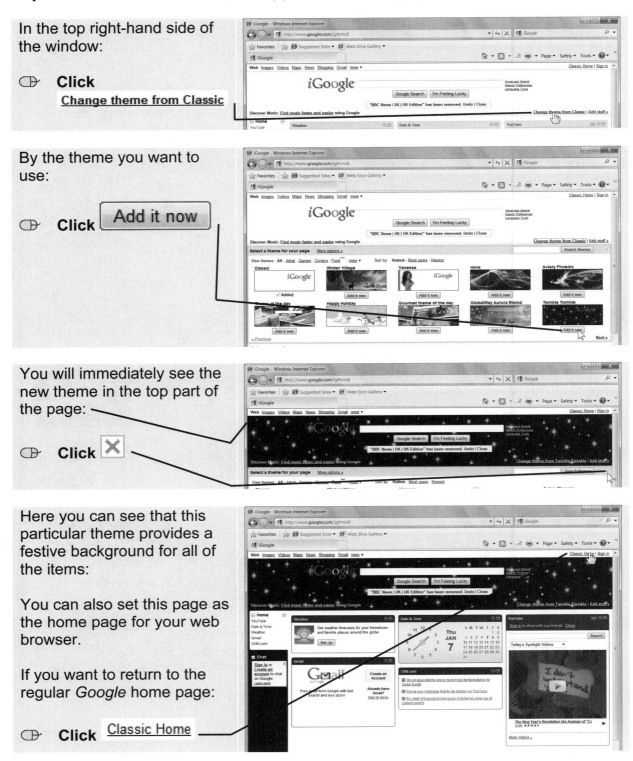

In the top right-hand side of the window:

☞ **Click**

Change theme from Classic

By the theme you want to use:

☞ **Click** Add it now

You will immediately see the new theme in the top part of the page:

☞ **Click** ✕

Here you can see that this particular theme provides a festive background for all of the items:

You can also set this page as the home page for your web browser.

If you want to return to the regular *Google* home page:

☞ **Click** Classic Home

Now you will see the regular *Google* home page:

1.6 Google Desktop

You are probably accustomed to using the *Windows* search engine to find items on your own computer. If you install *Google Desktop*, the contents of your computer will be indexed and you will be able to search your computer with *Google*. *Google Desktop* is a search program that allows you to search for text in e-mail messages, files, music files and photos. During the indexing process the program will search the files on your hard disk, and will store the search data in an index. This is how you install *Google Desktop*:

☞ **Browse to desktop.google.com** 🐾**2**

Click

Install Google Desktop

If the download does not start automatically:

Click

click here to get it going

Click Run

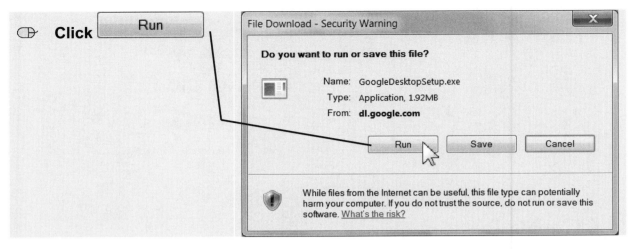

Now the files will be downloaded:

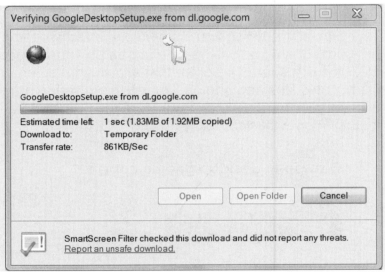

In *Windows Vista* and *Windows 7* your screen will now turn dark, and you will need to give permission to continue:

If necessary, click Continue **or** Yes

Here you will see the installation's progress:

Click [I agree]

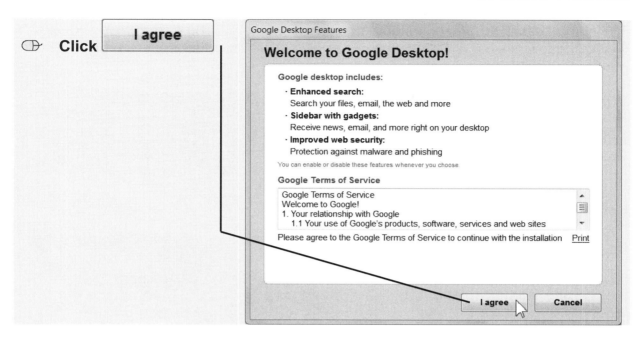

If you just want to install the *Desktop*:

 Uncheck the boxes ☑ **next to the other options**

If your computer is slow, also uncheck the box ☑ next to Enhanced Search :

 Click [Done]

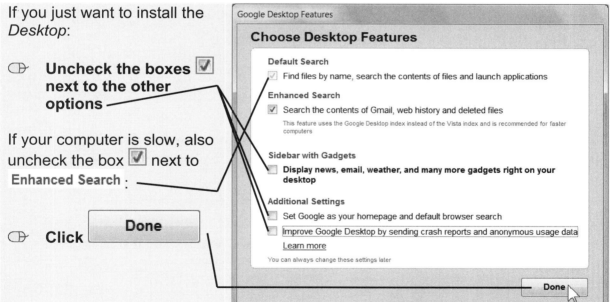

➥ Please note:

When *Google* searches your computer for the first time, this may take several hours, during which your computer might become extremely sluggish.

➥ Please note:

E-mail messages will only be indexed if your e-mail program has been open during the indexing process.

The computer will only be scanned and indexed once by *Google*. This may take a while, and this operation will only be executed if there are relatively few other programs open on the computer.

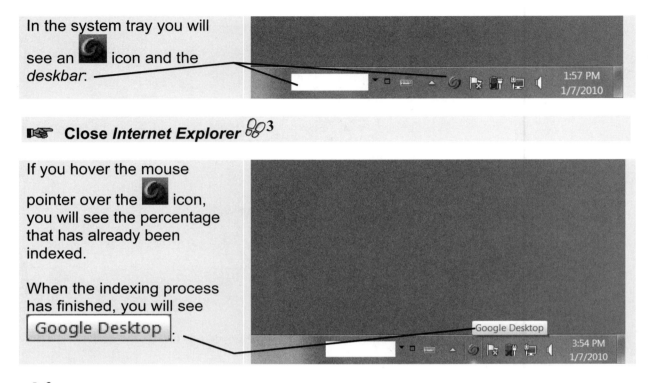

In the system tray you will see an ![icon] icon and the *deskbar*.

☞ **Close** *Internet Explorer* ✂³

If you hover the mouse pointer over the ![icon] icon, you will see the percentage that has already been indexed.

When the indexing process has finished, you will see | Google Desktop |.

![Badge] **HELP! At the bottom of the window I see a news message.**

Now and then you will see a newsflash at the bottom of your window, or an alert that e-mail has been received. For example:

Like these alerts?

Google Desktop can alert you of news, email, and more.

| Yes | | No |

‹ › 2 of 5   Customize Alerts...   ✕

Detroit attack: US border guards knew alleged terrorist was on flight

Telegraph.co.uk

Washington Post Detroit attack: US border guards knew alleged terrorist was on flight Telegraph.co...

| No |

If you do not want to see these alerts, click | No |.

After *Google* has indexed the contents of your computer, you can begin searching it with *Desktop*. There are two different ways of doing this. The quickest way is to type your search terms directly in the deskbar:

In the deskbar:

 Type the words

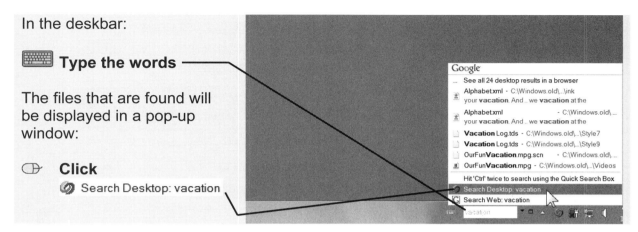

The files that are found will be displayed in a pop-up window:

⬤ **Click**

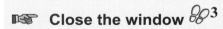 Search Desktop: vacation

💡 **Tip**

Directly open a file
You can also click the desired file and open it directly from the pop-up window.

The search results will be displayed in a *Google*-like window.

👉 **Close the window** ✂️*3*

💡 Tip

Floating deskbar

If you briefly press **Ctrl** twice, you will see a floating deskbar on the screen. You can drag this deskbar and move it anywhere you want on the desktop. It operates the same way as the deskbar on the taskbar below.

In the floating deskbar:

⌨ **Type the search term**

☞ **Click**
   🌀 Search Desktop: vacation

To close the floating deskbar, briefly press **Ctrl** twice.

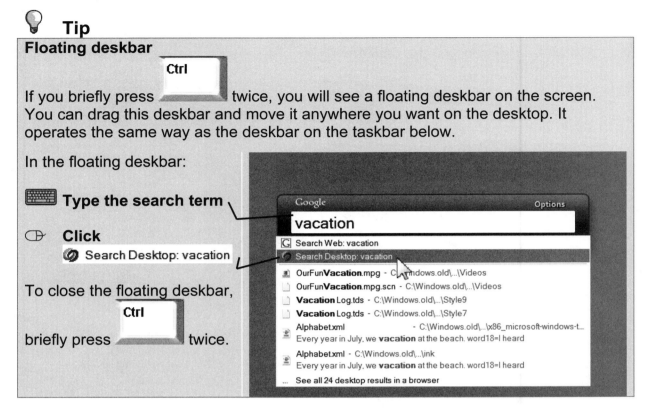

To use the second search method, you need to open the *Google Desktop* search page first:

At the bottom right-hand side of the window:

☞ **Click** 🌀

☞ **Click** Search Desktop

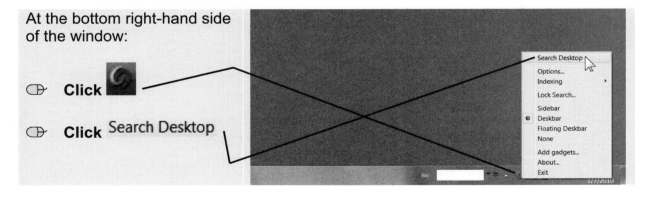

Type the search term

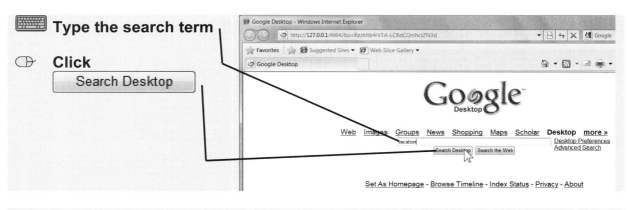

Click
Search Desktop

☞ **Close the window** 👣³

To disable the *Google Desktop*:

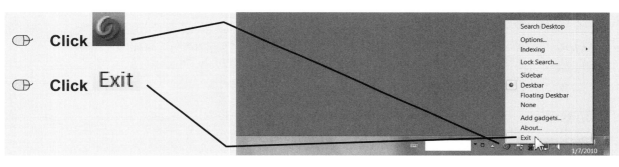

Click

Click Exit

If you want to permanently disable *Desktop*:

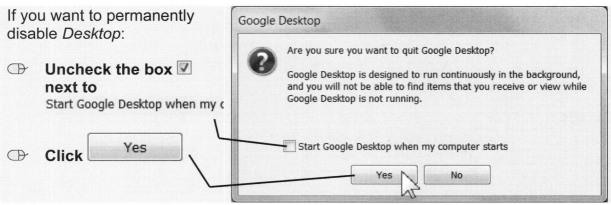

Uncheck the box ☑
next to
Start Google Desktop when my c

Click Yes

Now the icon in the system tray and the deskbar will have disappeared.

1.7 Background Information

Dictionary	
Advanced Search	Adding conditions or restrictions to a query.
Browser	A software program that is used to display web pages and surf the Internet. *Internet Explorer* is a web browser.
Cookie	A small text file that is placed on your computer by a website. This file contains data on your preferences while visiting the website.
Deskbar	Search box for *Google Desktop*. The deskbar can be located on the taskbar, on your desktop, or it can float. You can move a floating deskbar to a different location yourself.
Gadget	Literally: a smartly designed tool or item. Usually this is a small program that executes simple tasks.
I'm Feeling Lucky	When you enter your keywords and then click the I'm Feeling Lucky button, *Google* will take you directly to the first web page listed in the search results. You will not see the page with the other search results, but if you would view this page, the most relevant web page would be at the top.
SafeSearch filter	*Google's SafeSearch* filter will filter websites that contain pornography and will remove them from your search results. While no filter is 100 percent accurate, *SafeSearch* will block most of the inappropriate sites.
Theme	A collection of visual elements and sounds for your computer's desktop. A theme will determine the appearance of the various visual elements on your desktop, such as windows, icons, fonts, and colors.
Toolbar	A toolbar is a row, column, or block of buttons or icons representing tasks you can do within a program.

Source: Google Help, Windows Help and Support, Wikipedia

1.8 Tips

 Tip

Google Alerts
If you want to view the most current information about a certain topic or keyword, you can sign up for *Google Alerts*. Every time new search results have been found for this topic, you will automatically receive an e-mail message.

☞ **Open *Internet Explorer* ᵇᵖ1**

☞ **Browse to www.google.com/options ᵇᵖ2**

Click Alerts

At Search terms:

Type the words

If necessary, you can change the type or frequence of the search alerts.

Type your e-mail address

Click **Create Alert**

Now you will receive an e-mail at the address you have entered. This e-mail contains a link for you to click, to confirm the activation of *Google Alerts*.

Tip

Google Adwords

Do you want your company to stand out among the search results for your products or services? Go to the *Google* home page and click **Advertising Programs** to take a look at *Google Adwords*. This program will help you promote your products and services to the people who are really interested in them. Furthermore, you can restrict your advertisements to the region where you do business.

2. Exploring the World

Nowadays many people use a route planner to plan a trip or to look up a specific location. Apart from the built-in car navigation systems, such as the well-known *TomTom*, you can find various route planners on the Internet as well. One of the advantages of online route planners is that they are updated more frequently. And you do not have to be a subscriber to view the most recent information. There is also more local information and photos available then on a regular navigation system.

Google Maps is one of the free route planners on the Internet.

Every spot on earth is regularly photographed by satellites. With *Google Earth* you can display these photos on your computer. This way you can view your own neighborhood from above, or look at other interesting places.

Google Earth is not only entertaining. It can be a useful tool as well. Before booking your hotel room you can take a look at the hotel from above and check if it is really close to the beach that you want to be near to, or if the forest they promise is larger than just a few trees. Or you can see for yourself if the nearest landfill is not just around the corner. Before you sign the title deed for your new home, it cannot hurt to view the neighborhood from higher up.

In this chapter you will learn how to use the main functions of *Google Maps* and the free *Google Earth* version. In the *Background Information* at the end of this chapter you can read more about the paid versions of these programs.

In this chapter you will learn how to:

- find and view a location;
- plan a route;
- install *Google Earth*;
- navigate with *Google Earth*;
- view 3D buildings;
- fly to a location;
- measure distances;
- fly into space;
- open the flight simulator.

Please note:

In this chapter you will see screen shots from the *Google Maps* and *Google Earth* programs. Because these programs change regularly, these screen shots may differ from the images on your own screen. Usually this does not make any difference for the operation of the programs.

2.1 Find and View a Location

To use *Google Maps* you do not need to install software to your computer. All maps are stored on the *Google Maps* website, and you can view them on the Internet.

☞ **Open** *Internet Explorer* ⳗ¹

☞ **Browse to**

   maps.google.com ⳗ²

Please note: do not type 'www' in the web address.

You now see the opening window:

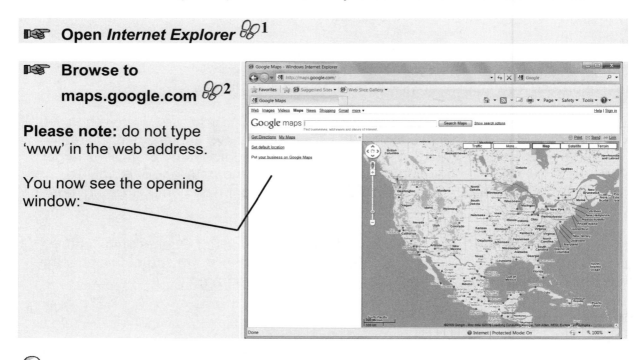

💡 **Tip**

Directly from the Google home page
You can also access *Google Maps* directly from the *Google* home page:

👉 **Click** Maps

In the search box:

Type:
```
1600 pennsylvania
ave nw 20500
```

Click
Search Maps

The address is indicated on the map:

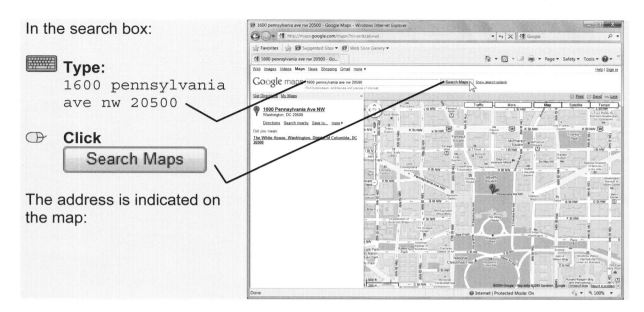

To find important buildings and organizations you only need to type their name:

In the search box:

Type: Statue of Liberty

Click
Search Maps

You will see the Statue of Liberty:

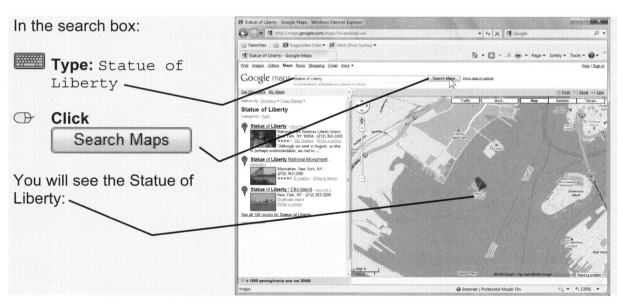

To zoom in (enlarge), you

click :

To zoom out (make smaller),

you click :

You can also use the mouse
pointer to drag the slider
along the zoom bar:

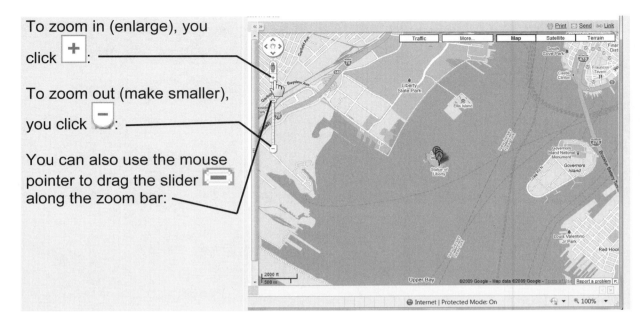

💡 **Tip**

Zooming in and out with the mouse
There are other ways of zooming in or out:
- Double-click the portion of the map you want to enlarge.
- If your mouse has a scroll wheel you can do it even faster:
  Roll the wheel forward (away from you) to zoom in, everything will be enlarged.
  Roll the wheel back (towards you) to zoom out, everything will become smaller.

💡 **Tip**

Viewing the neighborhood
When you zoom in, you lose the overall picture. In that case you can open the area
map:

At the bottom right-hand side
of the window:

⊕ **Click**

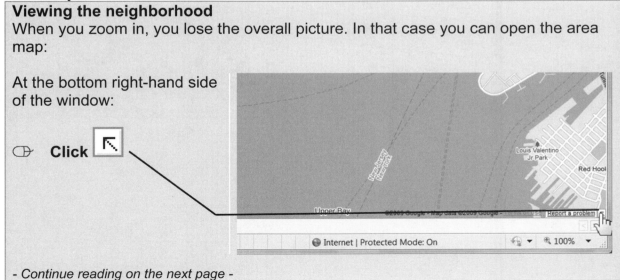

- Continue reading on the next page -

You now see an overview of the area:

To hide this map, you click 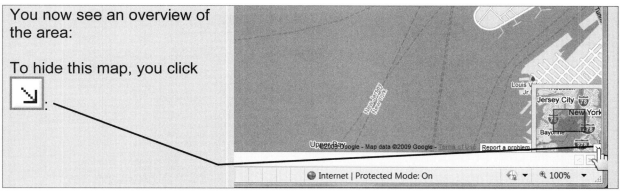:

With *Street View* you can view photos of the neighborhood:

👉 **Drag** 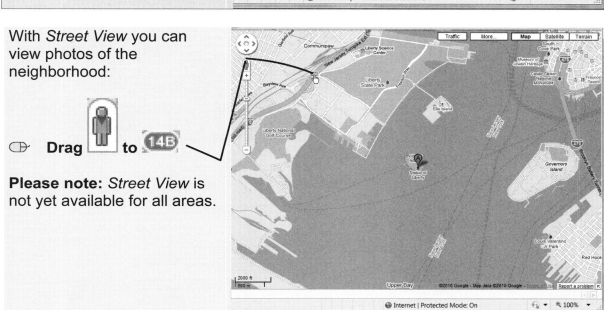 to 14B:

Please note: *Street View* is not yet available for all areas.

You now see the photo. To move horizontally, click ◀ or ▶: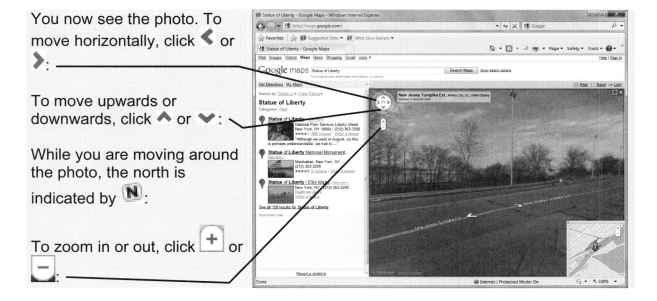

To move upwards or downwards, click ▲ or ▼:

While you are moving around the photo, the north is indicated by 🅽:

To zoom in or out, click ➕ or ➖:

Tip

Zoom in

By double-clicking a spot on the photo you can zoom in to this particular spot. This will only be possible if the marked spot appears in a lighter color, and if you see the  icon in the marked area.

To return to the map:

👉 **Click** ✖

💡 Tip

Move

To see a different part of the area, you need to move the map by dragging it to a different location:

👉 **Place the mouse pointer on the map**

The pointer will turn into 🖑:

👉 **Drag the mouse pointer until you see the right part of the area**

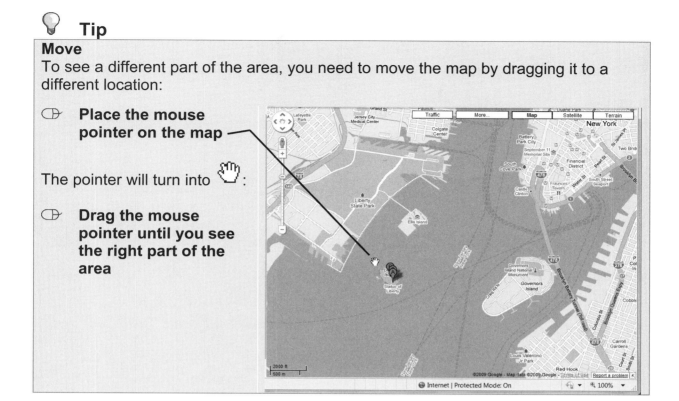

2.2 Planning a Journey

Google Maps not only helps you find places, but will help you plan your trips as well. This is how you plan your journey from Pennsylvania to New York:

👉 **Click** Get Directions

At 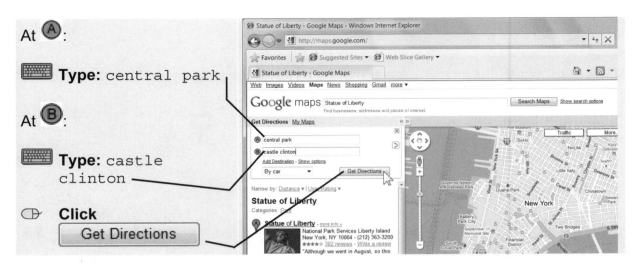Ⓐ:

⌨ **Type:** central park

At Ⓑ:

⌨ **Type:** castle clinton

☞ **Click**

     Get Directions

You will might see multiple locations called 'Castle Clinton'. First, you will need to indicate which location you want to use:

☞ **Click**

     ① **Clinton Castle** National Monument
        26 Wall Street, New York, NY 10004

Depending on the chosen destination, you may need to do the same thing for your final destination.

A path is drawn showing your journey on the map, along with the itinerary:

Click 🖶 Print to print these directions:

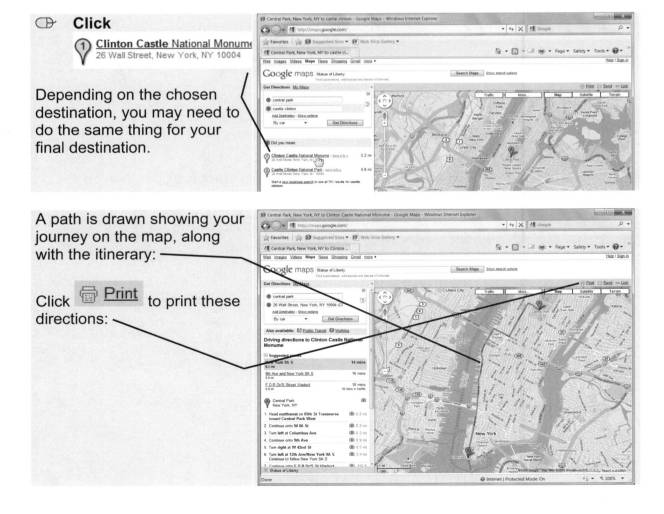

Tip

Change route

If you want to follow a different path, you need to drag the path shown on the map to a different location:

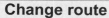 **Place the mouse pointer on a spot somewhere on the current path**

The pointer will turn into :

The route will display a white circle ⬡ :

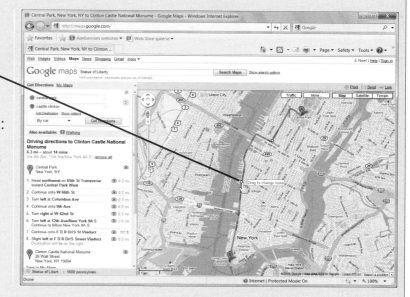

 Drag ⬡ to the place you want to include in your trip

The distance and time for the adjusted route is calculated and shown on the left.

You can also follow the route step-by-step:

 Drag the scroll bar downwards, until you see
　　3. Turn **left** at **Columbus Ave**

At 3. Turn **left** at **Columbus Ave** :

 **Click**

For all the spots marked with , a photo is available.

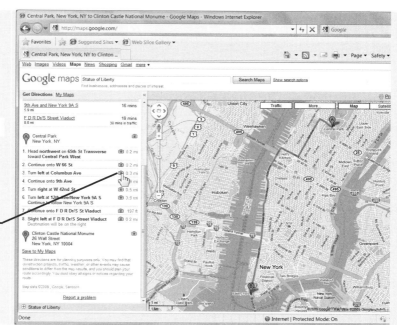

To move to the next point in the itinerary:

 Click [▷]

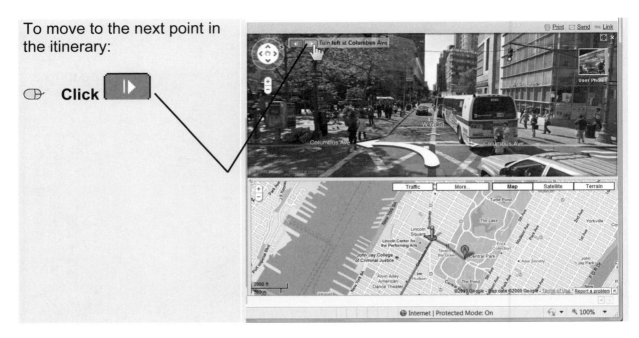

➡ Please note:

If a location is not marked by an 📷 icon, you will see the map or a satellite photo.

Now you are going to your final destination:

👉 **Drag the scroll bar downwards**

👉 **Click**

Ⓑ Clinton Castle National Mon
26 Wall Street
New York, NY 10004

You will see the final destination:

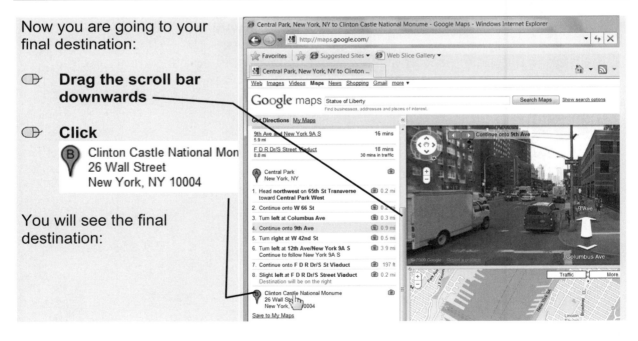

To close the *Street View* display:

⊕   **Click** ❌

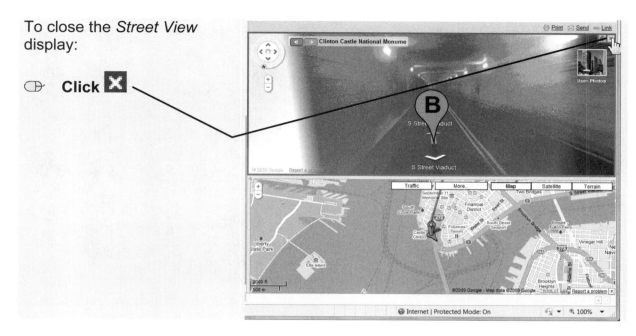

Instead of viewing the location on the map, you can also view a satellite photo:

⊕   **Click**

Satellite

You will see a satellite photo of the area:

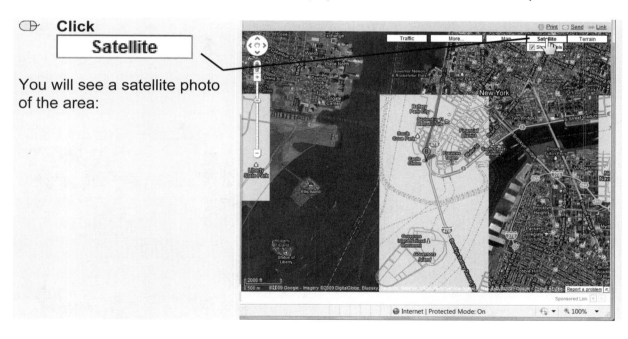

You can zoom in to see the details, just as on a map:

To zoom in:

☞ **Click** ➕ **three times**

By zooming in you will view a smaller, and sometimes, different part of the photo:

☞ **Move the photo around until you can clearly see Castle Clinton** 🐾⁶

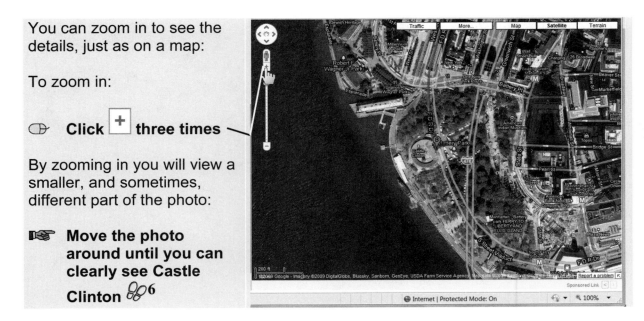

To make sure that you will always be able to view extra information from the *Wikipedia* Internet encyclopedia:

☞ **Click**
More... (1)

☞ **If necessary, check the box ☑ next to**
Wikipedia

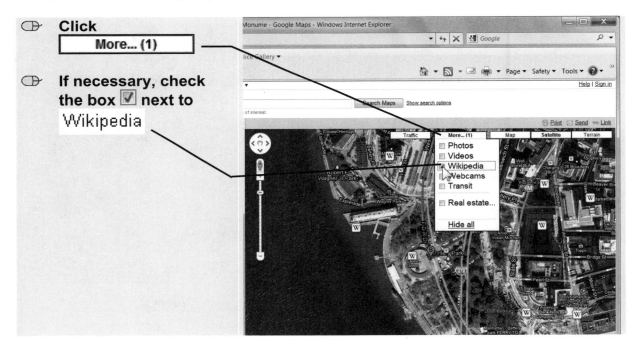

The 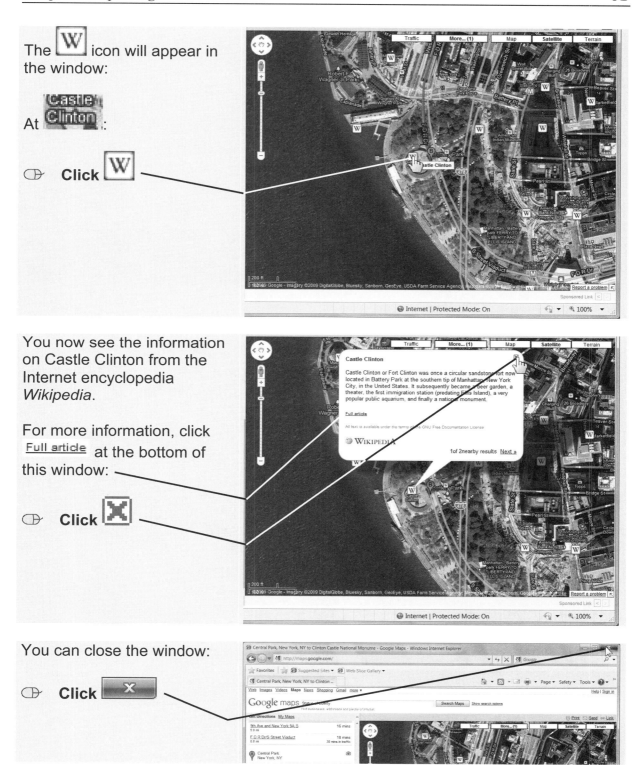 icon will appear in the window:

Castle Clinton

At **Clinton**:

☞ **Click** [W]

You now see the information on Castle Clinton from the Internet encyclopedia *Wikipedia*.

For more information, click **Full article** at the bottom of this window:

☞ **Click** [✕]

You can close the window:

☞ **Click** [X]

In the following section you will learn more about working with satellite images.

💡 **Tip**

Setting a default location

You can set your house or company as a default location, so you will not need to look up this location each time you start *Google Maps*:

Directly after opening *Google Maps*:

☞ **Click** Set default location

Now you can type and save the default address.

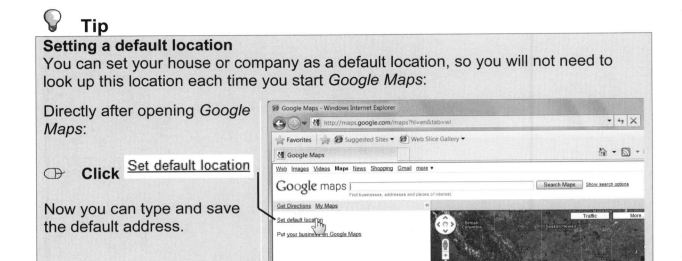

2.3 Installing Google Earth

Google Earth is a program that lets you view satellite photos of the earth. To use this program, you will need to install it to your computer first. This is how you install the program:

☞ **Open** *Internet Explorer* 🦶¹

☞ **Browse to earth.google.com** 🦶²

☞ **Click**

Download Google Earth 5

Please note: you might see a more recent version of this program on the screen.

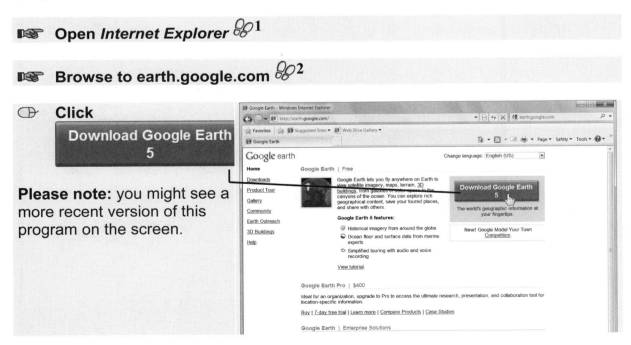

Uncheck the box ☑️
next to

Include Google Chrome, a fast ne

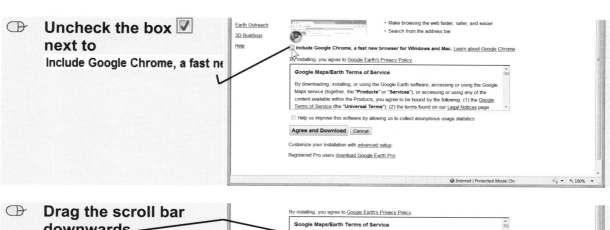

Drag the scroll bar
downwards

Click

Agree and Download

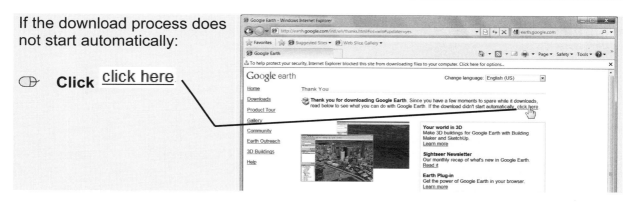

If the download process does
not start automatically:

Click click here

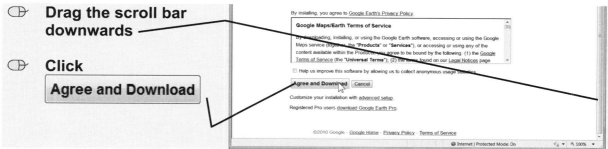

Click

Run

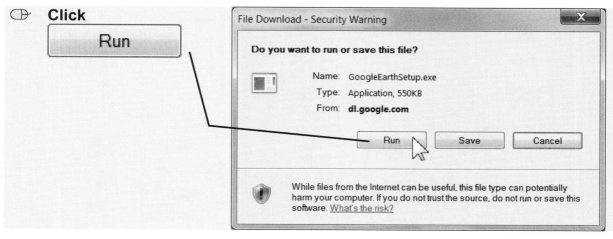

Click

In *Windows Vista* and *Windows 7* your screen will now turn dark and you will need to give permission to continue:

If necessary, click Continue **or** Yes

During the installation process you will see this window:

HELP! Google Earth starts directly.

If your *Google Earth* program opens directly, you can continue on the next page. Make sure to close *Internet Explorer* first.

☞ **Close *Internet Explorer*** ³

2.4 Navigation with Google Earth

This is how you open *Google Earth*:

You will see the *Google Earth* icon on your desktop:

☞ **Double-click**

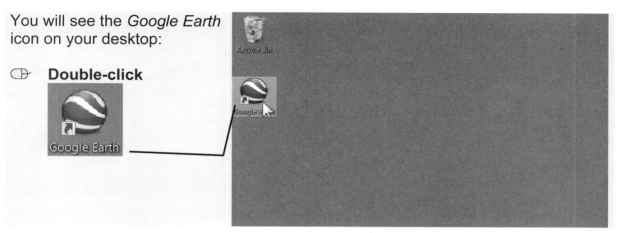

You will see the opening window with a *Start-Up Tip* on top. You can close the tip:

☞ **Click** [Close]

At the right-hand side of the window you will see a navigation tool:

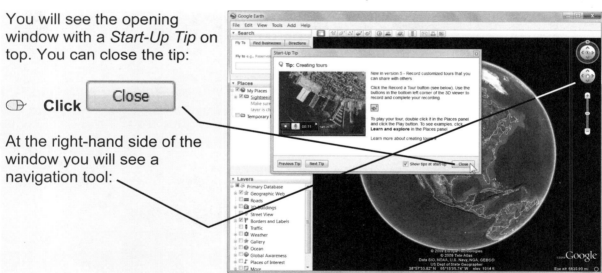

 HELP! I do not see a navigation tool.

If you do not see the navigation tool on the right side of your window, then do this:

☞ **Click** View , Show Navigation , Automatically

Now you will see the navigation tool when you place the mouse pointer in the right-hand side of your window.

Here you see the earth. To go to a specific location:

By Fly to:

⌨ **Type:** eiffel tower, paris, france

⌨ **Press** Enter ↵

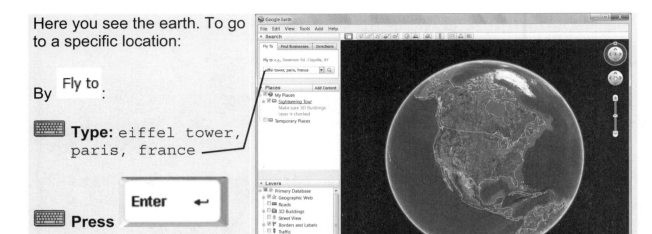

You now see the area surrounding the Eiffel tower. Just like in *Google Maps*, you can zoom in and out and move the photo:

👉 **Click** ➕ **a few times**

☞ **If necessary, move the photo around, until you can clearly see the Eiffel tower** 👣⁶

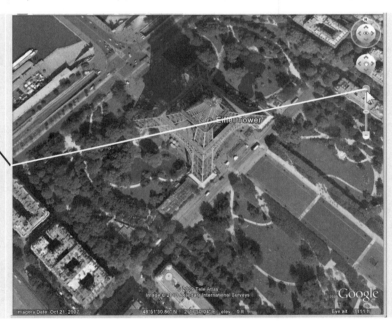

💡 Tip

Moving the photo with the navigation tool

You can also use the joystick with the small hand symbol [navigation tool] to move the photo. Click the navigation arrows to indicate in which direction you want to move the photo.

On the photo you will see a number of other icons and symbols. By clicking them you will see additional information or other photos:

By **Eiffel Tower**:

☞ **Click** ▪

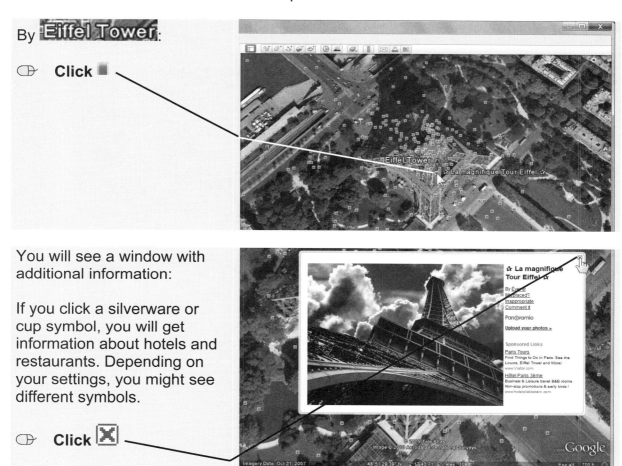

You will see a window with additional information:

If you click a silverware or cup symbol, you will get information about hotels and restaurants. Depending on your settings, you might see different symbols.

☞ **Click** ☒

These symbols are stored in layers that you can display or hide as you please. If you want to view the photo without all these symbols, you can disable the layers:

At the bottom left of the window, by **Layers** :

☞ **Click** ▣ **next to** Primary Database

▣ will turn into ☐:

If you do not see Primary Database, drag the scroll bar completely upwards.

2.5 Viewing Buildings in 3D

Usually, you will only see the picture and you can add all the layers you want to view. If you want to check if there are any 3D photos of the buildings available:

By :

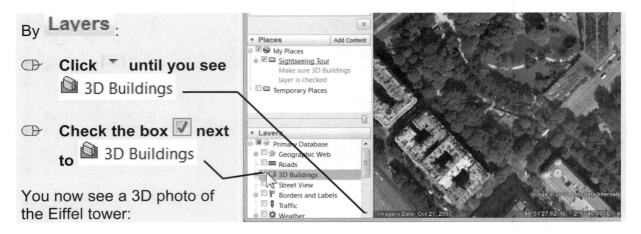

🖱 **Click** ▼ **until you see**
  🏢 **3D Buildings**

🖱 **Check the box** ☑ **next**
  to 🏢 **3D Buildings**

You now see a 3D photo of the Eiffel tower:

You can view 3D buildings from every possible angle.

Use the navigation arrows of the joystick ![joystick] to look around the object from a single viewpoint. With ◀ and ▶ you can look left or right. With ▲ and ▼ you can look up or down.

🐦 **Please note:**

While you rotate the viewpoint, the photo will move. If you cannot see the object anymore, drag the photo to a different position. If you place the mouse pointer on the object while you are moving it, the object will light up and you will keep seeing it.

💡 **Tip**

Finding the north

On the joystick, the **N** symbol indicates the north. Click **N** to position the north at the top of the photo.

Try to position the Eiffel tower the same way as shown in this example:

☞ **If necessary, use both joysticks and zoom in or out** 🦶5

☞ **If necessary, move the photo** 🦶6

 ## HELP! I have lost the Eiffel tower.

You will need to practice a bit, before you can maneuver the joysticks just the way you want to. If you do not succeed the first time, try again.

👆 **Click** [🔍]

Now the program will search for the Eiffel tower again.

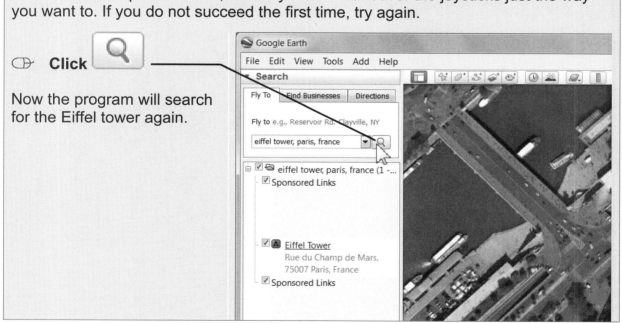

To look to the right:

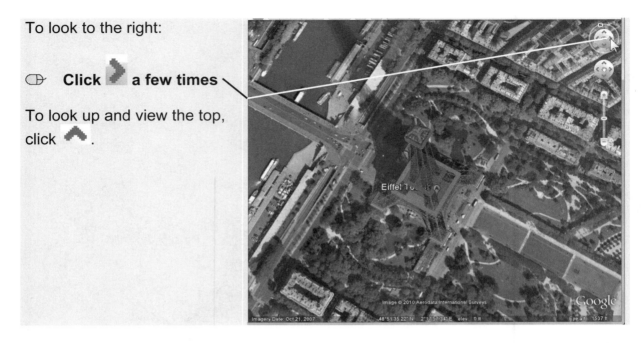

☞ **Click ▶ a few times**

To look up and view the top, click ⌃ .

There are not many 3D images of buildings available yet, but this number will surely increase in the future.

On the satellite images you can also display the public transportation services. To display the train, bus and subway stations, select the ⊞ Transportation layer:

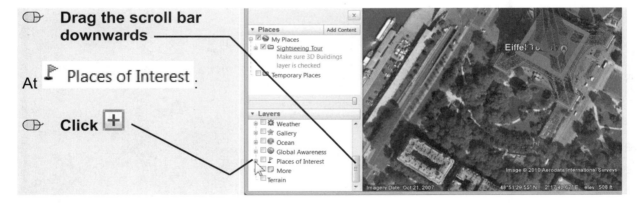

☞ **Drag the scroll bar downwards**

At ⚑ Places of Interest :

☞ **Click ⊞**

Click ▼ , until you see
⊕ Transportation

Check the box ☑ next to ⊕ Transportation

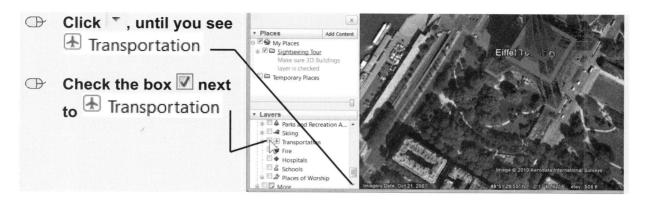

You may not see any public transportation icons on the satellite image yet. This is because in the current image you have zoomed in too far on the Eiffel Tower. First you will need to zoom out:

Drag the slider 🔲 downwards until the satellite image on your screen looks like this example

You will now see public transportation icons, such as

subways Ⓜ and railway

stations 🔲 :

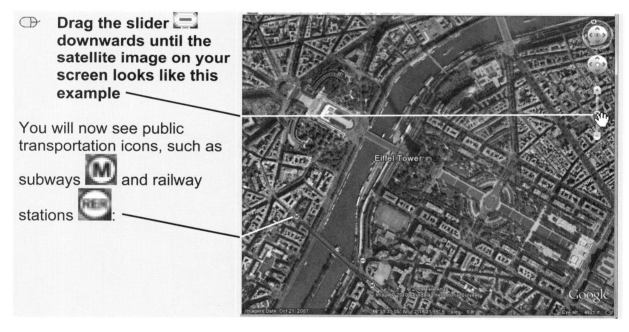

 HELP! I do not see these icons.

It is possible there are no stations in the area you are currently viewing. You can try moving the image, or zooming out some more. Make sure you do not zoom out too far, as that will make the icons disappear altogether.

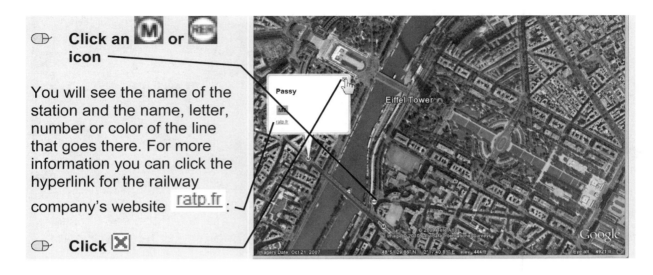

☞ **Click an 🅜 or ⓡ icon**

You will see the name of the station and the name, letter, number or color of the line that goes there. For more information you can click the hyperlink for the railway company's website ratp.fr :

☞ **Click ✖**

2.6 Fly a Route

If you want to go to another location, starting from the Eiffel tower, you can 'fly' this route on the screen. This is how you fly to the Arc de Triomphe:

☞ **Right-click 🅜**

☞ **Click**
    Directions from here

 Please note:

You will only find Directions from here in the menu if you place the mouse pointer on one of the symbols. If you want to plan a route from a different starting point, you need to use a marker. In the next section you will learn how to use markers.

The Directions tab will be opened and the starting point has already been entered:

At To :

⌨ **Type:** arc de triomphe

☞ **Click** 🔍

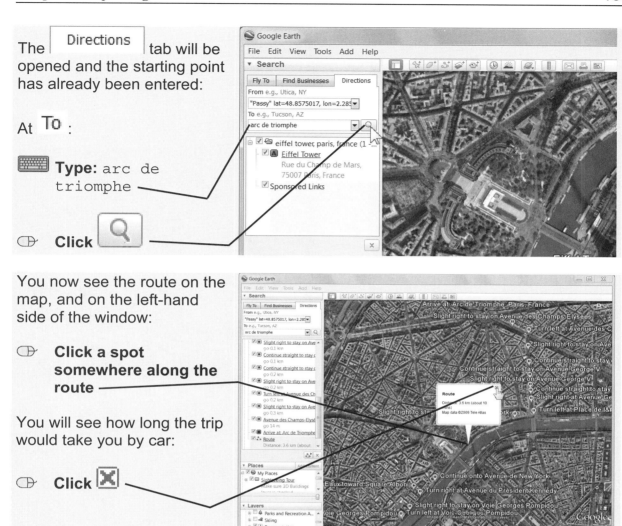

You now see the route on the map, and on the left-hand side of the window:

☞ **Click a spot somewhere along the route**

You will see how long the trip would take you by car:

☞ **Click** ☒

Tip

Measure the distance as the crow flies

The route planner will measure the distance by road. If you want to measure the distance between two locations in a straight line, you can use the ruler:

↪ **Click**

The mouse pointer will turn

into   :

↪ **Click** M

↪ **Click the Arc de Triomphe**

You will see the distance:

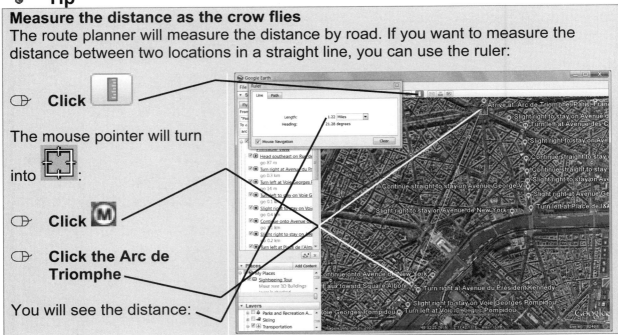

↪ **Click**

Now you will fly this route:

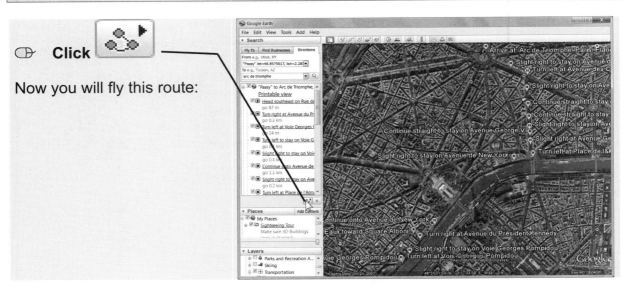

When you place the mouse pointer on a photo, you will see a video bar:

To stop the flight, you click . With you will fly forwards, with you fly backwards.

To remove the video bar:

☞ **Click** ✖

To delete the route:

☞ **Click** ✖

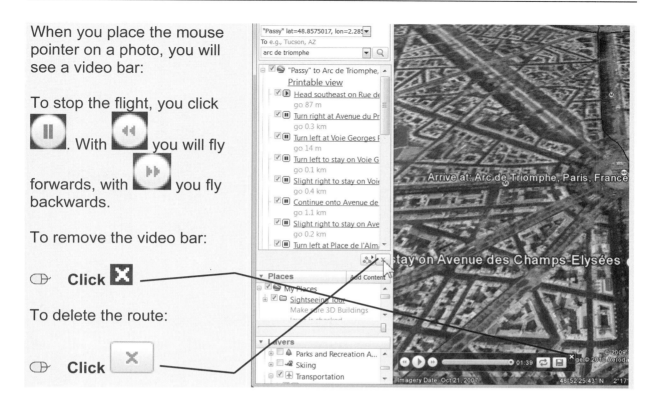

2.7 Marking Places

If you want to remember important places, you can add a placemark to them. This will make it easier to find them again:

☞ **Zoom in until you clearly see the Arc de Triomphe** 🐾5

☞ **If necessary, move the photo** 🐾6

By **Places**:

☞ **Click** 🌐 My Places

☞ **Click** 📌

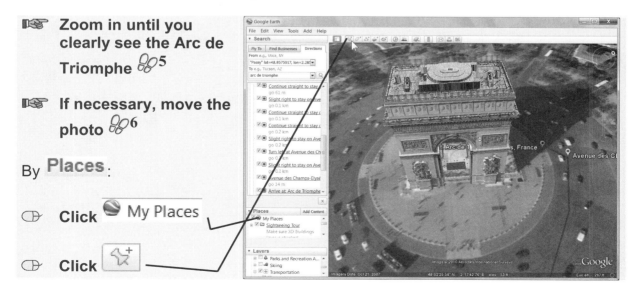

You now see a window:

By Name: .

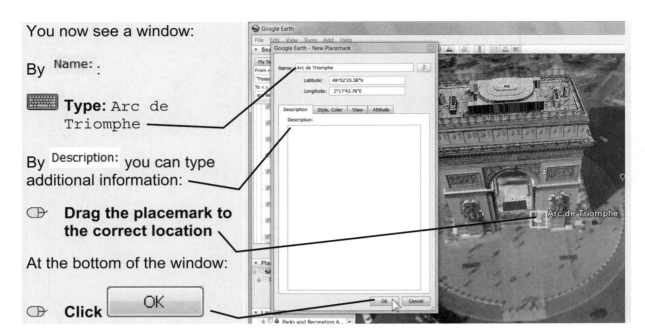

 Type: Arc de
Triomphe

By Description: you can type
additional information:

⊕ **Drag the placemark to
the correct location**

At the bottom of the window:

⊕ **Click** OK

💡 **Tip**

Mark your house or business
Add a placemark to your house or business. This way it will be easy to use these
locations as a starting point for your route.

Now you are going to visit another place first, for instance Disneyland Paris:

⊕ **Click the** Fly To **tab**

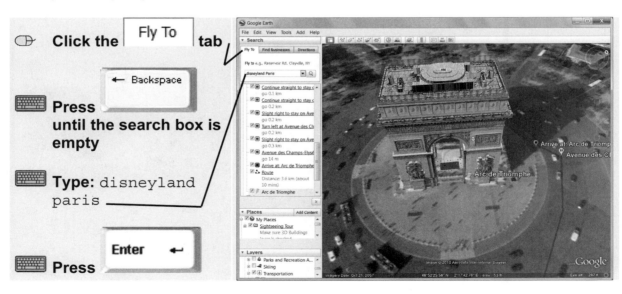

⌨ **Press** ← Backspace
**until the search box is
empty**

⌨ **Type:** disneyland
paris

⌨ **Press** Enter ↵

You now see different
locations again, but you want
to return directly to the Arc de
Triomphe:

By  :

☞ **If necessary, click ▼
until you see**
  🚩 Arc de Triomphe

☞ **Double-click**
  🚩 Arc de Triomphe

Now you will fly back to the
Arc de Triomphe.

To delete the information on
Disneyland Paris:

☞ **Click** ⎡×⎤

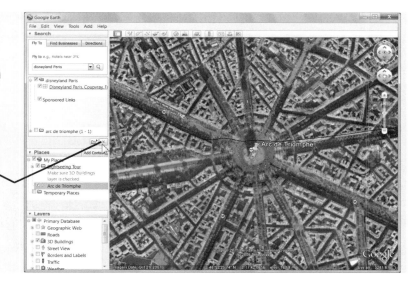

2.8 Up In Space

Google Earth does not just offer views of the earth, but you can also take a look at the moon, Mars, or the starry sky:

Click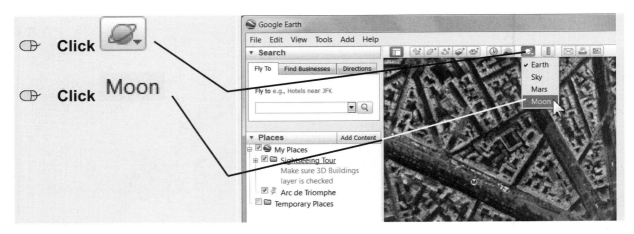

Click Moon

To hide the *Start-Up Tip*:

Click Close

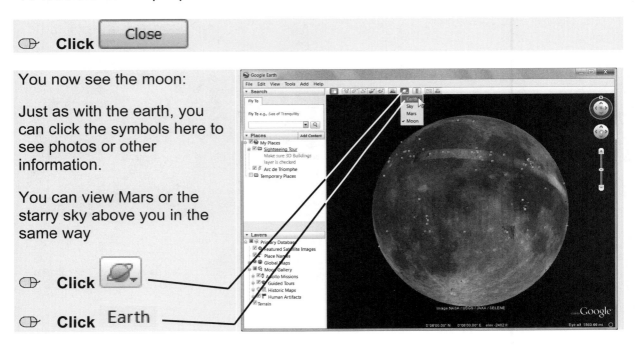

You now see the moon:

Just as with the earth, you can click the symbols here to see photos or other information.

You can view Mars or the starry sky above you in the same way

Click

Click Earth

To hide the *Start-Up Tip*:

Click Close

You now see the earth once more:

☞ **Click** [image]

This will display the day and night time areas on earth.

On the time bar:

☞ **Drag the slider to the left or to the right**

You will see a night shadow covering the earth.

☞ **Click** [image]

You can also go back in time a few years:

☞ **Click** [image]

☞ **Drag the slider to the left**

You will see the changes in the vegetation and the polar caps:

☞ **Click** [image]

☞ **Close** *Google Earth* ³

⚲ Tip

To Google Maps
You can switch directly from *Google Earth* to *Google Maps*:

⊕ **Click**

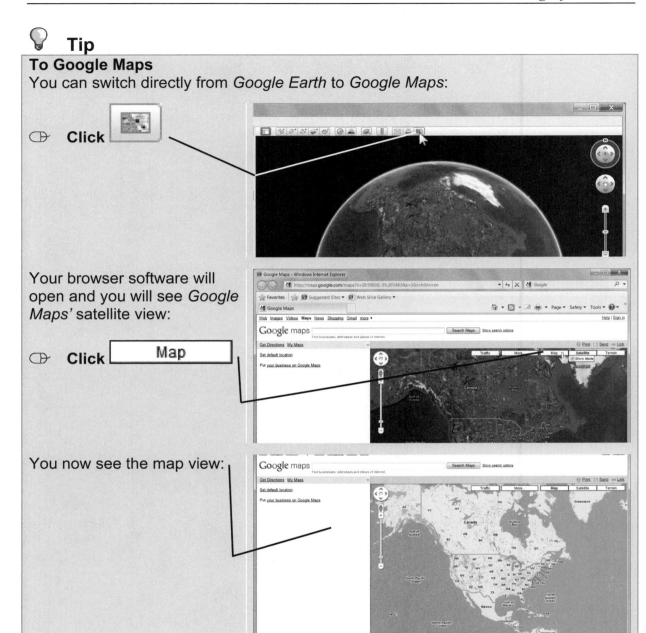

Your browser software will open and you will see *Google Maps'* satellite view:

⊕ **Click** | Map |

You now see the map view:

💡 Tip

Flight simulator
Google Earth contains a simple flight simulator.

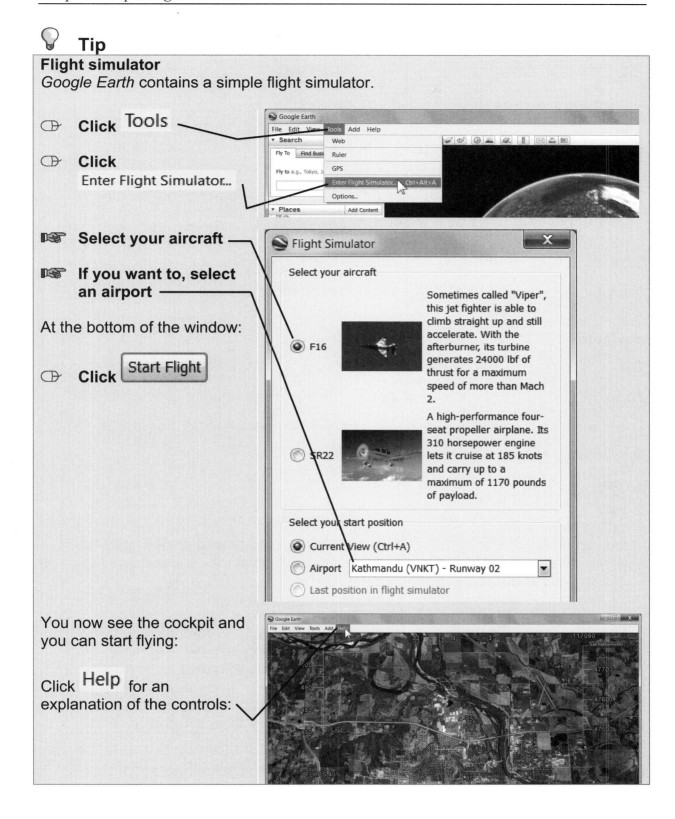

👉 **Click** Tools

👉 **Click**
Enter Flight Simulator...

☞ **Select your aircraft**

☞ **If you want to, select an airport**

At the bottom of the window:

👉 **Click** Start Flight

You now see the cockpit and you can start flying:

Click Help for an explanation of the controls:

2.9 Background Information

Dictionary	
Blur	To change parts of images or objects in such a way that they cannot be recognized (make them fuzzy or unfocused).
Default location	The starting point for your routes. You can set this location yourself and it will be displayed each time you open *Google Maps*.
Layers	Additional information which is projected on to a map or photo.
Mark	Add a placemark to a spot on the map or photo, so you can easily find it again.
Navigate	Move yourself around the map or photo.
Tilt	Change the angle for viewing an object.
Zoom in	Enlarge part of a map or image, to get a more detailed view.
Zoom out	Make part of a map or image smaller and less detailed.

Source: Google Help, Windows Help and Support, Wikipedia

Satellite photos
In the last few years the quality of satellite photos has improved so much, that you now can clearly recognize even the smallest detail. Sometimes you can even see your own car standing outside your door.

Google Earth acquires the best imagery available, which is also used by manufacturers of navigation systems. Most images are approximately one to three years old. It is not yet possible to render all the cities in high resolution (where you can distinguish individual buildings and cars). Currently more images are available of the United States than of other countries. Because the images are supplied by many different sources and need to be reassembled in a kind of mosaic, it is not easy to pin an exact date to the photos of a particular city or region. A city can consist of images that are made throughout a period of several months.

Some strategic objects, such as military facilities, are blurred. These objects will be displayed in a low resolution, as a result of which they will not be recognizable.

Google Earth versions
Google Earth offers entertainment and information for personal use. *Google Earth Pro* offers powerful functions for professional and commercial use. Although both products use the same images, their functions are quite different.

Google Earth (free version)
Intended for personal, non-commercial use, the free version of *Google Earth* sends you on an interactive, 3D exploration of the planet through terabytes of aerial and satellite imagery. You can zoom in on locations and display terrain and buildings in 3D, or look for hotels and restaurants. Apart from that, you can view various interesting data layers. The results are displayed in a 3D view of the earth. You can easily execute searches, save the results to folders, and share data with others. You can also import GPS data, which allows you to read tracks and waypoints from select GPS devices.

Google Earth Pro
For professional and commercial uses, *Google Earth Pro* is the ultimate research, presentation, and collaboration tool for geographic information. If you are using *Google Earth* for business purposes, *Pro* is the version for you. *Pro* includes all features available in the free version of *Google Earth*, plus the following:
- An area-measurement tool (that measures square feet, miles, acres, radii, etcetera).
- Data importing, which allows you to ingest up to 2,500 locations by address or by latitude/longitudinal coordinates.
- The highest resolution printing and saving capabilities, which enable larger, clearer printouts (up to 4,800 pixels).
- *Movie maker*, which allows you to export movies of zooms and tours.
- GIS data import, which allows you to drag and drop SHP files, *GeoTiffs*, etcetera.
- Premium printing, which enables you to print high-resolution images up to 11" x 17" (4,800 pixels).

At http://earth.google.com you will find more information on *Google Earth Pro*.

Source: Google Help

2.10 Tips

 Tip

Plan the return journey
To plan the journey home you do not need to enter the route all over again:

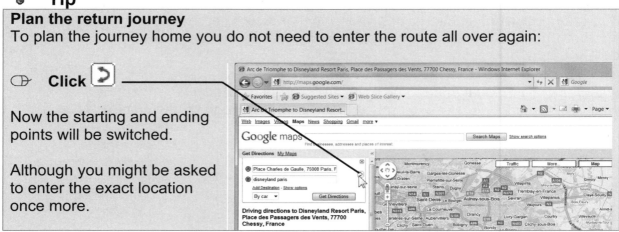

☞ **Click** [↰]

Now the starting and ending points will be switched.

Although you might be asked to enter the exact location once more.

 Tip

Different routes
If it is possible to use different routes, *Google Maps* will display the shortest route. If you want, you can select one of the other routes:

You will see the route that is displayed:

If you want to use a different route, click one of the routes at **Suggested routes**.

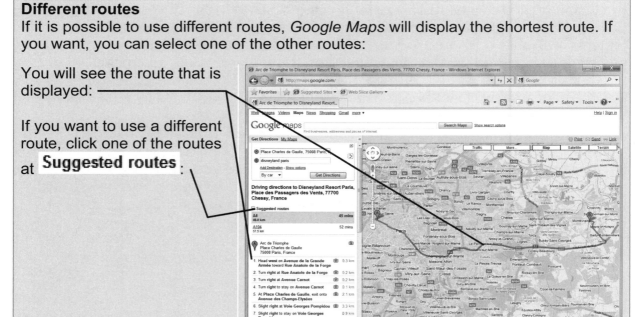

Tip

Creating, editing, and sharing 3D models
With *Google SketchUp* you can create your own 3D models for *Google Earth*, but you can also use this program to design a building. At http://sketchup.google.com you can download *Google SketchUp* for free.

 Tip

Layers
Google Earth is put at the user's disposal for free, by the *Google* company. This huge investment is financed by a number of commercial activities. For instance, businesses must pay advertizing fees in order to be listed in *Google Earth*.

At the bottom left of your window, under **Layers** and ⌐ **Places of Interest**, you can select the restaurants, shopping malls, etcetera and view them: —

 Tip

Sightseeing
You can also take a trip to various well-known places on the planet. These places have already been marked in *Google Earth*.

By **Places** :

☞ **Check the box ☑ next to** Sightseeing Tour

☞ **Click** 📁▸

Now a tour will start which will guide you to various places of interest:

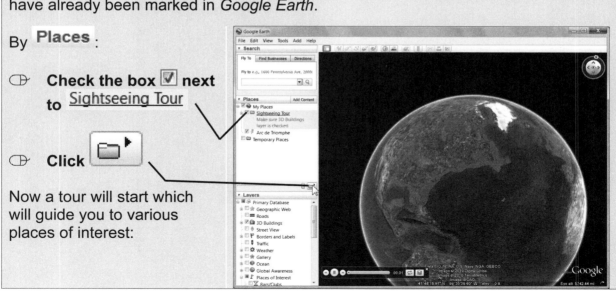

Tip

Photos in Google Earth
You can also view many photos (made by other users) of different locations. First, you will need to activate the *Panoramio* (photo-sharing community) layer:

At the bottom left of your window, under **Layers**, the ▣ Panoramio option should be checked.

The photos in *Google Earth* are indicated by ▮:

On the www.panoramio.com webpage you can upload your own photos to *Google Earth*.

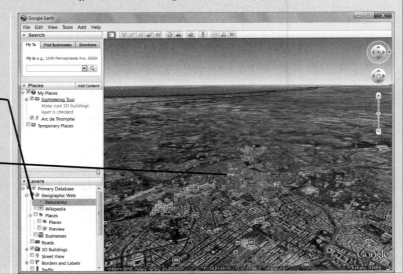

3. Mail and Surf with Google

Internet Explorer is one of the best-known programs for surfing the Internet. Many people who use webmail often have a *Hotmail* or *Live Mail* e-mail address. Since both of these tasks can be accomplished just as easily with free *Google* programs, why not give them a try?

You can use your *Google* account to create a *Gmail* e-mail address. It is very easy to manage, store and organize your messages in *Gmail*. You can even store the same message in different subject folders, so you will not have to worry where to store the message. You can add references to the message in all folders, so you can always retrieve the message from each folder. Important messages are marked by a star. Also, you can gather various messages that are part of the same conversation, and keep them together. In *Gmail*, you can follow all the e-mail messages that are part of the same conversation, because *Gmail* groups these messages for you.

Google has also created a web browser application called *Chrome*. You can use *Chrome* to surf the Internet. The program has a nice interface and is easy to use. If you already have experience with *Internet Explorer* or one of the other web browsers, learning how to use *Google Chrome* will be a snap. Since the program is much smaller than *Internet Explorer* it also operates faster. And you can customize the program yourself by changing its appearance.

In this chapter you will learn how to:

- sign up for *Gmail*;
- create and send messages;
- open messages and send a reply;
- categorize your e-mail messages by using labels and stars;
- store messages;
- delete and restore messages;
- filter your e-mail messages;
- add and group contacts;
- install *Google Chrome*;
- set a new home page;
- select a theme;
- bookmark a page;
- delete your browser history.

➥ Please note:

You will need a *Google* account to perform the operations in this chapter. If you do not yet have one, read *Appendix A Creating a Google Account* first, and learn how to create an account.

➥ Please note:

The exercises in this chapter require some experience in the use of e-mail programs and web browsers. This is why the basic operations will not be fully explained, and will only be referred to if they differ from other programs.

➥ Please note:

In this chapter you will see screen shots from the *Gmail* and *Google Chrome* programs. Because these programs are subject to regular changes, the screen shots may differ from your own screen. Usually this does not affect the operation of the programs.

3.1 Sign Up for Gmail

Gmail is *Google's* e-mail program. If you want to use this program, you will need to sign in first:

☞ **Open** *Internet Explorer* ¹

☞ **Browse to www.google.com** ²

 Click Gmail

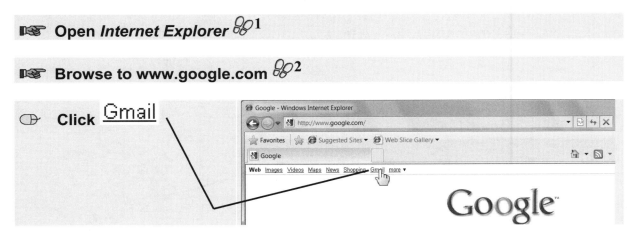

In the right-hand side of the window:

By Username:.

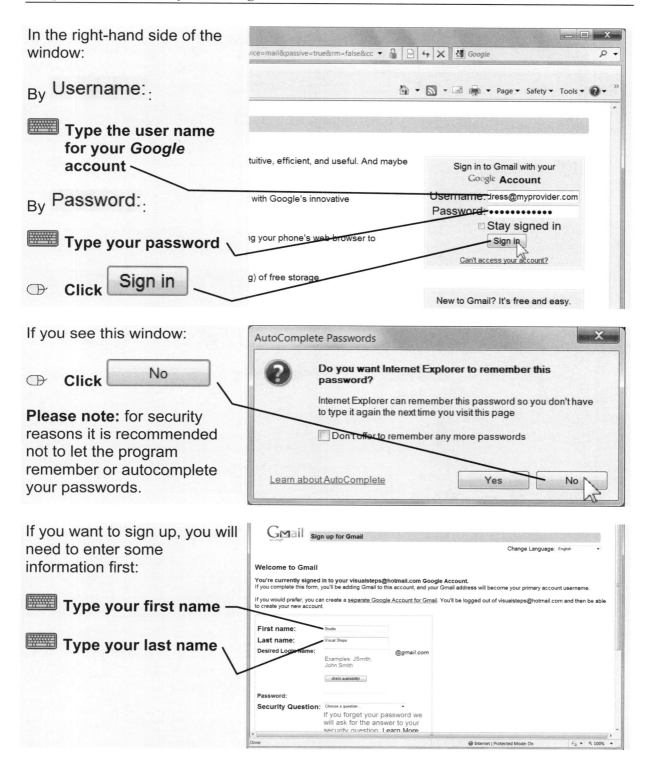

⌨ **Type the user name for your *Google* account**

By Password:.

⌨ **Type your password**

☞ **Click** Sign in

If you see this window:

☞ **Click** No

Please note: for security reasons it is recommended not to let the program remember or autocomplete your passwords.

If you want to sign up, you will need to enter some information first:

⌨ **Type your first name**

⌨ **Type your last name**

⌨ **Type the desired user name for this account**

The *Gmail* domain name, *@gmail.com*, will complete the potential new account:

☞ **Click**

  check availability!

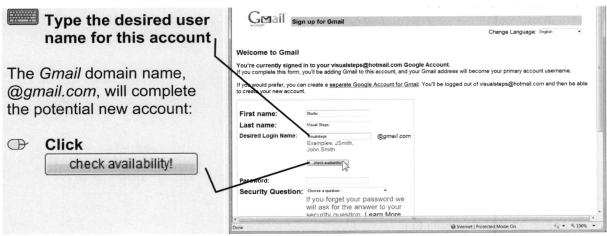

☞ **Drag the scroll bar downwards**

If the name is already in use, you will see
visualsteps is not available, but the following usernames are:
followed by some alternative suggestions:

⌨ **Type a different user name**

☞ **Click**

  check availability!

Or:

☞ **Click a radio button ⦿ next to one of the suggested user names**

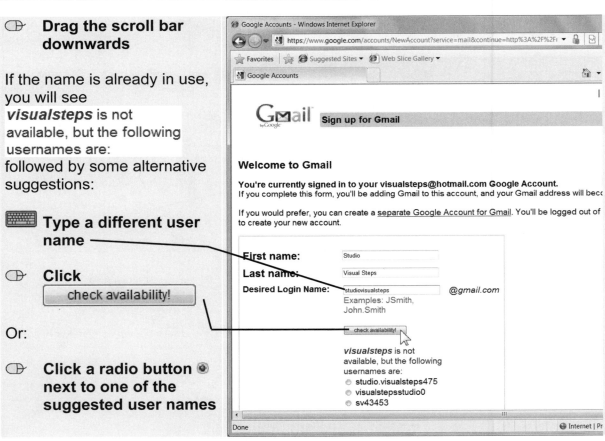

If that name is still available,
you will see

visualsteps1 is available .

☞ **Drag the scroll bar
downwards**

⌨ **Type a password**

☞ **Click**
Choose a question ...

☞ **Click**
Write my own question

⌨ **Type your question**

⌨ **Type the answer**

☞ **Click** Continue

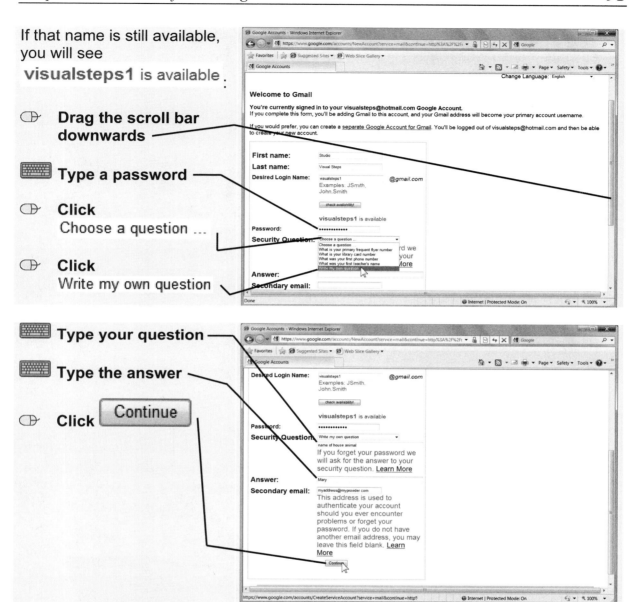

First, you will need to request a verification code which will be sent to your mobile phone:

☞ **Select your country**

⌨ **Type your mobile phone number**

👆 **Click**

> Send verification code to

Now you will receive an SMS message containing your code:

⌨ **Type the code**

👆 **Click** Verify

If you have successfully signed up, you will see:

👆 **Click**

> **Show me my account »**

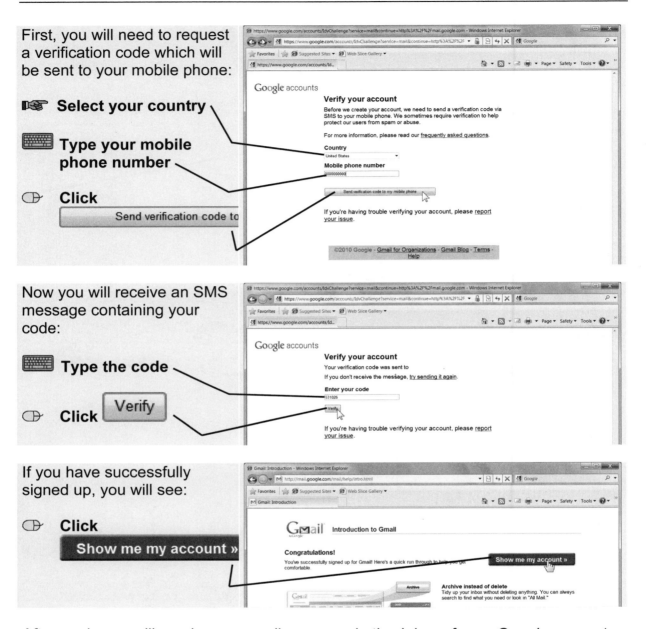

Afterwards you will receive an e-mail message in the *Inbox* of your *Google* account. You will not see the message in this window, because it will be placed in the *Inbox* of the *Google* account you have just created.

You may see this window:

👆 **Click**
Nah, go to my inbox

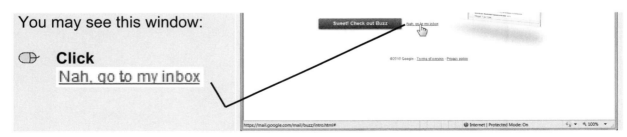

Now you will see the *Inbox*:

In the *Inbox* you will see a welcome message:

☞ **Click the first message**

Please note: you might see multiple or different messages on your own screen.

You will see the contents of the message:

To return to the *Inbox*:

☞ **Click « Back to Inbox**

Or:

☞ **Click Inbox**

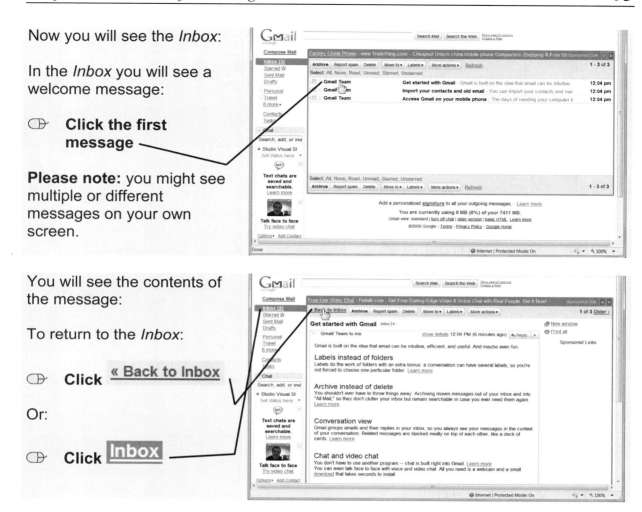

3.2 Send and Receive Mail

Now you are going to send a message to yourself:

☞ **Click Compose Mail**

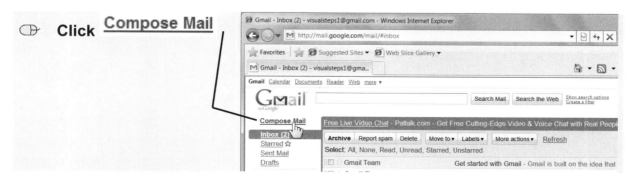

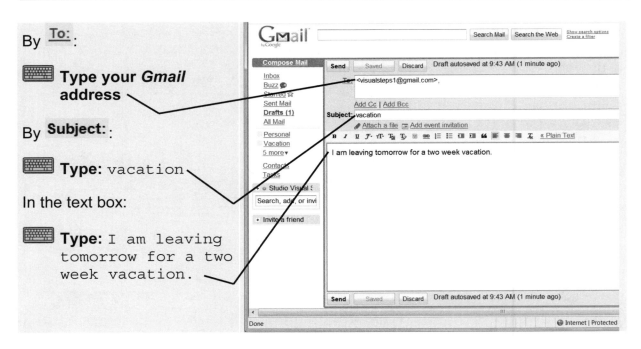

By **To:** :

Type your *Gmail* address

By **Subject:** :

Type: vacation

In the text box:

Type: I am leaving tomorrow for a two week vacation.

While composing a message you can use the text formatting buttons on the bar above the message. Most of these buttons should look familiar. They are similar to several other e-mail programs and text editors.

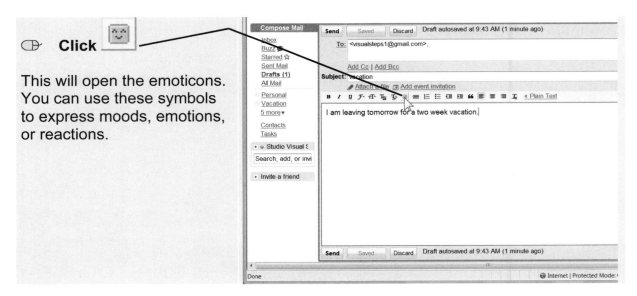

☞ **Click**

This will open the emoticons. You can use these symbols to express moods, emotions, or reactions.

⟡ **Click an appropriate emoticon, for instance**

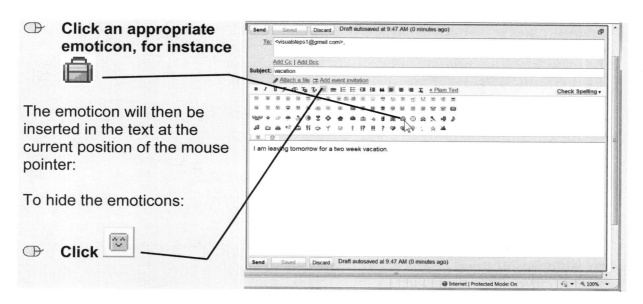

The emoticon will then be inserted in the text at the current position of the mouse pointer:

To hide the emoticons:

⟡ **Click**

Before sending the message, you can check the spelling. To try this out, first make a spelling mistake:

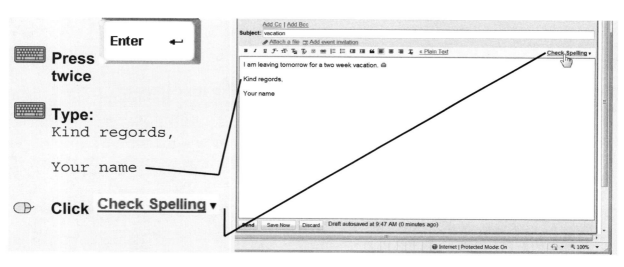

⌨ **Press** **Enter** ⏎ **twice**

⌨ **Type:**
Kind regords,

Your name

⟡ **Click Check Spelling ▾**

💡 **Tip**

Other language

To select a different language, first click ▼ by **Check Spelling ▾**.

Unknown words will be marked in yellow:

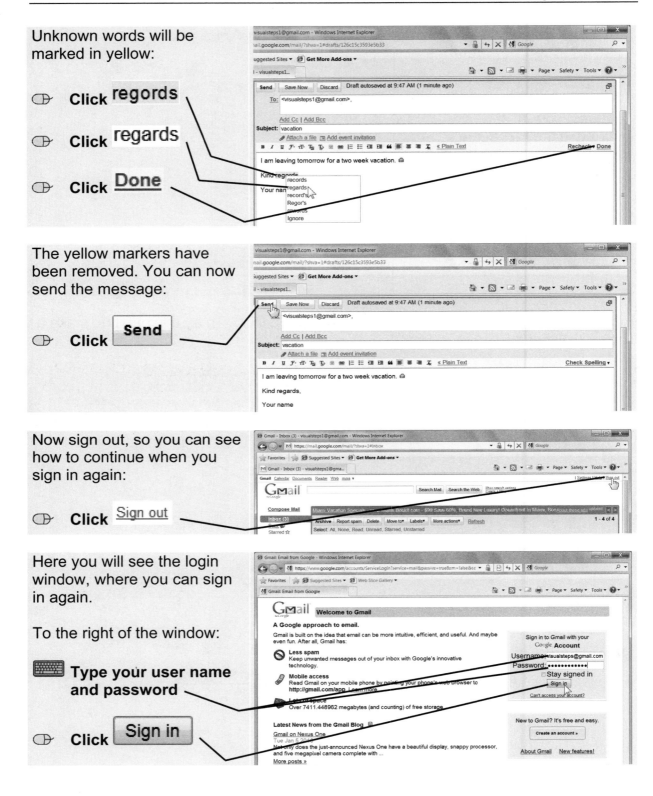

Click regords

Click regards

Click Done

The yellow markers have been removed. You can now send the message:

Click Send

Now sign out, so you can see how to continue when you sign in again:

Click Sign out

Here you will see the login window, where you can sign in again.

To the right of the window:

Type your user name and password

Click Sign in

Tip

Disable password autocomplete
Do you see the *AutoComplete Passwords* window each time you sign in? This is how you disable this function:

☞ **Check the box** ☑ **next to**
    Don't offer to remember any

☞ **Click** [No]

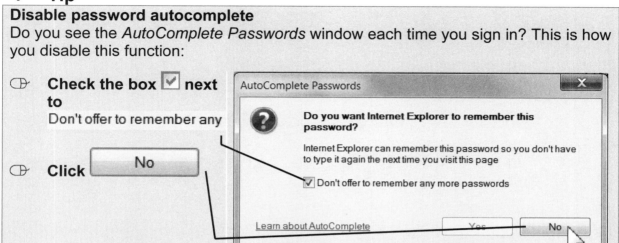

Here you see the message you have sent to yourself:

At the top of the *Inbox* you will see a bar with some ads. The *Gmail* service is financed by advertizing.

Here the sender has been automatically changed to **me** , but that line could have contained an e-mail address as well.

☞ **Click your message**

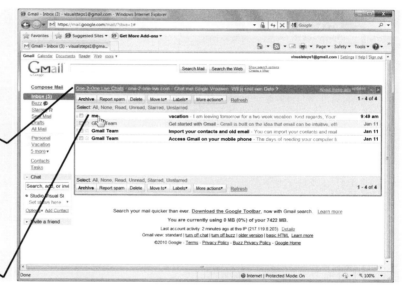

You will see your message:

Now you are going to reply to this message:

👆 **Click** ↰ <u>Reply</u>

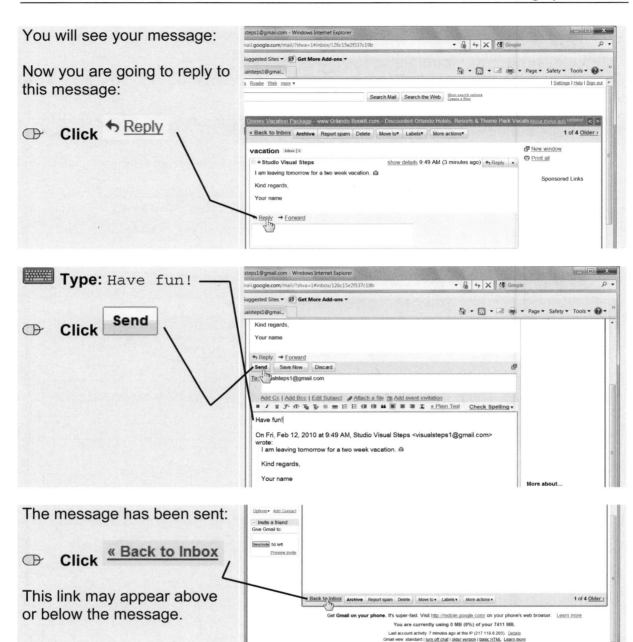

⌨ **Type:** Have fun!

👆 **Click** **Send**

The message has been sent:

👆 **Click** **« Back to Inbox**

This link may appear above or below the message.

You now see a (2) appended
to the message:

☞ **Click your message**

A group of messages that belong together is called a conversation.
In *Gmail*, messages that belong together will automatically be saved together. This
allows you to follow the full conversation regarding a particular subject very easily.

Here you can see the original message and the reply to this message:

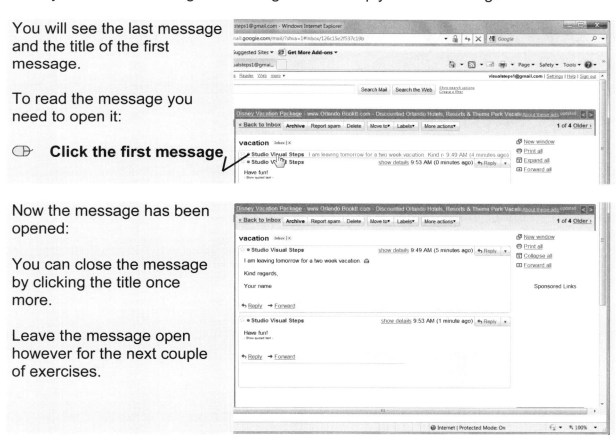

You will see the last message
and the title of the first
message.

To read the message you
need to open it:

☞ **Click the first message**

Now the message has been
opened:

You can close the message
by clicking the title once
more.

Leave the message open
however for the next couple
of exercises.

In this example you have seen that *Google* can easily group and store messages that
are part of the same conversation. This may come in handy when you send the same
message to a large number of people who are all going to reply to your message.
You will find all these messages in the same conversation.

3.3 Categorizing with Labels and Stars

You can categorize your e-mail messages in a variety of ways. In *Gmail* you can use labels and stars for this purpose:

- Use labels to categorize your messages by subject.
- Use stars to mark important messages, or messages that need your attention.

 Please note:

Labels and stars are merely references to certain messages. The original message will always be stored in the *All Mail* folder (which you will learn to use later on). So, by classifying a message you will not move the message to a different location.

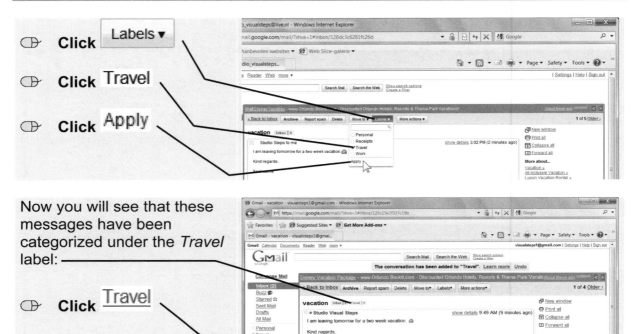

Click Labels ▾

Click Travel

Click Apply

Now you will see that these messages have been categorized under the *Travel* label:

Click Travel

A message can contain multiple labels. You can even create your own labels:

First, you need to select the message or the conversation for which you want to create a new label:

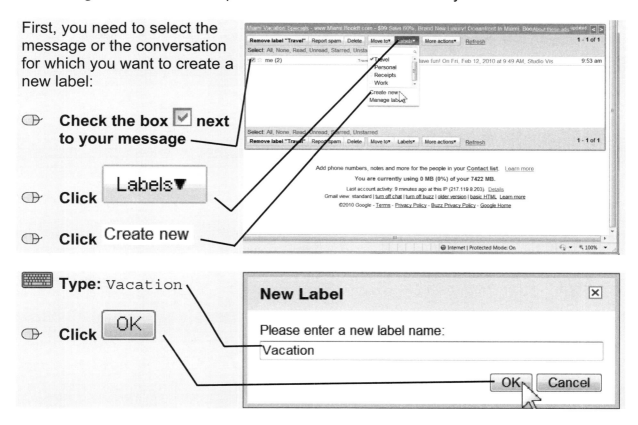

☞ **Check the box ☑ next to your message**

☞ **Click** Labels▼

☞ **Click** Create new

⌨ **Type:** Vacation

☞ **Click** OK

Now the full conversation has acquired the *Vacation* label as well. You can remove the *Travel* label from this conversation:

☞ **Click**

Remove label "Travel"

Please note: make sure the conversation is still selected.

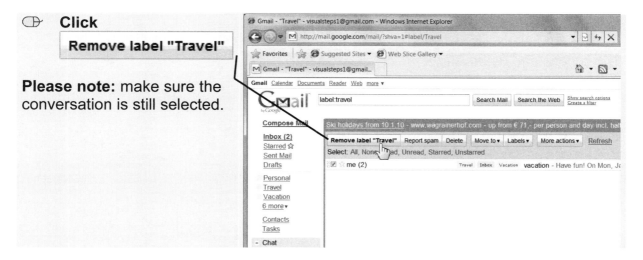

Tip

Removing labels from open messages
If a message has been opened, you can also remove the labels in this way:

Above the message you will
see the labels:

Next to the label you want to
remove:

☞ **Click** ✕

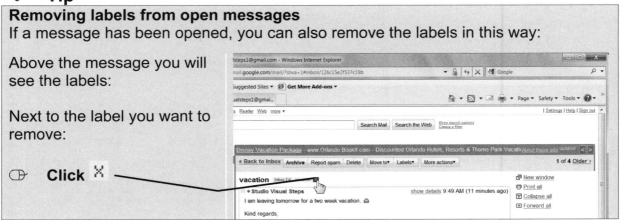

The *Travel* label does not
refer to a conversation
anymore:

☞ **Click** Vacation

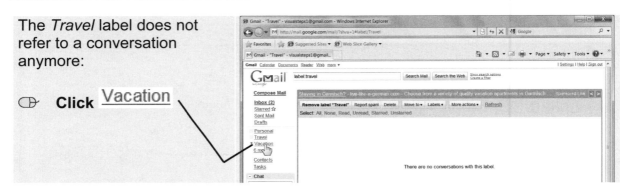

Here you will still see the
conversation.

If, from now on, you want to
use *Vacation* instead of
Travel, you can delete the
Travel label:

☞ **Click** Labels▼

☞ **Click** Manage labels

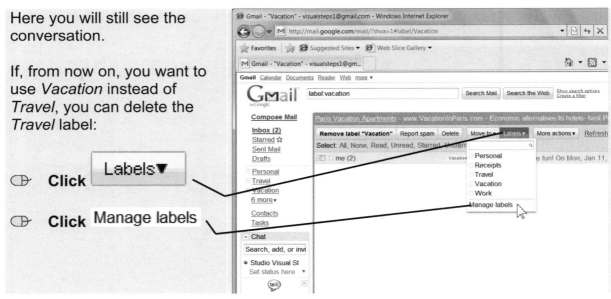

Here you will see the labels which are shown and the ones that are hidden:

First you will see the system labels. You cannot delete them, only show or hide them.

By **All Mail** :

☞ **Click** show

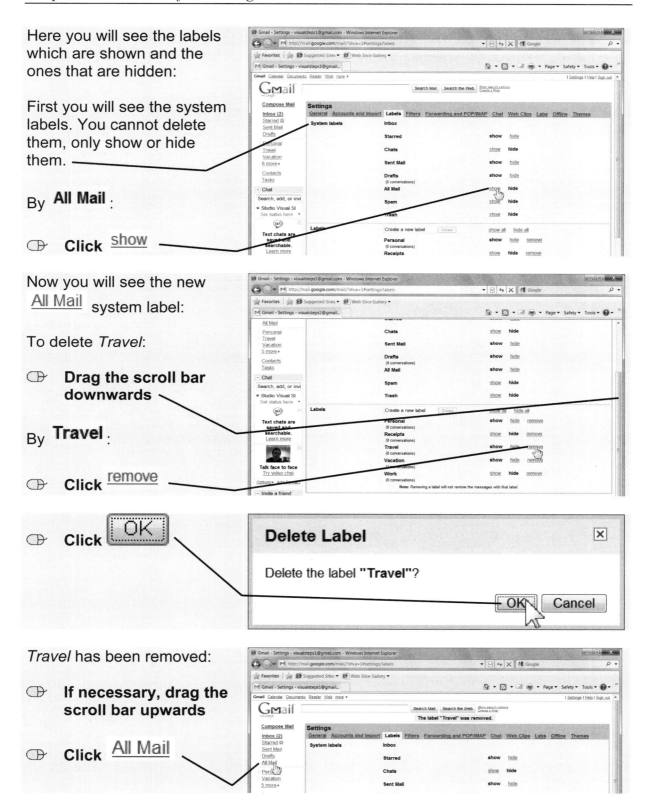

Now you will see the new All Mail system label:

To delete *Travel*:

☞ **Drag the scroll bar downwards**

By **Travel** :

☞ **Click** remove

☞ **Click** OK

Delete Label   ✕

Delete the label **"Travel"**?

                                          OK   Cancel

Travel has been removed:

☞ **If necessary, drag the scroll bar upwards**

☞ **Click** All Mail

In the *All Mail* folder you will find all sent and received messages which have not been deleted. If you think a specific message or conversation is important, you can mark it with a star:

You will see all messages and conversations:

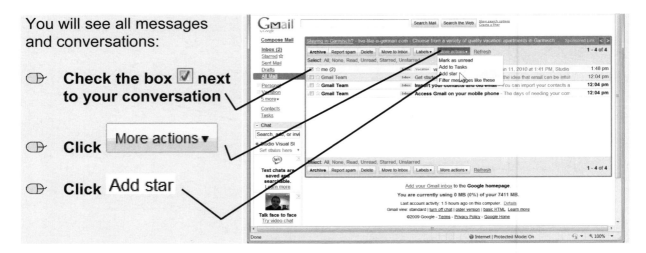

☞ **Check the box ✓ next to your conversation**

☞ **Click** More actions ▼

☞ **Click** Add star

The star will be added to the conversations and messages you have selected.

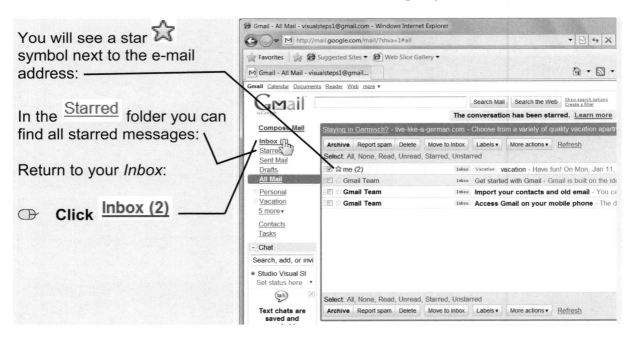

You will see a star ☆ symbol next to the e-mail address: ──────

In the Starred folder you can find all starred messages:

Return to your *Inbox*:

☞ **Click** Inbox (2)

Now you will see the messages in the *Inbox*:

After you have read the messages, you can archive them. You will need to select them first:

☞ **Click** **All**,

☞ **Click** **Archive**

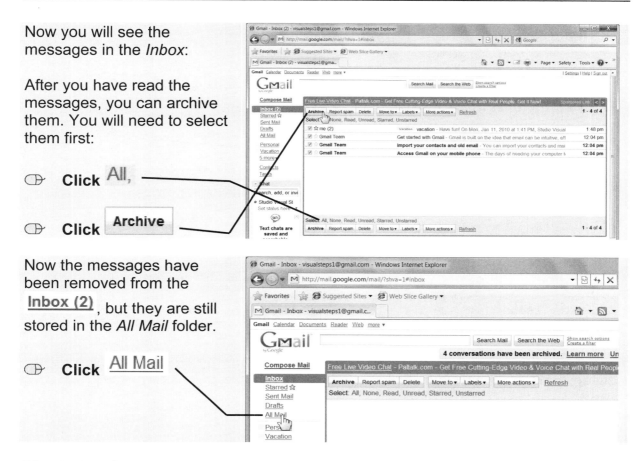

Now the messages have been removed from the **Inbox (2)**, but they are still stored in the *All Mail* folder.

☞ **Click** All Mail

The *All Mail* folder contains all the messages you have sent and received, but have not yet deleted. To remove a single message from a conversation, you need to open the conversation first:

In the *All Mail* folder you will still see the messages:

☞ **Click your conversation**

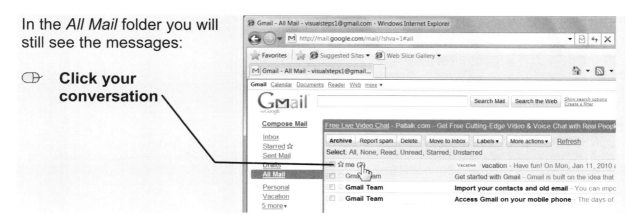

Open the message you want to delete. Now you are going to delete the first message:

⊕ **Click the first message**

⊕ **Click** ▼

⊕ **Click**
      Delete this message

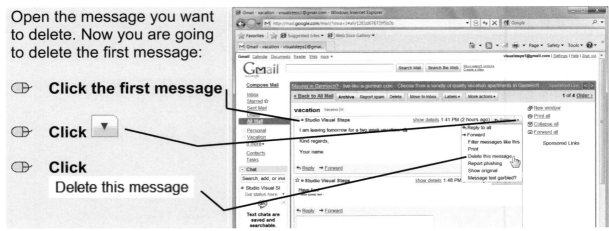

The message has been deleted. The other message in this conversation has not been deleted.

You will find the deleted messages in the *Trash* folder:

⊕ **Click** 5 more▼

You may see a different number on your screen, or the Trash folder may already be visible.

⊕ **Click** Trash

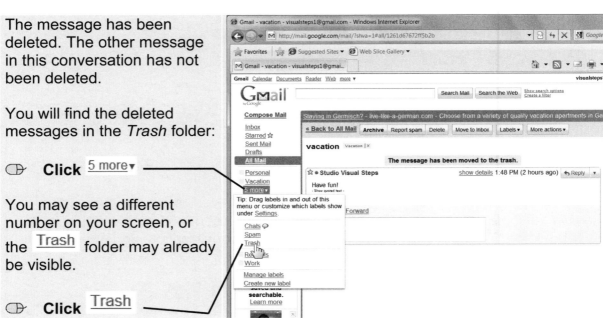

➜ **Please note:**

After 30 days, *Gmail* will automatically and permanently delete all messages in the *Trash* folder.

To empty the entire *Trash* folder, click
Empty Trash now :

If you want to delete one of the messages manually, you need to check the box ☑ next to the message, and then click **Delete forever** :

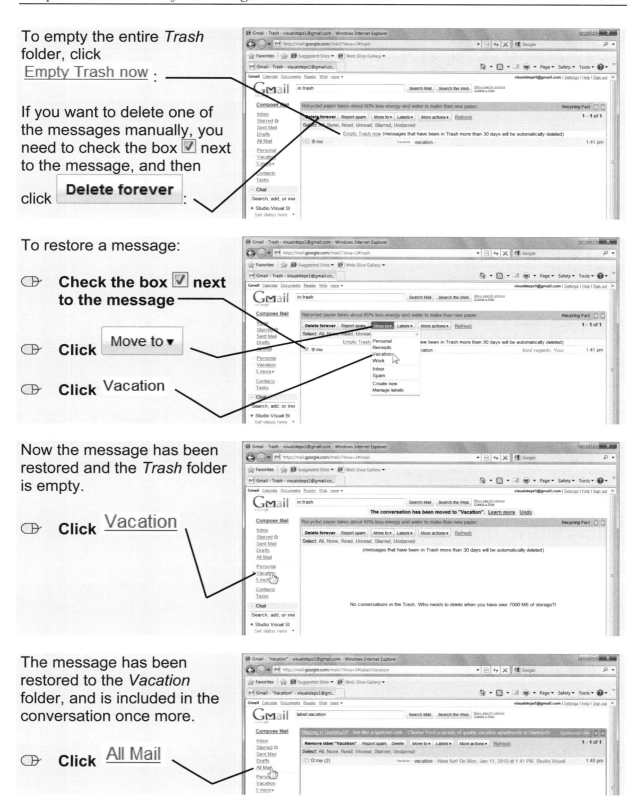

To restore a message:

☞ **Check the box ☑ next to the message**

☞ **Click** Move to ▾

☞ **Click** Vacation

Now the message has been restored and the *Trash* folder is empty.

☞ **Click** Vacation

The message has been restored to the *Vacation* folder, and is included in the conversation once more.

☞ **Click** All Mail

In the *Vacation* folder you will only see a reference. The actual message can be found in All Mail. The message has automatically been restored to that folder:

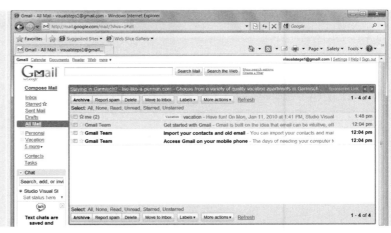

🩹 HELP! I can only find a single message.

If you have restored a message to the *All Mail* folder and afterwards see only a single message, the information in the window most likely needs to be refreshed:

☞ **Click** Refresh

3.4 Creating Filters

Filters will search your messages for specific words, subjects, addressees, or senders. When the message is found, *Gmail* can directly save it to the correct folder, and add a label or a star to the message.

☞ **Click** Create a filter

By **Subject:** :

⌨ **Type:** Vacation

☞ **Click** Test Search

Now you will see the
messages and conversations
with 'vacation' as a subject:

☞ **Click** Next Step »

Here you can determine what
to do with the messages that
match your filter's criteria:

You can select multiple
options.

☞ **Click** Choose label...

☞ **Click** Vacation

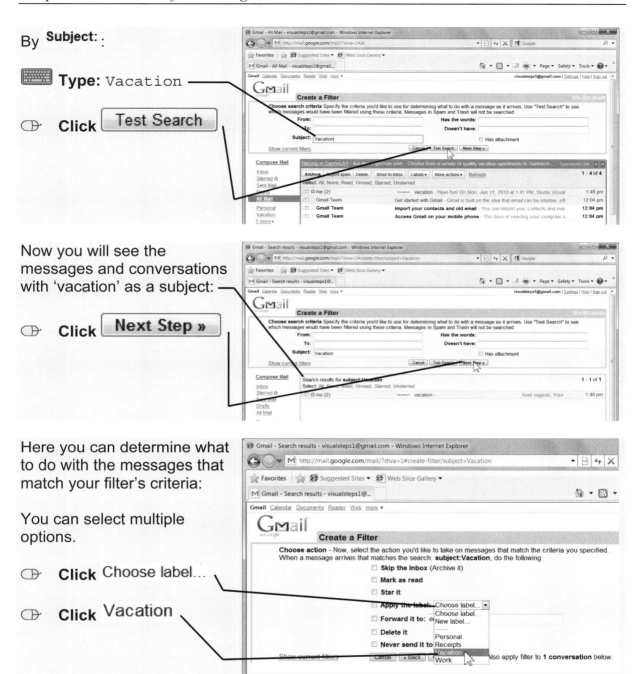

The existing messages with this subject are already labeled *Vacation*. If that is not yet the case, check the box ☑ next to
Also apply filter to **1 conversation** bel

☞ **Click** Create Filter

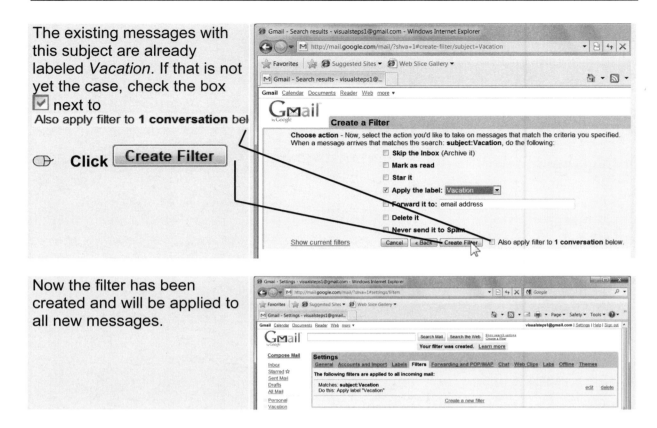

Now the filter has been created and will be applied to all new messages.

3.5 Contacts

You can save all persons or companies with whom you have regular correspondence as *contacts*. This means you will not have to type their full address every time you want to send them a message.

☞ **Click** <u>Contacts</u>

You most likely will not see any contacts yet. But your window may already show a few contacts.

You are going to add your own name as a family member:

Click **Family**

Click **+ &**

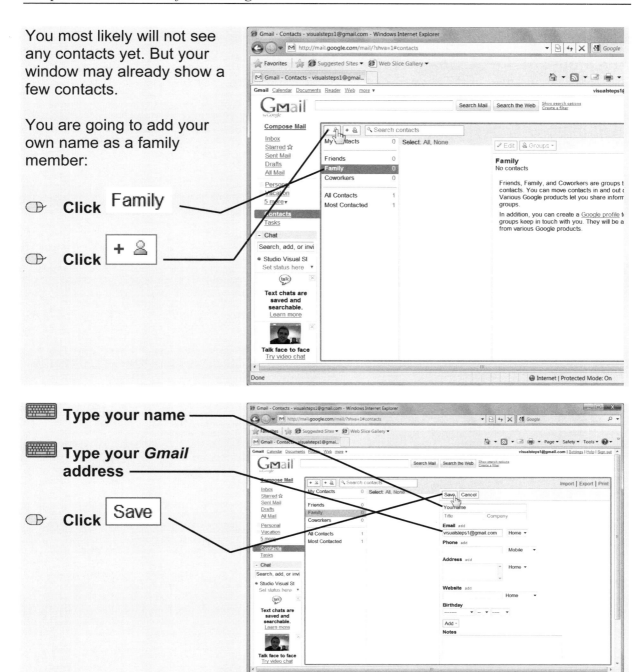

Type your name

Type your *Gmail* address

Click **Save**

💡 Tip

Add groups
The *Friends*, *Family* and *Coworkers* groups are standard groups. This is how you create new groups:

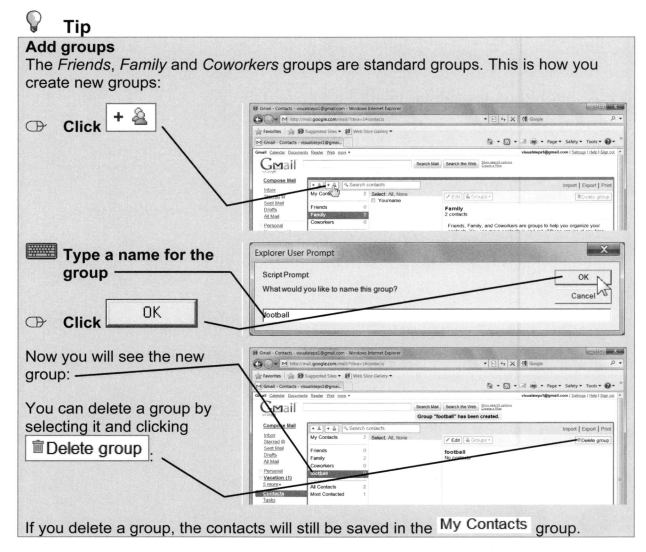

⊕ **Click**

⌨ **Type a name for the group**

⊕ **Click** OK

Now you will see the new group:

You can delete a group by selecting it and clicking 🗑 Delete group :

If you delete a group, the contacts will still be saved in the My Contacts group.

Your information have been added:

Now you can select this group when you compose a new message:

⊕ **Click** Compose Mail

Click To:

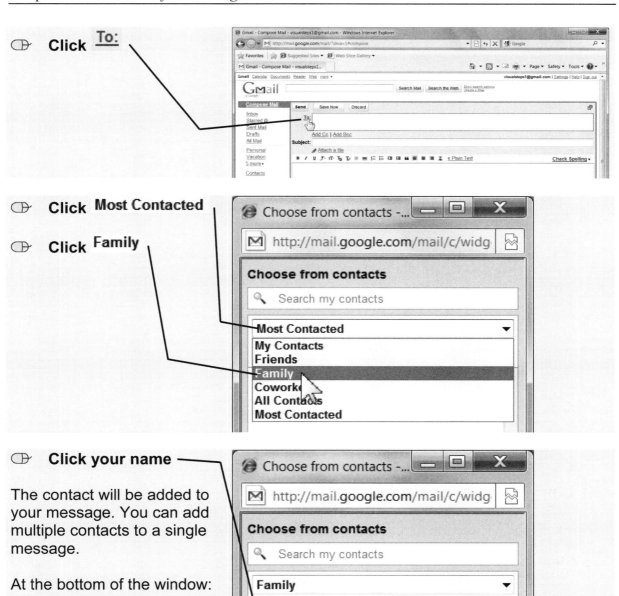

Click Most Contacted

Click Family

Click your name

The contact will be added to your message. You can add multiple contacts to a single message.

At the bottom of the window:

Click Done

Tip

Finding contacts
If you do not know in which group your contact is located, you can search for it:

By 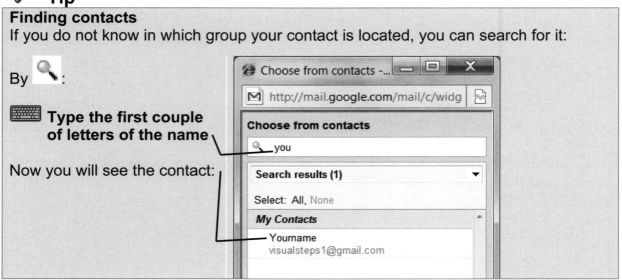 :

⌨ **Type the first couple of letters of the name**

Now you will see the contact:

The contact is now set to receive this message:

By **Subject:** :

⌨ **Type:** Vacation

⌨ **Type:** Have a nice holiday!

☞ **Click** Send

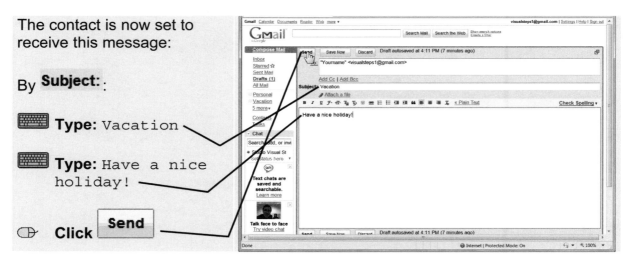

Now you will see the *All Mail* window, and after a short while you will see the message you have sent:

☞ **Click** Vacation (1)

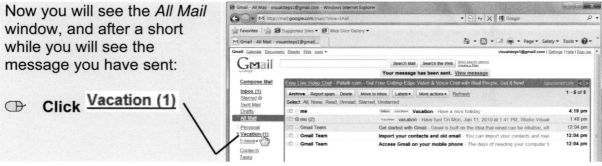

The *Vacation* filter created in the previous section places the message in the *Vacation* folder:

☞ **Click** Inbox (1)

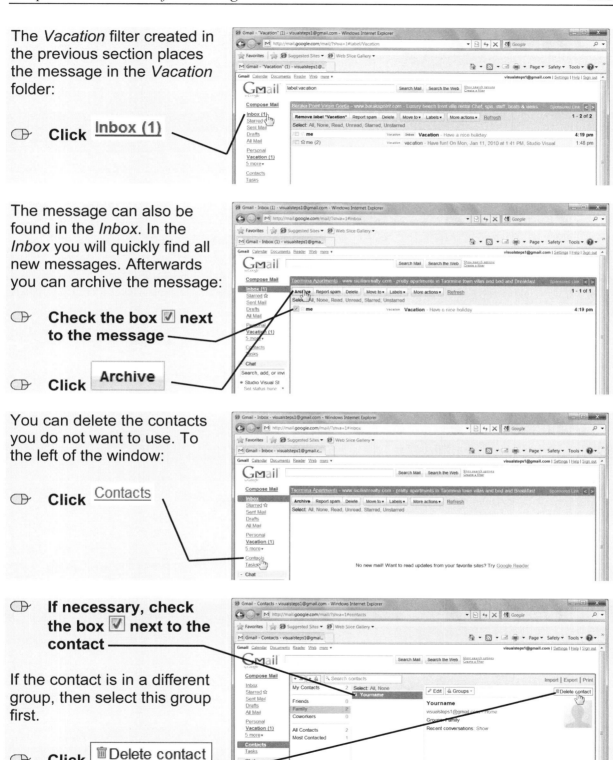

The message can also be found in the *Inbox*. In the *Inbox* you will quickly find all new messages. Afterwards you can archive the message:

☞ **Check the box ☑ next to the message**

☞ **Click** **Archive**

You can delete the contacts you do not want to use. To the left of the window:

☞ **Click** Contacts

☞ **If necessary, check the box ☑ next to the contact**

If the contact is in a different group, then select this group first.

☞ **Click** 🗑 Delete contact

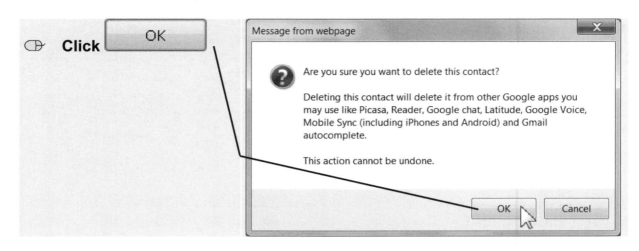

Click `OK`

Message from webpage

Are you sure you want to delete this contact?

Deleting this contact will delete it from other Google apps you may use like Picasa, Reader, Google chat, Latitude, Google Voice, Mobile Sync (including iPhones and Android) and Gmail autocomplete.

This action cannot be undone.

`OK` `Cancel`

💡 **Tip**

Use the search box
Here you can search for the contact as well:

At :

⌨ **Type the first couple of letters of the name**

Now you will see the contact:

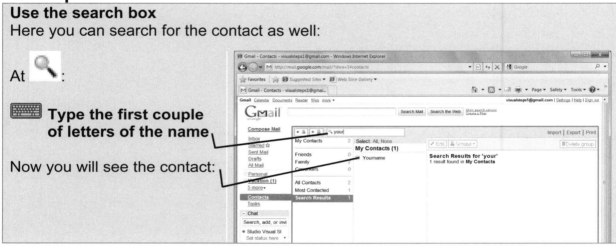

At this point you have learned to use *Gmail's* main functions. When you have finished, you can sign out:

Click `Sign out`

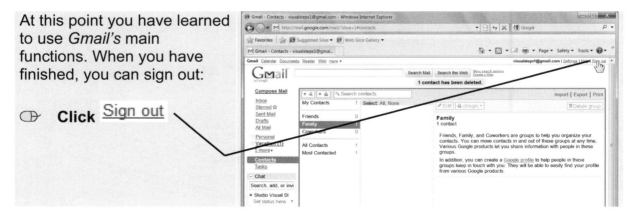

3.6 Set Google Chrome As Your Web Browser

In addition to the well-known, popular web browsers such as *Internet Explorer* and *Firefox*, you may find it fun and interesting to surf the web with a new kid on the block: *Google Chrome*. This is how you install the web browser application:

☞ **Browse to www.google.com/options** ᏗᏗ2

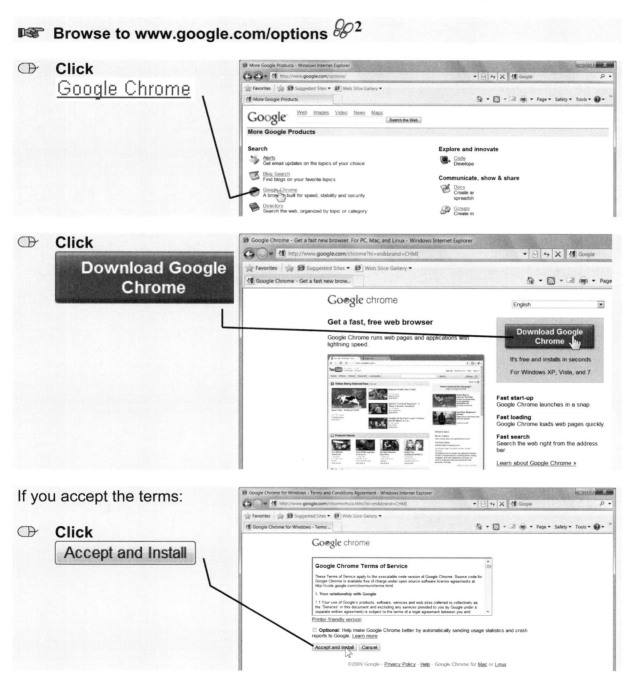

Click
Google Chrome

Click
Download Google Chrome

If you accept the terms:

Click
Accept and Install

During the download and install process, you will see this window:

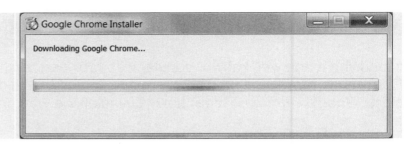

If you want to try out *Google Chrome* first, do not set it as your default browser:

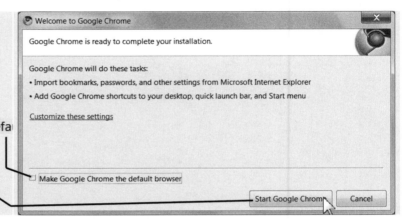

☞ **Uncheck the box** ☑
next to
Make Google Chrome the defa

☞ **Click**

    Start Google Chrome

Now the favorites and a number of other settings will automatically be imported from *Internet Explorer*.

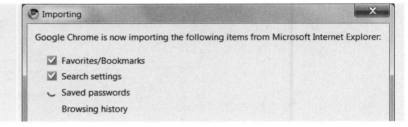

You will see the web browser and its home page:

First, close *Google Chrome* and all other windows:

☞ **Close all windows** ⏀³

3.7 Setting a Home Page

Using *Google Chrome* to surf the web is much the same as using any of the other web browsers, such as *Internet Explorer* and *Firefox*. By clicking the icons you will quickly learn how to use the program. In the next section you will learn about some of the operations and functions that are different from the other web browsers.

On your desktop you see a shortcut to *Google Chrome*:

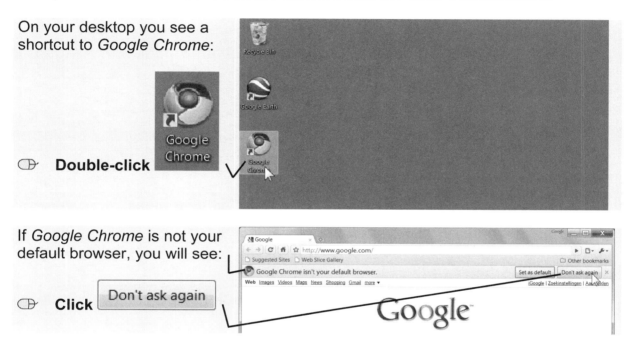

☞ **Double-click**

If *Google Chrome* is not your default browser, you will see:

☞ **Click** Don't ask again

Now you are going to change the home page:

In the address bar:

⌨ **Type:** visual steps

⌨ **Press** Enter ↵

The address bar is also a search box. If you do not type a web address, you will see the search results for your keyword:

⊕ **Click**

    Visual Steps, books for the beginni

Now you will see the Visual Steps website. To set this web page as your home page:

⊕ **Click**

⊕ **Click** Options

⊕ **Click the radio button next to** ◉
    Open the following pages:

⊕ **Click** Use Current

You will see the Visual Steps website address:

To set *Google* as a second home page:

⊕ **Click** Add...

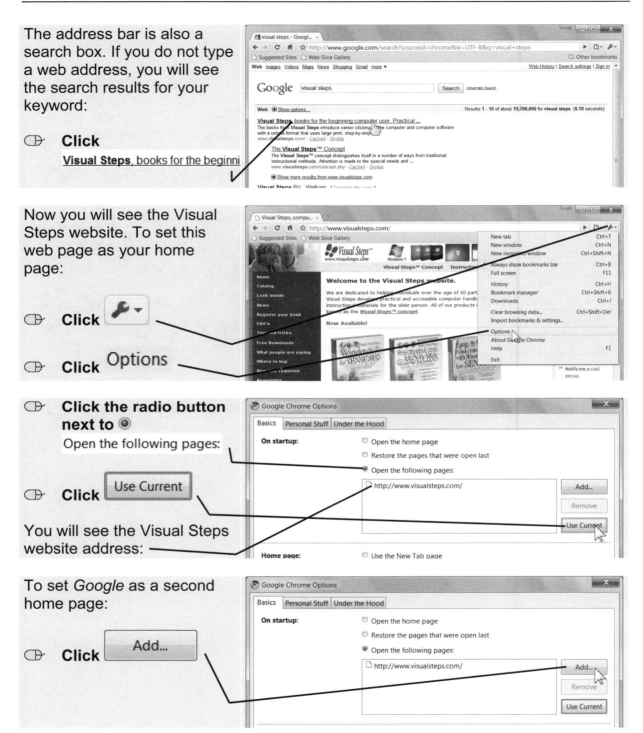

Now you will see the web pages you have recently visited:

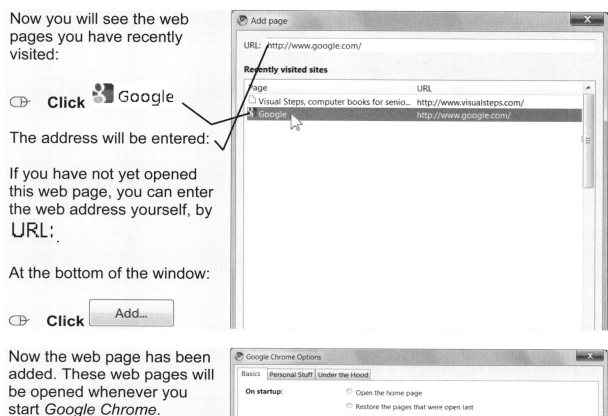

☞ **Click** Google

The address will be entered:

If you have not yet opened this web page, you can enter the web address yourself, by URL:

At the bottom of the window:

☞ **Click** Add...

Now the web page has been added. These web pages will be opened whenever you start *Google Chrome*.

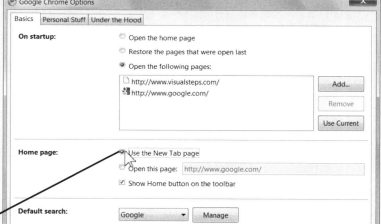

You can also select the web page by clicking 🏠 :

☞ **Click the radio button ⊙ next to**
Use the New Tab page

🢒 **Please note:**

The 🏠 button lets you browse to a different page other than the startup home page(s). You can enter this other page by Open this page: .

If you want to personalize
your web browser, you can
select a theme:

⊕ **Click the** | Personal Stuff |
    tab

⊕ **Click** | Get themes |

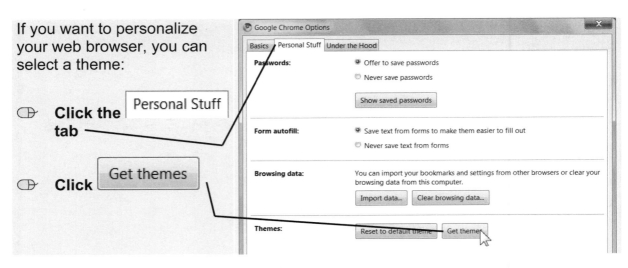

⊕ **Click** Themes by Google

⊕ **Click** **Desktop**

Or select a different theme
yourself.

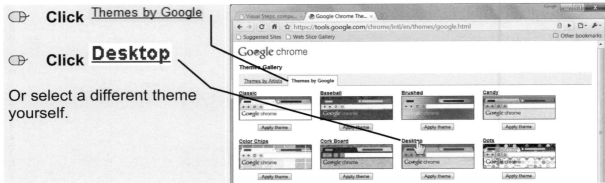

You will see an example of
the theme you have selected:

⊕ **Click**

| Apply this theme |

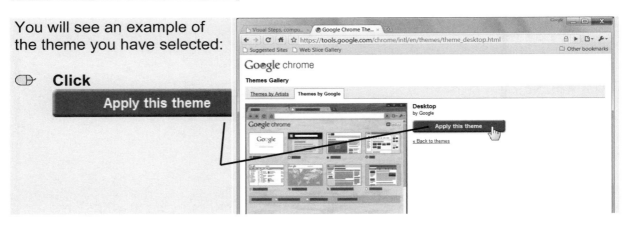

After a short while the theme will have been applied:

☞ **Open the *Google Chrome Options* window** ✇14

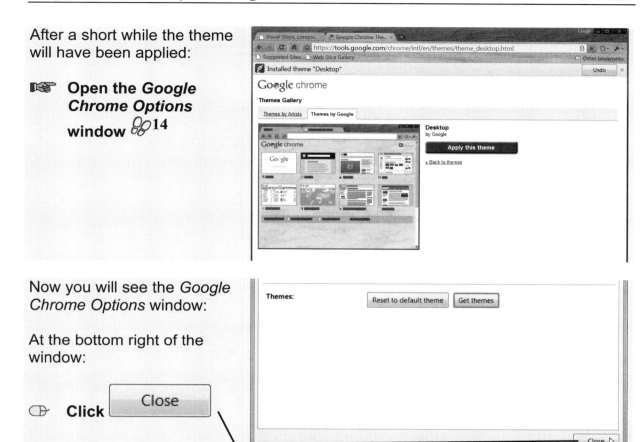

Now you will see the *Google Chrome Options* window:

At the bottom right of the window:

☞ **Click** `Close`

3.8 Bookmarks

In *Google Chrome* you can use *bookmarks* to quickly browse to frequently visited web pages. This is how you add a bookmark:

☞ **Browse to www.google.com/options** ✇2

☞ **Click** ☆

You can also type a different name for this bookmark:

For now, this will not be necessary.

You can add the most important bookmarks to the bookmarks bar, and less important bookmarks to the Other bookmarks folder:

☞ **Click**

Bookmarks bar ▾

☞ **Click** Bookmarks bar

☞ **Click** [Close]

Now you will see this bookmark appear on the bookmarks bar:

Try out the new settings:

☞ **Click** [X]

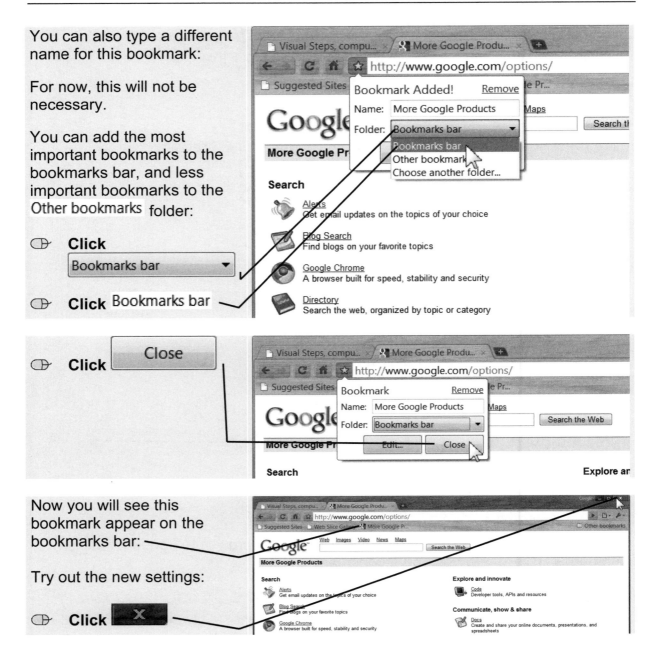

3.9 Surfing with Google Chrome

After you have set your home pages and bookmarks, you will discover that using *Google Chrome* to surf the Internet is similar to using other web browsers. It takes a

little while to get used to the new icons and to the different functionality of the button. But in no time at, you will find that *Google Chrome* is easy to use.

☞ **Open *Google Chrome***

Now you will see the home pages you have set:

Open a new tab:

☞ **Click**

You will see a new tab which contains thumbnails of the web pages you last visited:

Please note: you may see different thumbnails on your own screen.

You can click a thumbnail to open the website.

☞ **Click a thumbnail**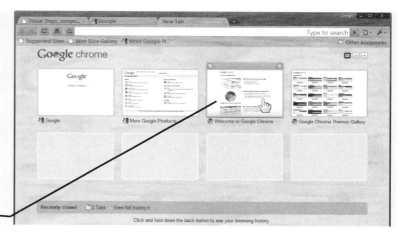

Now you will see the web page:

Click a bookmark to directly open a page:

☞ **Click**

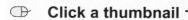

The web page that has been bookmarked will be opened:

To use the bookmarks in the Other bookmarks folder you need to click Other bookmarks first:

To view the web pages you have recently visited:

⊕ **Click** 🏠

The thumbnails will be displayed in the current tab:

To delete a bookmark:

⊕ **Right-click**
   🔲 More Google Pr...

⊕ **Click** Delete

You can close the unused tabs:

⊕ **Click** ✖

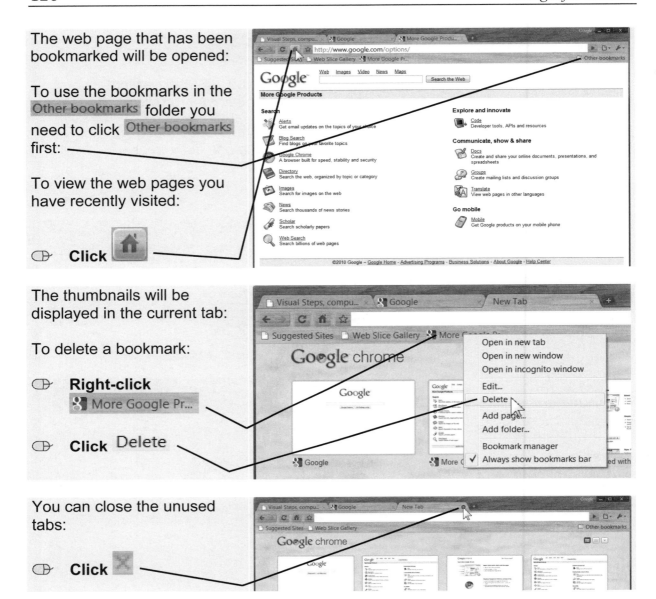

You will see that *Google Chrome* remembers your browsing history and will save cookies, just like the other web browsers. This is how you delete this information:

At the top right of the window:

☞ **Click** 🔧▾

☞ **Click** Options

☞ **Click the**
Personal Stuff **tab**

☞ **Click**
Clear browsing data...

☞ **Check the box** ☑ **next to the items you want to clear**

☞ **Click**
Clear Browsing Data

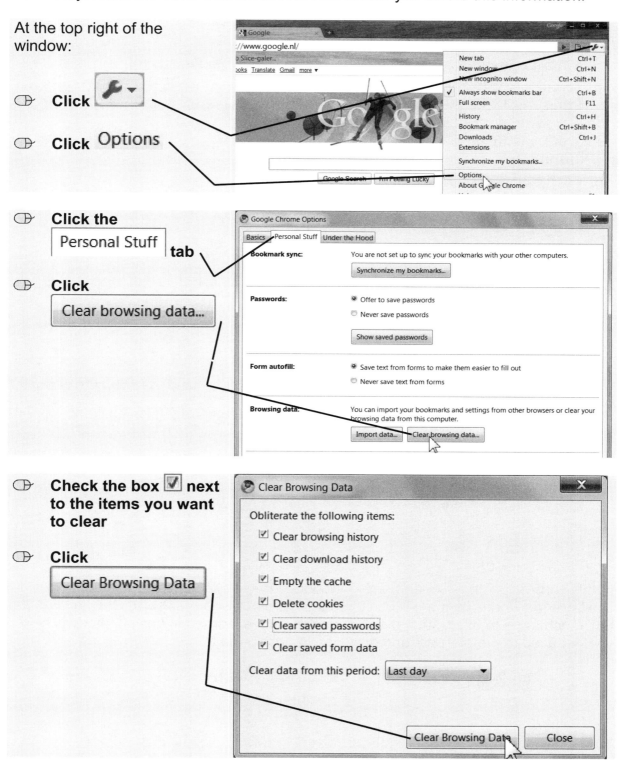

☞ **Close the *Google Chrome Options* window** 👣³

💡 **Tip**

Clearing browsing data for a specific period
You can also clear the browsing history for a specified amount of time:

◫ **Click** Last day

◫ **Click the desired period**

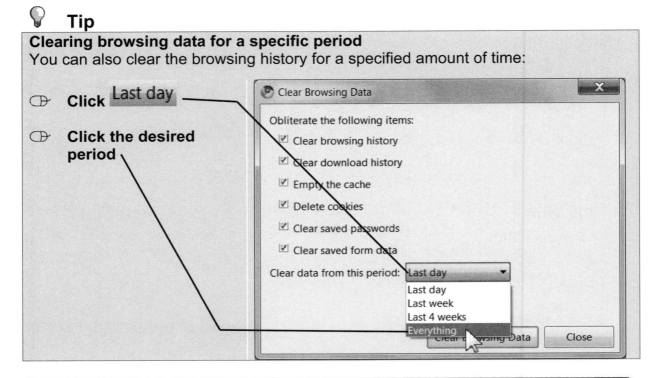

◫ **Click** 🏠

You now will see a number of empty thumbnails:

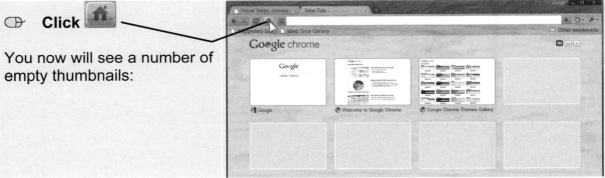

In this chapter you have been briefly introduced to *Google Chrome*. The options available in this program are much the same as other web browsers. *Google Chrome* has much more to offer, but the operations you have learned in this chapter will help you get used to the program and discover its possibilities.

◫ **Click** X

3.10 Background Information

Dictionary	
BCC	This abbreviation stands for *Blind Carbon Copy* (a so-called 'blind' copy). The advantage of sending an e-mail message to multiple recipients using BCC is that they will not be able to see each other's e-mail address.
Bookmark	Link to a website. You can create bookmarks for your favorite web pages, which you frequently visit.
CC	This abbreviation stands for *Carbon Copy*. This means you are sending a copy of the e-mail message to more than one e-mail address.
Contact	Information about a certain person. It will at least include the e-mail address, but may contain other data as well. The data is saved in the *Contacts* folder.
Download	Copying a file to your computer. This can be from another computer, USB-stick or other external memory device or from the Internet.
Home page	The page you visit by clicking ⌂. In *Google Chrome* this does not need to be the same page as the page you see when you open the program.
Web browser/ browser	A software program that can be used to view web pages and surf the Internet. *Internet Explorer*, *Firefox*, *Opera*, *Safari* and *Google Chrome* are web browsers.

Source: Google Help, Google Chrome, Windows Help and Support, Wikipedia

3.11 Tips

 Tip

Surfing the net in disguise

If you want to surprise your partner with a holiday trip, you may not want him or her to see your browsing history and find out about your recent searches. An incognito window lets you surf without recording your browse history. For this you need to open a separate window:

 Click

Click
New incognito window

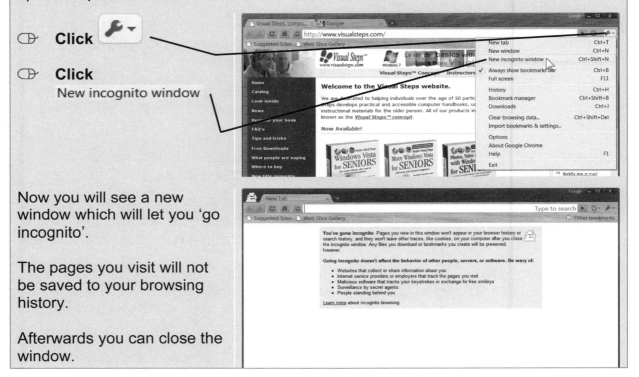

Now you will see a new window which will let you 'go incognito'.

The pages you visit will not be saved to your browsing history.

Afterwards you can close the window.

 Tip

Additional storage space for your e-mail messages

Gmail offers 7.3 GB of space for your e-mail messages. The exact amount of space increases regularly.

If you have used up all your storage space, you can buy extra space, which will be distributed among the various *Google* products. For instance, you will be able to use this space for your *Picasa* web albums as well. You can choose one of these storage options (pricing is from November 2009):

- 10 GB - 20 USD per year
- 40 GB - 75 USD per year
- 150 GB - 250 USD per year
- 400 GB - 500 USD per year

You can find more information about storage space on the *Google* support pages.

Tip

Importing bookmarks
If you decide to use *Google Chrome* as your web browser, you can easily import your favorite bookmarks from *Internet Explorer*:

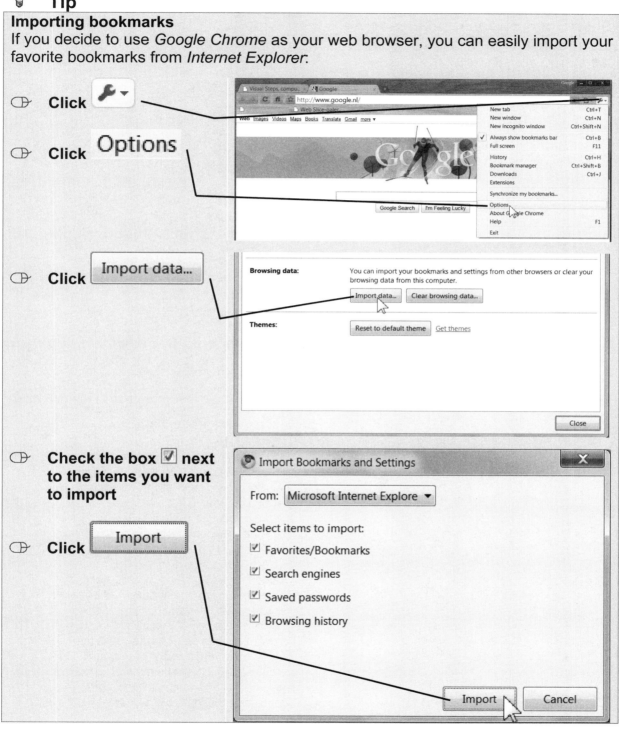

💡 Tip

Shortcut to a website

If you want to access a website directly from your desktop, or from the quick start taskbar, you can add a shortcut:

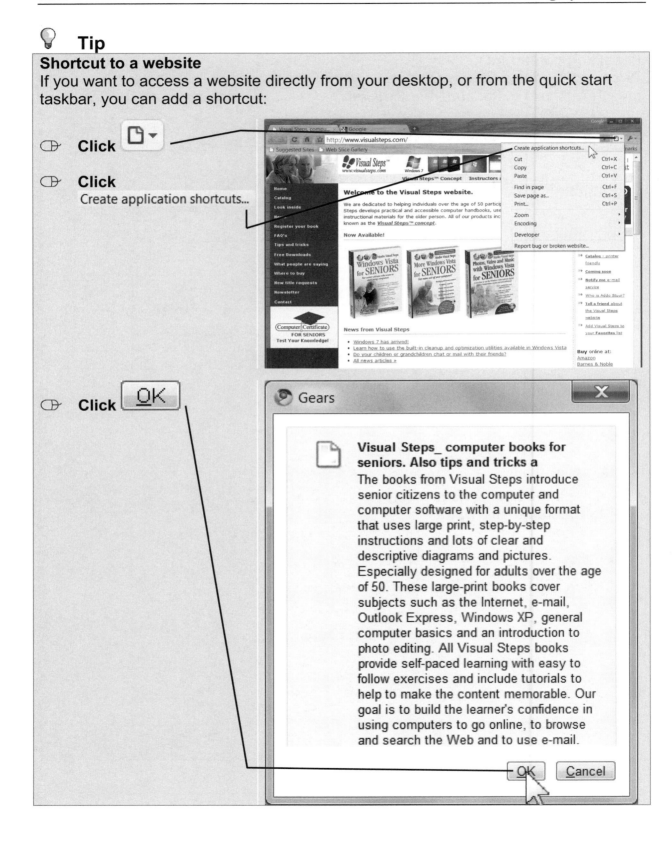

☞ **Click**

☞ **Click**
   Create application shortcuts...

☞ **Click** ⟨OK⟩

4. Your Online Calendar

Many people are rather hesitant about keeping an online diary or calendar. But these fears are misplaced. If you use the correct security settings, you need not be worried. You can compare it to using *Gmail* or *Hotmail* for sending and receiving messages. In those programs your private messages are also displayed online, but you are the only person who can access them.

An online calendar has the same advantages as online e-mail. If you need to work in several different locations and use different computers, an online calendar is just the thing for you. No matter where you are, you can always check your calendar on the Internet.

You can also share your online calendar with others. In this way your family members or colleagues can keep track of upcoming events. You can also create public calendars that are accessible to a specific group. For instance, this could be a good way to share information with all the members of your club or organization.

In this chapter you will learn how to:

- make appointments;
- edit appointments;
- make repeat appointments;
- search for appointments;
- view your calendar offline;
- add a public calendar;
- share calendars.

 Please note:

You will need a *Google* account to perform the operations in this chapter. If you do not yet have an account, read *Appendix A Creating a Google Account* first and learn how to create one.

 Please note:

The *Google* programs are subject to regular changes. The screen shots in this book may differ somewhat from what appears on your screen due to these modifications. This should not affect the operation of the program.

4.1 Entering and Editing Appointments

Before you can use the calendar, you need to sign in first. You can sign in with your *Google* account:

☞ **Open *Internet Explorer*** 👣¹

☞ **Browse to www.google.com/calendar** 👣²

In the right-hand side of the window:

By **Email:.**

⌨ **Type the user name for your *Google* account**

By **Password:.**

⌨ **Type your password**

🖰 **Click** | **Sign in** |

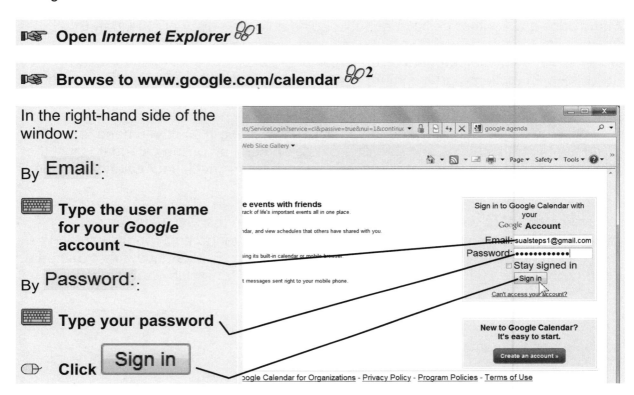

Please note:

In the next few exercises you will need to use the exact same weekday as in this example. In your case, the dates of these days will be different.

You will see a welcome window:

🖰 **Click** | **Continue** |

Now you see an empty calendar:

☞ **On Friday, click 9:00am** ———

If you are editing this calendar in the afternoon or in the evening, look for the scroll bar on the right-hand side of the window and drag it up until you can see the morning hours.

You will see a small window:

By What: :

⌨ **Type:** dentist

The default duration for an appointment is one hour. To change this:

☞ **Click** edit event details »

⌨ **Delete 10:00am**

⌨ **Type:** 9:30am

If necessary, you can type a location by **Where** and additional information by **Description**.

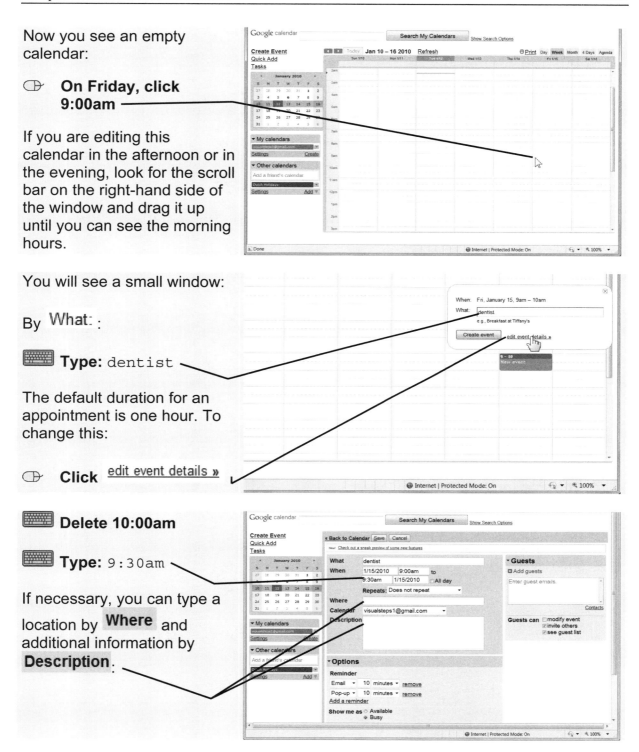

Drag the scroll bar downwards

You can enter various reminders. They will appear in pop-up windows or be sent to you by e-mail.

By E-mail :

Click remove

By Pop-up :

Double-click 10

Type: 1

Click minutes

Click days

Click the radio button next to Private

Click Save

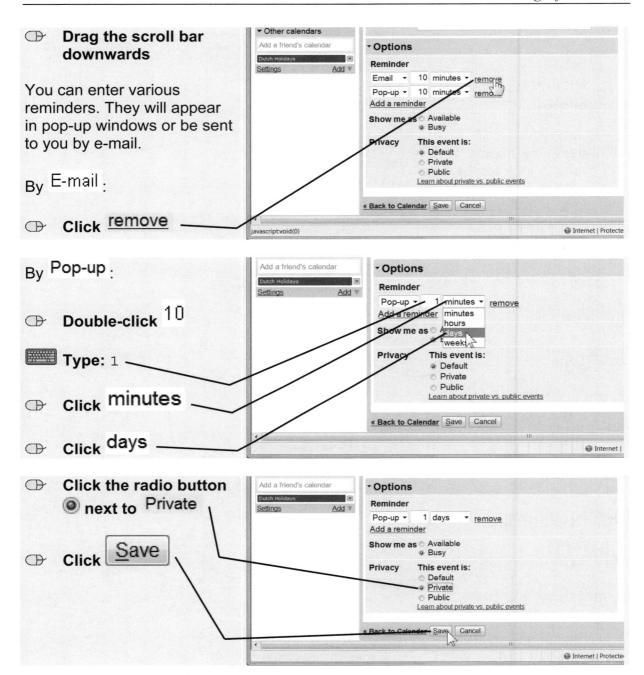

Tip

Change the time of an appointment
You can also edit the duration of an appointment in the calendar itself:

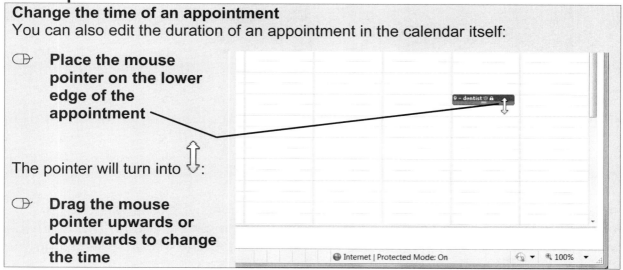

▷ **Place the mouse pointer on the lower edge of the appointment**

The pointer will turn into ⇕:

▷ **Drag the mouse pointer upwards or downwards to change the time**

You can move an appointment by dragging it to a new day and time:

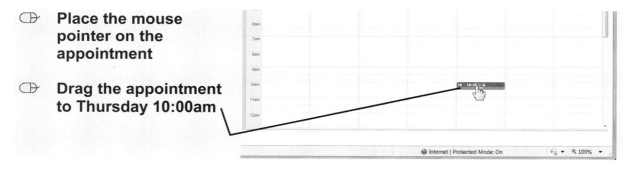

▷ **Place the mouse pointer on the appointment**

▷ **Drag the appointment to Thursday 10:00am**

 Tip

Changing appointments
If you want to change an existing appointment, you need to open the details window:

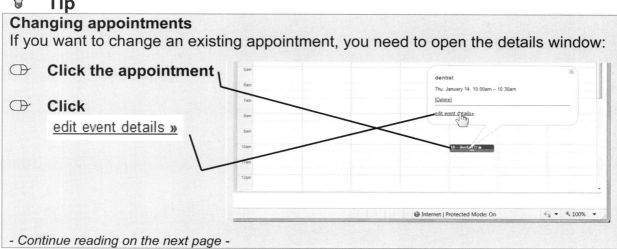

▷ **Click the appointment**

▷ **Click**
 edit event details »

- Continue reading on the next page -

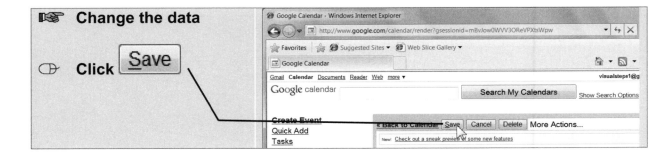

☞ Change the data

☞ Click Save

4.2 Recurring Appointments

In the details window you can also add appointments directly. This is especially useful if you need to enter an appointment outside of the current period. This way, you will not have to look up the date in your calendar first. There is a disadvantage however with this method. You cannot see if you have any other appointments already scheduled on or around that date.

☞ Click **Create Event**

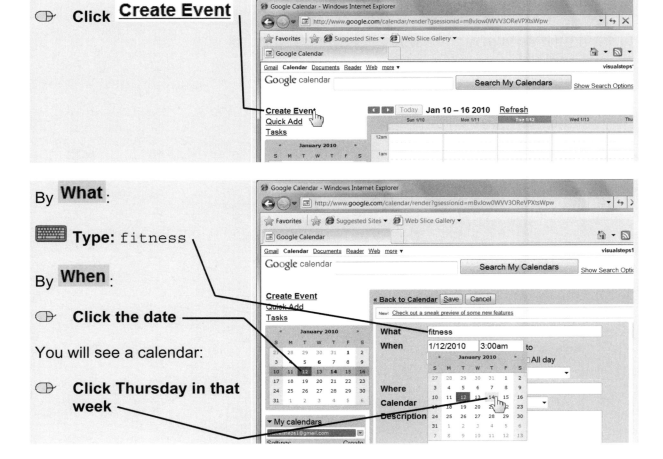

By **What**:

⌨ **Type:** fitness

By **When**:

☞ Click the date

You will see a calendar:

☞ Click Thursday in that week

By **When** :

⌨ **Delete the time**

⌨ **Type:** 9:00am

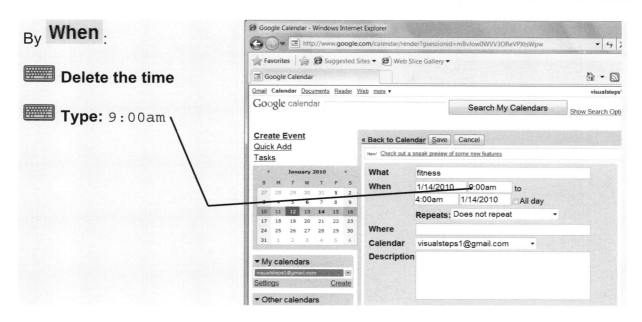

If you like to work out the same time each week, you can set this appointment as a repeat appointment:

By **Repeats:**.

☞ **Click**
Does not repeat

☞ **Click Weekly**

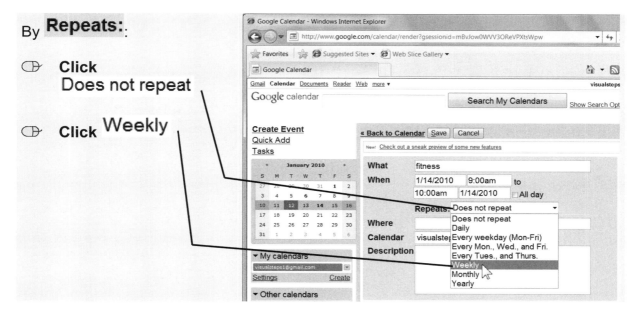

Now you see that the appointment is set to occur on a weekly basis:

⊂☞ **Click** Save

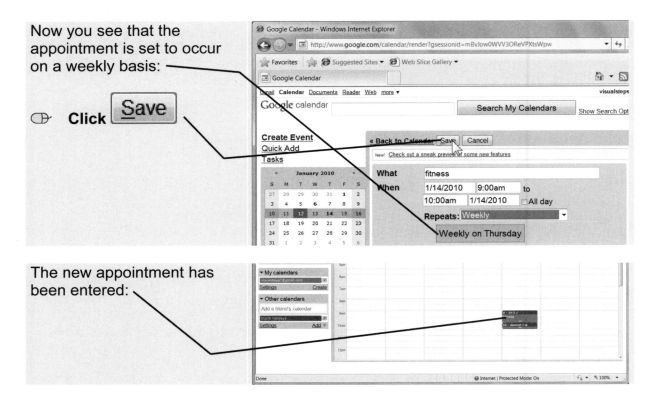

The new appointment has been entered:

4.3 Searching for Appointments

Have you forgotten when your next dentist appointment is? Here is how to look it up:

In the search box:

⌨ **Type:** dentist

⊂☞ **Click** Search My Calendars

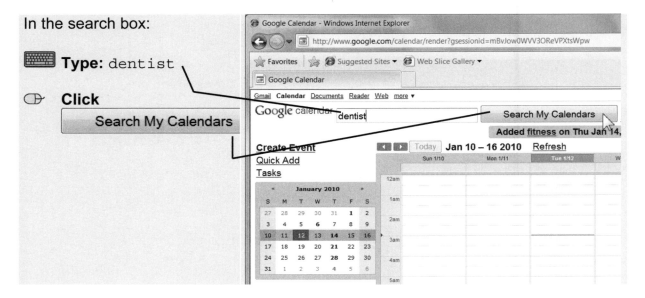

Tip

Extensive search

In the exercise above you searched for an appointment by its name. You can use other search options as well, such as the name of the location or any other attributes of the appointment:

☞ **Click**
   Show Search Options

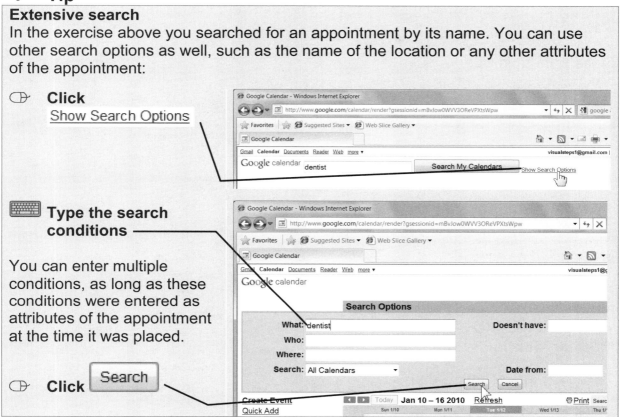

⌨ **Type the search conditions**

You can enter multiple conditions, as long as these conditions were entered as attributes of the appointment at the time it was placed.

☞ **Click** Search

You will see the appointment:

☞ **Click**
   « Back to Calendar

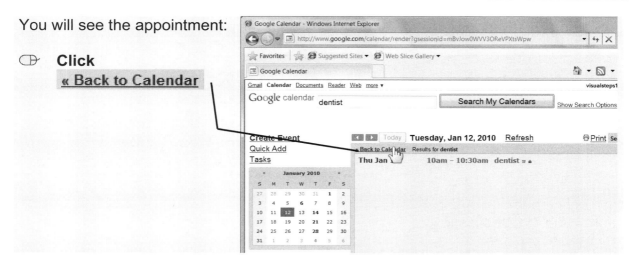

In this example the calendar is displayed as a list. This is a clear and simple way to view appointments over long periods. You can also view the full calendar in the same way:

In the right-hand side of your window:

☞ **Click** Agenda

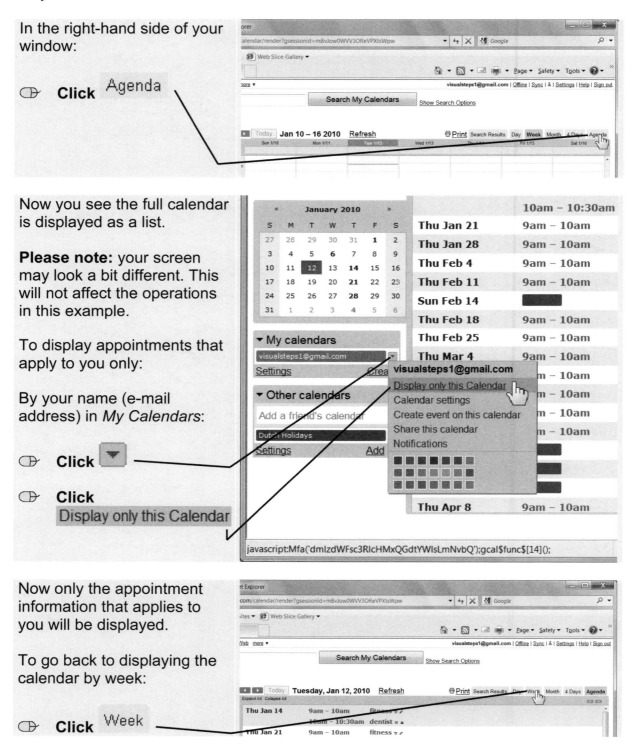

Now you see the full calendar is displayed as a list.

Please note: your screen may look a bit different. This will not affect the operations in this example.

To display appointments that apply to you only:

By your name (e-mail address) in *My Calendars*:

☞ **Click** ▼

☞ **Click**
Display only this Calendar

Now only the appointment information that applies to you will be displayed.

To go back to displaying the calendar by week:

☞ **Click** Week

4.4 Viewing Your Calendar Offline

The calendar is stored and maintained on one of *Google's* servers. But you can view your calendar offline as well. First, you will need to install a program from *Google* called *Gears*. *Gears* will enable offline access to your calendar.

In the top right of the window:

☞ **Click** Offline

The window will turn dark.
Then you will see this:

At the bottom of the window:

☞ **Click** Get Gears now

You will see a new window:

☞ **Click** Install Gears

☞ **Uncheck the box** ☑
next to
Help us improve Gears by se

☞ **Click** Agree and Download

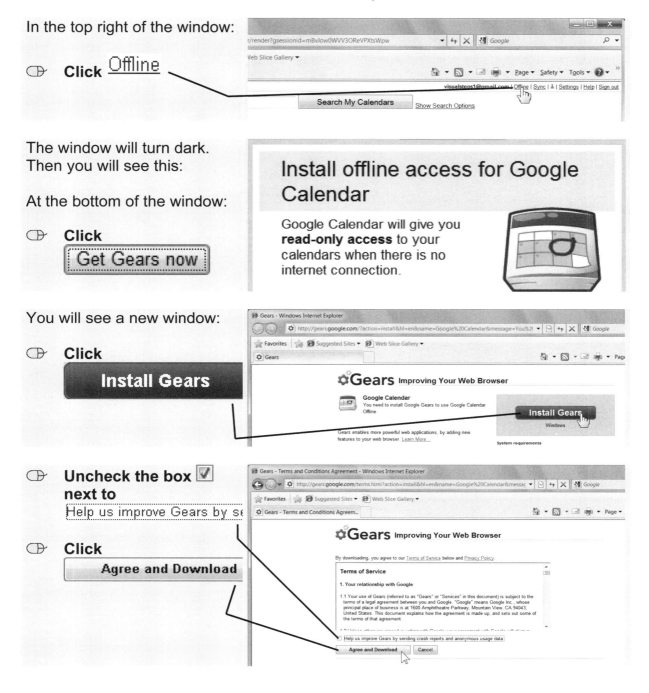

If the installation program does not start automatically:

☞ **Click** Click here.

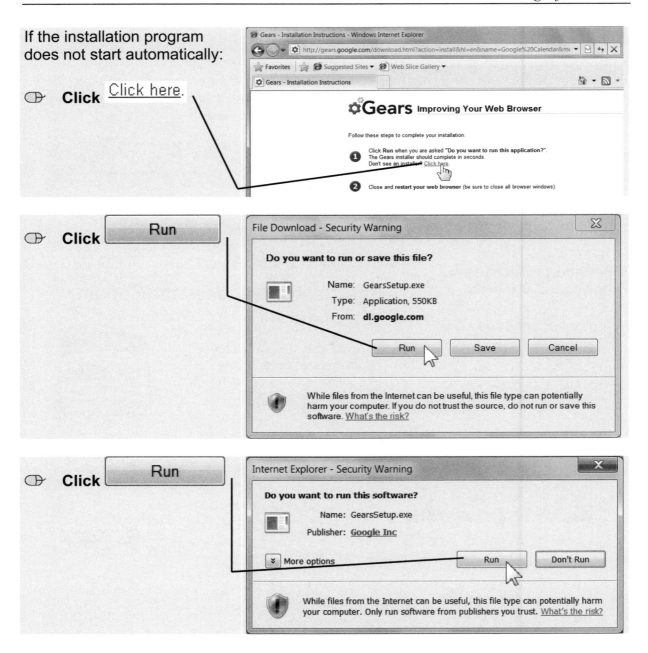

☞ **Click** Run

☞ **Click** Run

In *Windows Vista* and *Windows 7* your screen will now turn dark and you will be asked for permission to continue:

☞ **If necessary, click** Continue **or** Yes

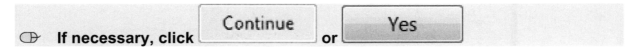

During the installation you will see:

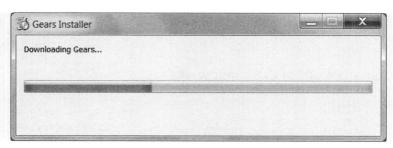

⊕ **Click**
  Restart Browsers Now

Your web browser will be closed and then reopened:

☞ **If necessary, sign in to *Google Calendar*** ⬤⬤7

You will see the calendar settings:

⊕ **Click**
  « Back to Calendar

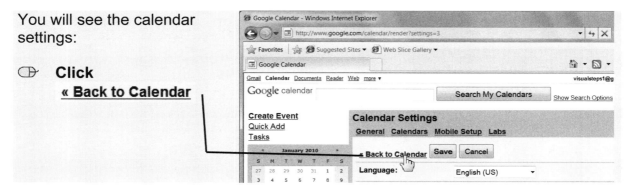

In the top right of the window:

⊕ **Click** Offline

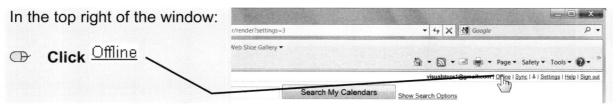

The window will turn dark again:

At the bottom of the window:

⊕ **Click**

Enable offline access

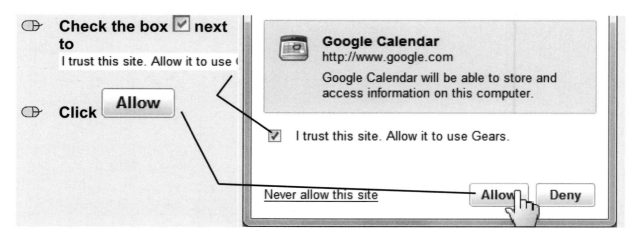

⊕ **Check the box** ☑ **next to**

I trust this site. Allow it to use (

⊕ **Click** **Allow**

Install offline access for Google Calendar

Google Calendar will give you **read-only access** to your calendars when there is no internet connection.

This feature will download your

Google Calendar
http://www.google.com

Google Calendar will be able to store and access information on this computer.

☑ I trust this site. Allow it to use Gears.

Never allow this site · · · · · · Allow · · · · Deny

⊕ **Check the box** ☑ **next to** Desktop

⊕ **Click** **OK**

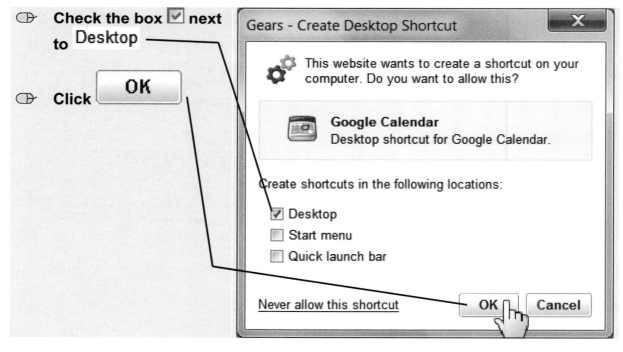

Gears - Create Desktop Shortcut ✕

This website wants to create a shortcut on your computer. Do you want to allow this?

Google Calendar
Desktop shortcut for Google Calendar.

Create shortcuts in the following locations:

☑ Desktop
☐ Start menu
☐ Quick launch bar

Never allow this shortcut · · · · · OK · · · Cancel

Now the software will be updated:

The link *Offline* is replaced by the ✅ in the list of links in the upper part of the page:

☞ **Close *Internet Explorer*** ❧3

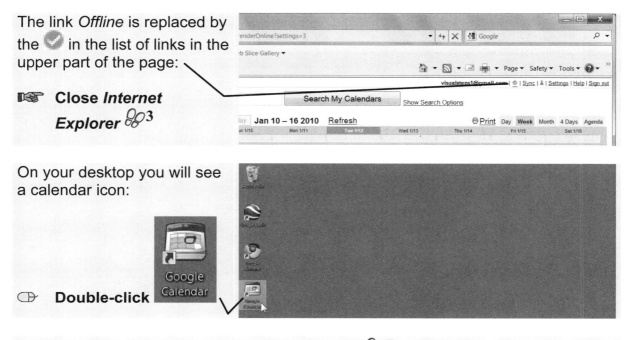

On your desktop you will see a calendar icon:

👆 **Double-click**

☞ **If necessary, sign in to *Google Calendar*** ❧7

You will see your calendar. From now on you can also use it offline.

In the list of links in the upper part of the window:

👆 **Click** ✅

👆 **Click** Go offline

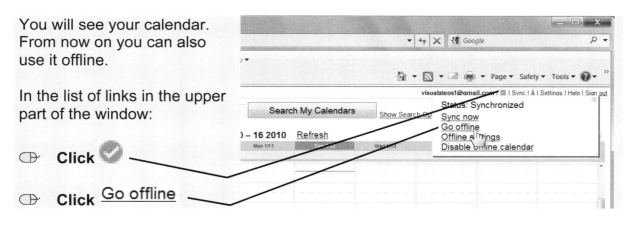

HELP! I see a login window.

If you have not signed in yet, do so now:

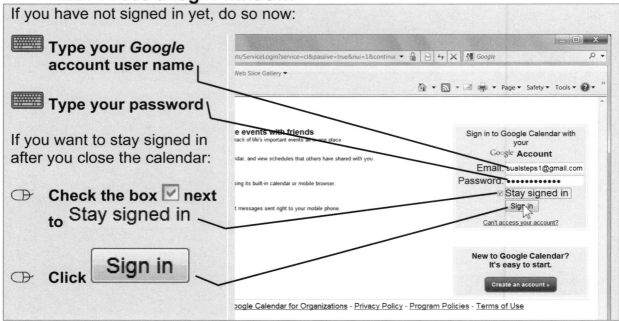

Type your *Google* account user name

Type your password

If you want to stay signed in after you close the calendar:

⊕ **Check the box ☑ next to Stay signed in**

⊕ **Click** **Sign in**

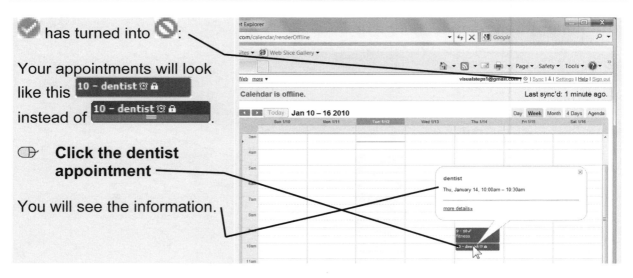

✅ **has turned into** 🚫:

Your appointments will look like this `10 - dentist ☺ 🔒` instead of `10 - dentist ☺ 🔒`.

⊕ **Click the dentist appointment**

You will see the information.

 Please note:

While you are working offline you cannot change or delete appointments.

To go online again:

⊕   **Click**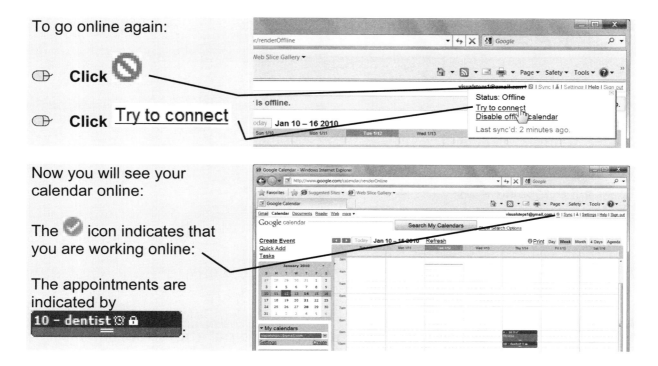

⊕   **Click Try to connect**

Now you will see your calendar online:

The ✓ icon indicates that you are working online:

The appointments are indicated by
`10 - dentist ☺ 🔒`

4.5 Public Calendars

One of the advantages of an online calendar is that you can easily share it with others. This way, you can create a calendar for your club, company, or board that is accessible to all people involved. You can copy the data from a shared sample calendar into your own calendar:

By **Other calendars**:

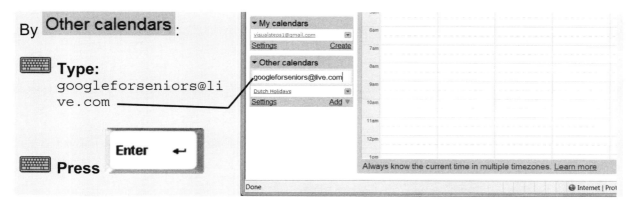

⌨   **Type:**
googleforseniors@li
ve.com

⌨   **Press** Enter ←

Now a meeting has been set in your calendar for Friday:

Under Other calendars you will also see the new calendar. By the color you can tell to which calendar an appointment belongs.

To hide the appointments:

 Click
googleforseniors@live.com

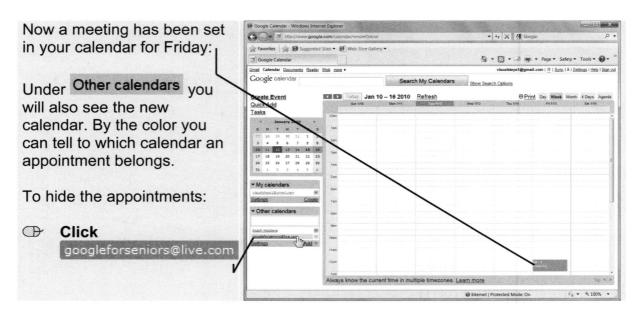

HELP! My most recent appointments are not included.

The data for the shared calendar will be retrieved as soon as you open the calendar. You will not see any changes right away. If you want to check whether anything has changed:

 Click

The calendar will be updated:

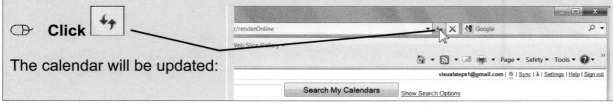

googleforseniors@live.com
has changed into
googleforseniors@live.com :

To view the calendar again:

 Click
googleforseniors@live.com

When you no longer want to have the information in this calendar synchronized to your own calendar, you can unsubscribe.

In the bottom left-hand side of
the window:

☞ **Click** Settings

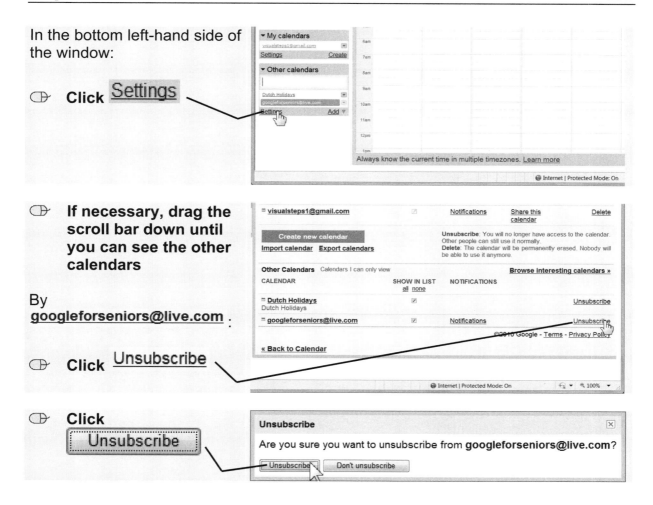

☞ **If necessary, drag the
scroll bar down until
you can see the other
calendars**

By
googleforseniors@live.com :

☞ **Click** Unsubscribe

☞ **Click**
Unsubscribe

4.6 Sharing Calendars

To share your own calendar with others, you need to take the following steps:

In your calendar:

☞ **Click** ▼

☞ **Click**
Share this calendar

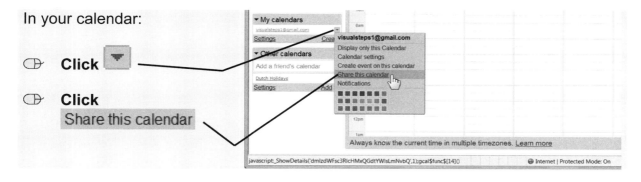

By **Person** :

 **Type the *Gmail* address of the person who is allowed to view your calendar**

Now you can set the permissions:

☞ **Click**
See all event details

☞ **Click**
See only free/busy (hide deta

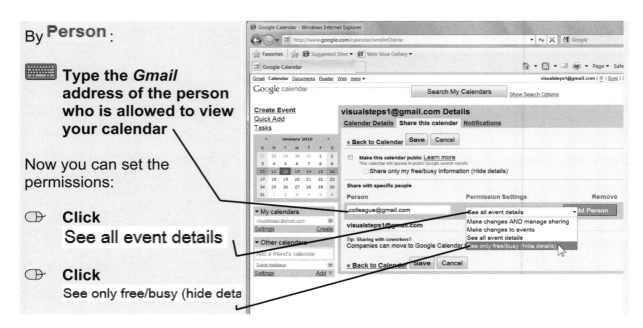

Please note:

If you check the box ☑ next to **Make this calendar public** , this calendar can be viewed by anyone who knows your *Gmail* address:

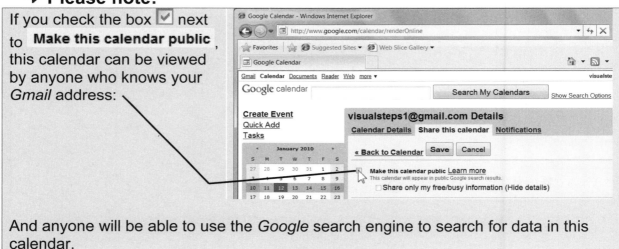

And anyone will be able to use the *Google* search engine to search for data in this calendar.

⬩ **Click** **Save**

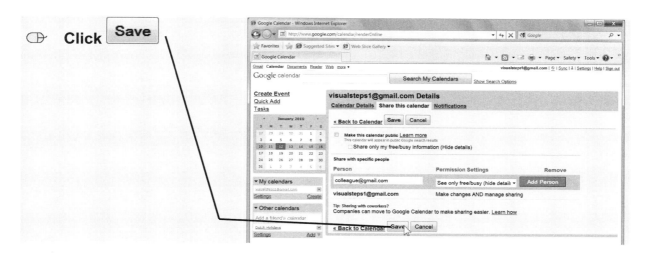

If this person does not yet have a *Google* calendar, you can send them an invitation:

⬩ **Click** **Invite** or **Don't invite**

If you no longer want to give someone access to your calendar, you can remove their e-mail address:

In your calendar:

⬩ **Click** 🔻

⬩ **Click** **Share this calendar**

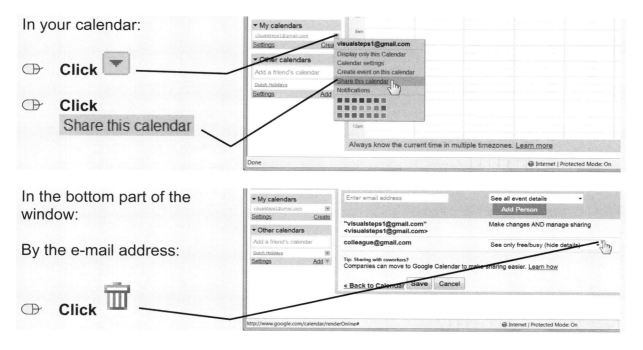

In the bottom part of the window:

By the e-mail address:

⬩ **Click** 🗑

Now the address has been removed:

⊕ **Click** **Save**

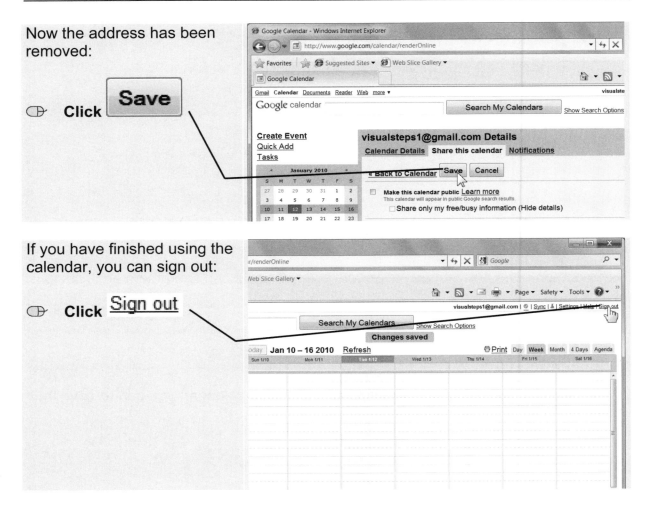

If you have finished using the calendar, you can sign out:

⊕ **Click** Sign out

It is your choice to update your calendar online or not. *Google Calendar* is a free program that allows you a safe way of maintaining a calendar online. You can create a calendar for yourself as well as a calendar for a club, business or a special event. Members or participants can view the calendar and be reminded of important information, registration dates, necessary subscriptions, or other details.

☞ **Close** *Internet Explorer* ✂³

4.7 Background Information

Dictionary	
Gears	Browser program that is required and needs to be installed before viewing *Google* calendars offline.
Online/offline	If you are connected to the Internet, you are online. If you are not connected, you are offline.
Public calendar	Calendar that can be viewed and modified by anybody else. You can access this calendar by clicking a hyperlink in an e-mail message or on a web page. The information listed in a public calendar can be found by Internet search engines.
Repeat appointments	Reoccurring appointment. For instance weekly or monthly. You enter the details about the appointment just once. It then appears automatically in the designated time.
Share calendar	Provide access to somebody else's calendar, or share your own calendar with others. The access may be limited, for instance read-only, or you can allow changes to be made. You can share a calendar with specific users, or create a public calendar.

Source: Google Help, Windows Help and Support, Wikipedia

4.8 Tips

 Tip

Import a calendar
In many cases you can also import data from your current online calendar, such as *Windows Calendar*. First you will need to export the data from that calendar. Be sure to take note or write down where you have stored the file and what the file name is.

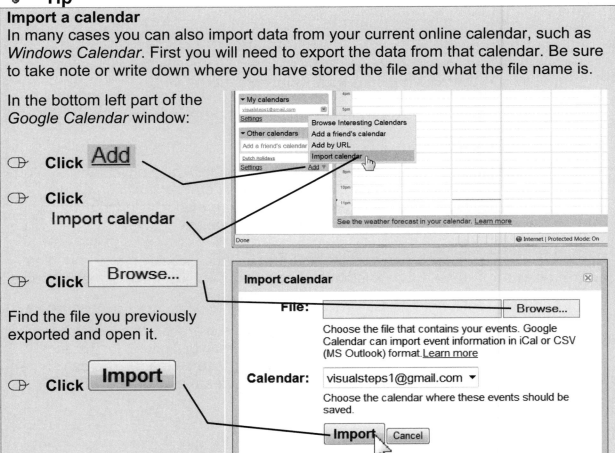

In the bottom left part of the *Google Calendar* window:

☞ **Click** Add

☞ **Click**
    Import calendar

☞ **Click** Browse...

Find the file you previously exported and open it.

☞ **Click** Import

You will see how many appointments have been imported. This calendar will not be updated when you change appointments in the *Windows Calendar*.

In the same way you can import various other calendars, such as the *Microsoft Outlook* calendar. *Google Calendar* is able to import appointments in the ICAL and CSV file format.

5. Communication

Google offers several programs that can be used to communicate with others.

For instance, with Google Talk you can chat in small groups, or even call each other by phone. Since these calls are conducted over the Internet, they are free of charge.

If your main goal is to spread information about a club or activity, a discussion group can be a really useful tool. You can use groups to publish information in a number of different ways. You can create a group that has restricted access to members only or you can create a public group. When you set up a group, you can decide whether to allow comments or reactions to the posts.

With Blogger you can create a blog. This medium is often used to publish a diary or travel journal. You can post your thoughts and reflections anytime you wish to do so. In Blogger, you can also decide whether to allow comments or reactions to the posts.

In this chapter you will learn how to:

- create a group;
- start a discussion;
- react to a discussion;
- add and delete members;
- add pages and files to a group;
- install Google Talk;
- send and receive express messages;
- use Google Talk for phone calls;
- create a blog;
- add messages and images to a blog;
- invite people to visit your blog;
- react to blog messages;
- restrict the access to your blog.

 Please note:

In this chapter you will see screen shots from the Google Talk and Blogger programs. Because these programs are subject to frequent changes, the screen shots may differ from your own screen. This should not affect the operation of these programs.

Please note:

> To perform the operations in this chapter, you will need to download the corresponding practice files to your computer's hard disk. You can read how to do this in *Appendix C Download Practice Files* at the end of this book.

5.1 Creating Groups

Discussion groups are a modern and effective way to share information and news within a club, school, company or just about any group of people that is interested in a certain subject. Creating a group is easy:

☞ **Open** *Internet Explorer* 🦶[1]

☞ **Browse to www.google.com/options** 🦶[2]

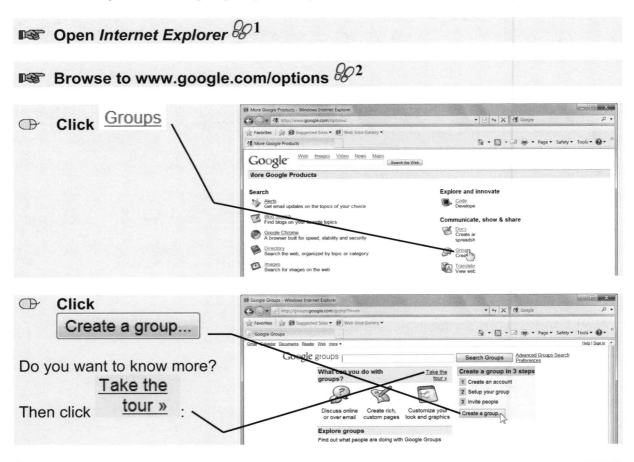

☞ **Click** Groups

☞ **Click** Create a group...

Do you want to know more? Take the tour

Then click tour » :

☞ **If necessary, sign in to your** *Google* **account first** 🦶[9]

First, you will need to enter some information:

By **Nickname:**.

⌨ **Type the name you want to use in the group**

☞ **Click** Continue

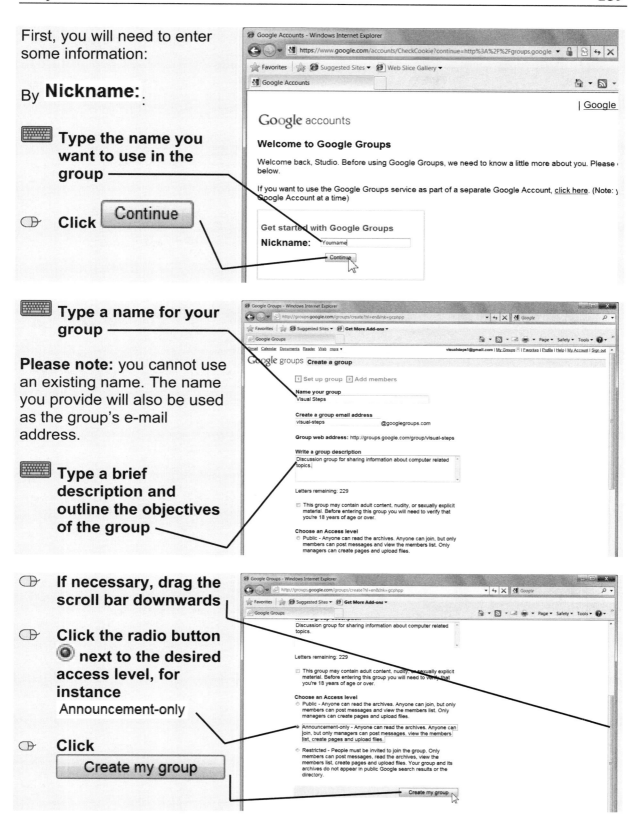

⌨ **Type a name for your group**

Please note: you cannot use an existing name. The name you provide will also be used as the group's e-mail address.

⌨ **Type a brief description and outline the objectives of the group**

☞ **If necessary, drag the scroll bar downwards**

☞ **Click the radio button ⦿ next to the desired access level, for instance** Announcement-only

☞ **Click** Create my group

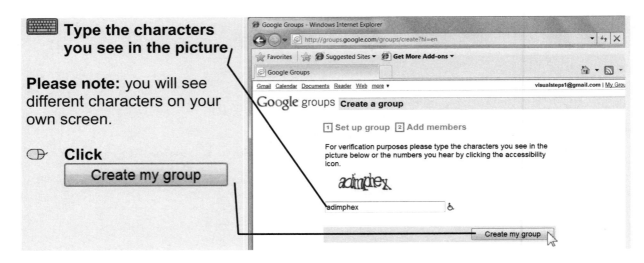

⌨ **Type the characters you see in the picture**

Please note: you will see different characters on your own screen.

🖰 **Click**

    Create my group

Now the group has been created and you can start adding members:

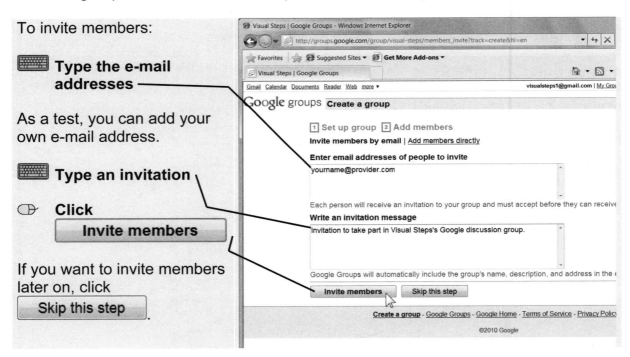

To invite members:

⌨ **Type the e-mail addresses**

As a test, you can add your own e-mail address.

⌨ **Type an invitation**

🖰 **Click**

    Invite members

If you want to invite members later on, click

    Skip this step.

Tip

Add members directly
Instead of inviting people, you can also add them as a member right away. For example, all the members of a specific club.

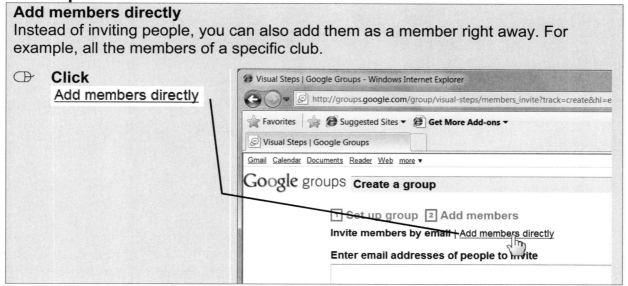

⊕ **Click**
 Add members directly

The members you have invited will receive an e-mail message:

They can accept the invitation by clicking the link:

To visit the group:

☞ **Click**
   Visit your new group »

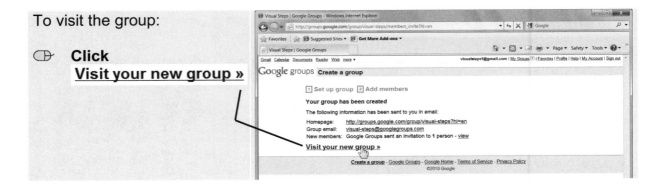

5.2 Access and Appearance Settings

Because you have created this discussion group, you are its owner. This means you can change the settings for its appearance and decide on the level of access. First, you are going to check the group settings and then modify the group's appearance:

You are the owner:

☞ **Click** Group settings

Now you will see the general settings. If you want to change these settings, click Edit .

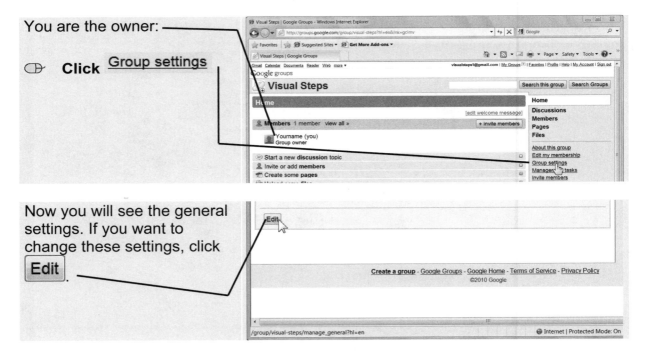

⊕ **Click** **Access**

Here you can set the access rights for the members and the administrator. The owner is also an administrator, but you can appoint other administrators if you want.

After you have changed the settings, drag the scroll bar downwards and click **Save Changes**.

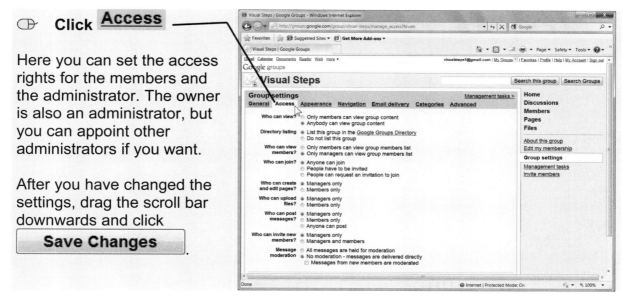

➡ **Please note:**

An administrator is also called a *moderator*. Usually the term moderator is used to indicate the person who screens and admits the member's messages to the group.

⊕ **Click** **Appearance**

To select a different appearance:

⊕ **Click** Select a different look

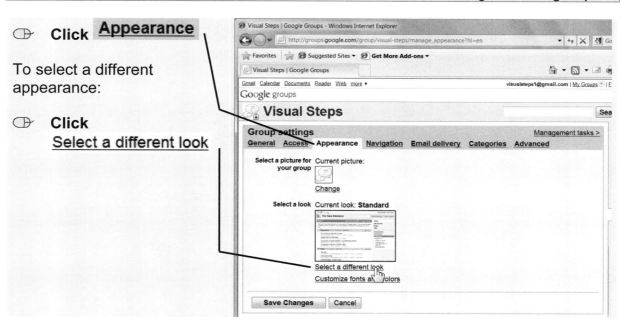

☞ **Click the desired look**

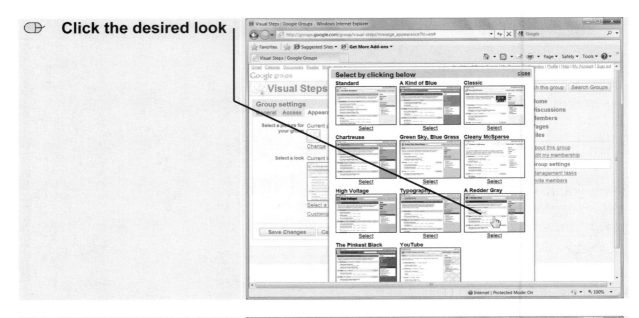

You can also select a different picture for your group, for example, the logo of your club:

☞ **Click** _Change_

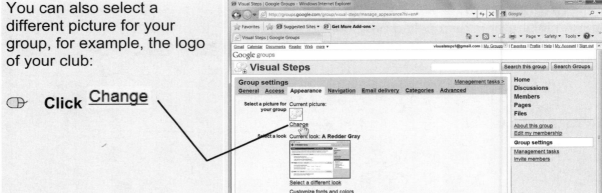

☞ **Click a picture**

If you want to use a picture from your computer's hard disk, click | **Browse...** |. After that you open the picture and click | **Upload picture »** |:

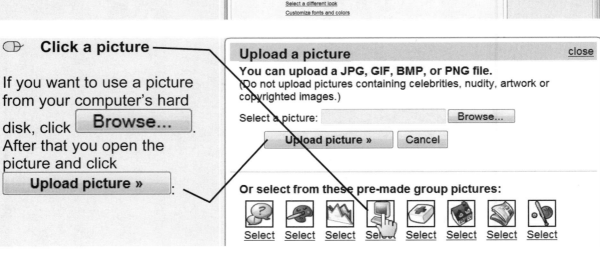

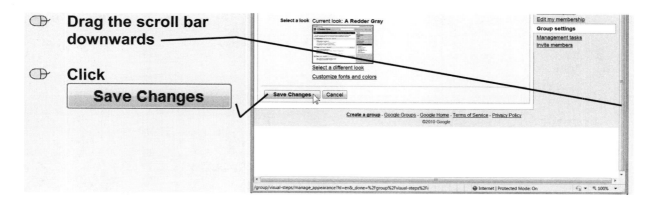

☞ **Drag the scroll bar downwards**

☞ **Click** **Save Changes**

5.3 Start a Discussion

A discussion group contains messages and comments from its members. These are called *discussions*. This is how you start a discussion:

At the right-hand side of the window:

☞ **Click** **Discussions**

☞ **Click** **+ New post**

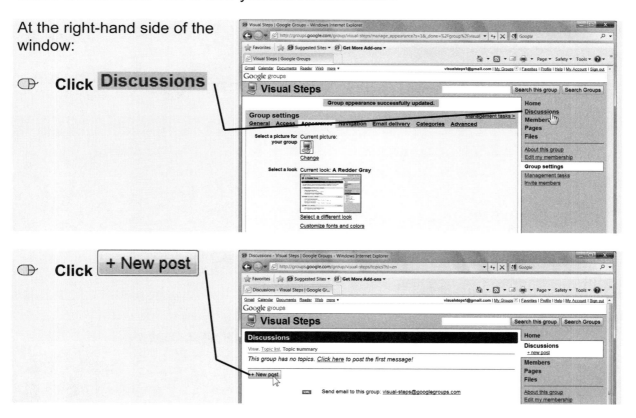

By **Subject:** :

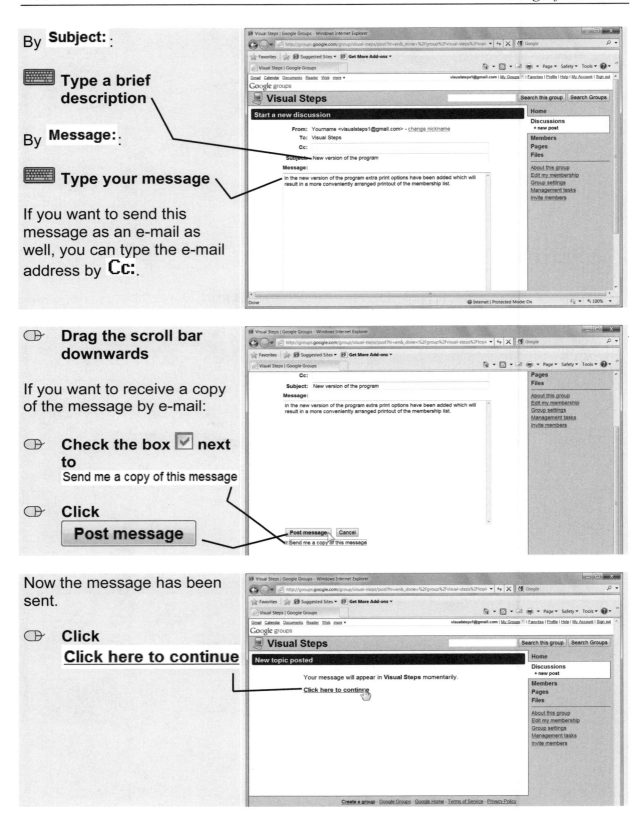

⌨ **Type a brief description**

By **Message:** :

⌨ **Type your message**

If you want to send this message as an e-mail as well, you can type the e-mail address by **Cc:**.

👆 **Drag the scroll bar downwards**

If you want to receive a copy of the message by e-mail:

👆 **Check the box ☑ next to**
Send me a copy of this message

👆 **Click**
Post message

Now the message has been sent.

👆 **Click**
Click here to continue

Here you will see the message. To reply:

- Click the topic's title

Click <u>Reply</u>

By clicking <u>Reply to author</u> you can send a reply directly to the author of the message:

- Type your reply

This reply will be inserted above the original message:

- Click

  Send

The message has now been posted.

- Click

  <u>« Back to Discussions</u>

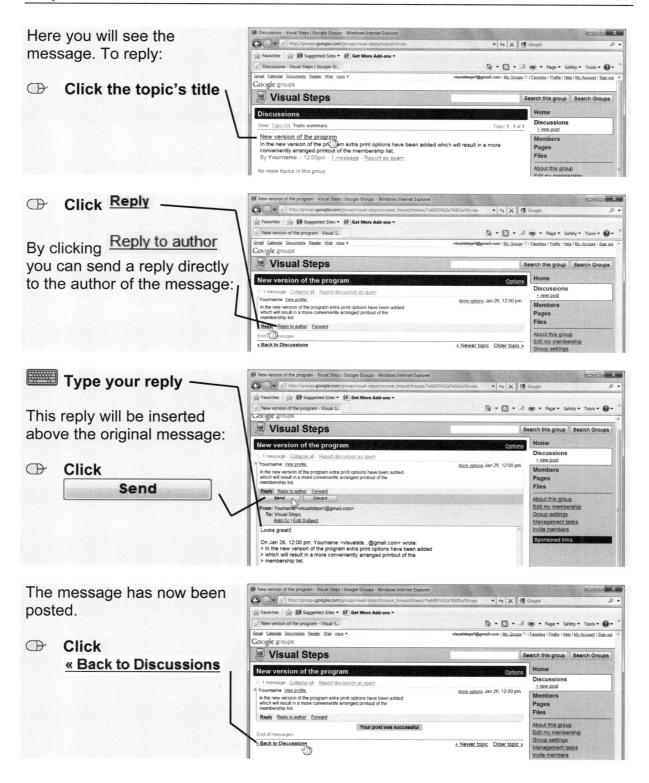

Here you see two messages. The original message and your reply:

To view all messages, you click the message title again, or click

1 new of 2 messages .

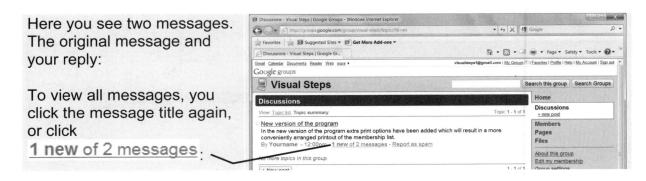

5.4 Create Pages

Pages contain information for members. The members will be able to react to this information.

In the right-hand side of the window:

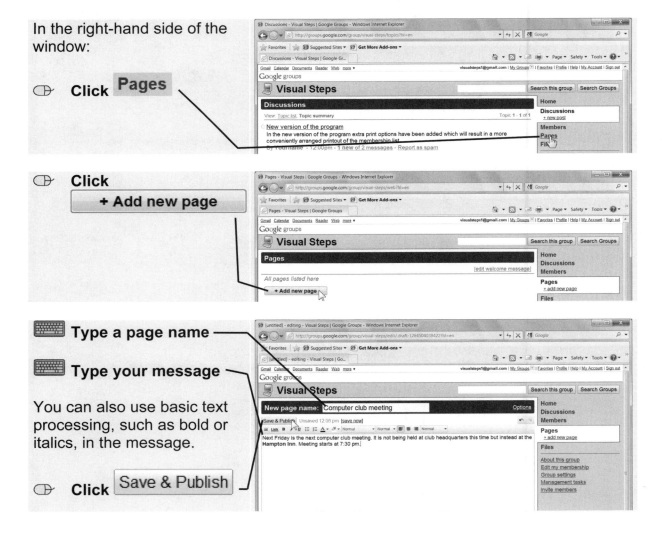

Click **Pages**

Click **+ Add new page**

Type a page name

Type your message

You can also use basic text processing, such as bold or italics, in the message.

Click **Save & Publish**

Now the page has been published:

☞ **Click** <u>View the page</u>

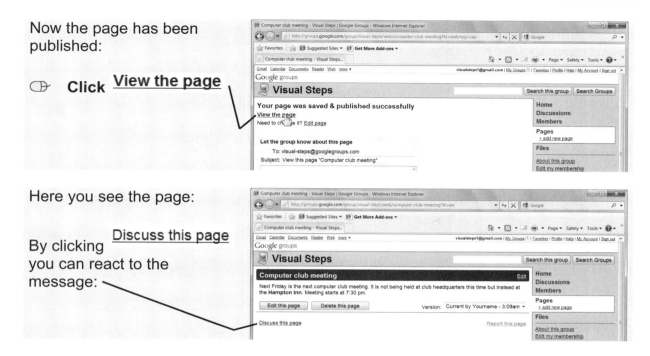

Here you see the page:

By clicking <u>Discuss this page</u> you can react to the message:

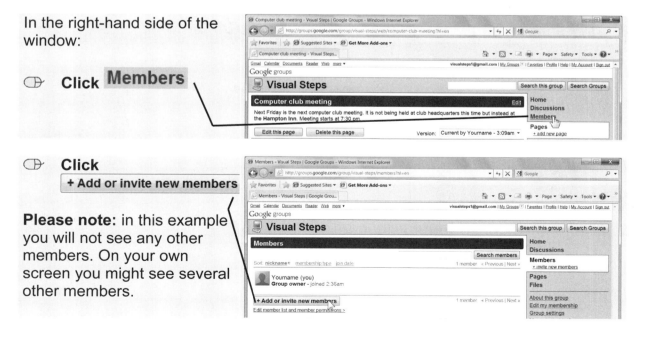

5.5 Member Administration

One of the owner's important tasks is administering the group members. You can add and remove members or change their access rights.

In the right-hand side of the window:

☞ **Click** **Members**

☞ **Click**
+ Add or invite new members

Please note: in this example you will not see any other members. On your own screen you might see several other members.

Add the members as described in *section 5.1 Creating Groups*. When you are done, you can invite them by clicking

Invite members :

To view the members' list:

☞ **Click** **Members**

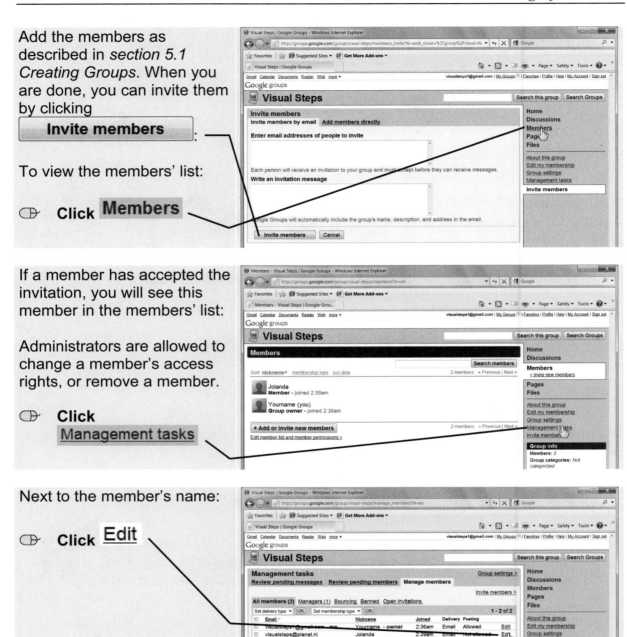

If a member has accepted the invitation, you will see this member in the members' list:

Administrators are allowed to change a member's access rights, or remove a member.

☞ **Click** **Management tasks**

Next to the member's name:

☞ **Click** **Edit**

⏻ **Drag the scroll bar downwards** ⎯

Here you can set the access rights for this member. When you are done, click **Save Changes**.

To remove the member:

⏻ **Click** Unsubscribe

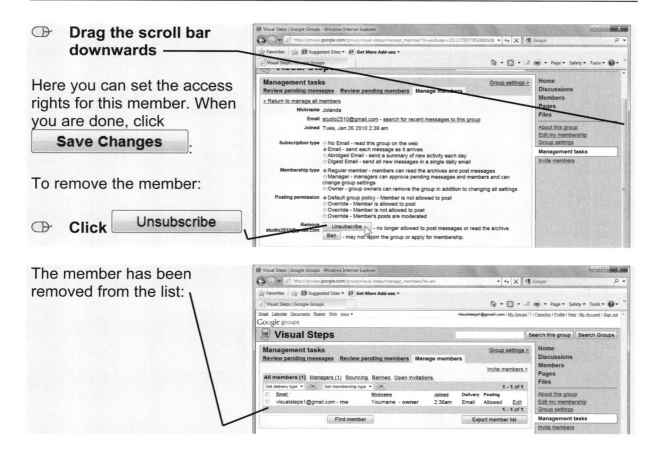

The member has been removed from the list:

5.6 Uploading Files

In the previous section you have learned how to use a discussion group for discussions and messages. You can also add files to the group, such as a picture or a document containing the minutes of a meeting. In this way, the group members are able to print or download these files.

In the right-hand side of the window:

⏻ **Click** Files

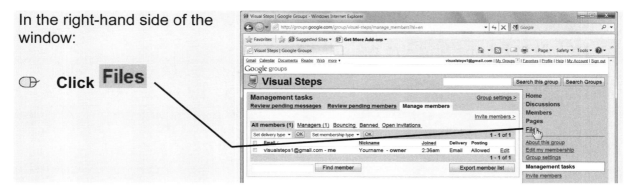

Click

+ Upload file

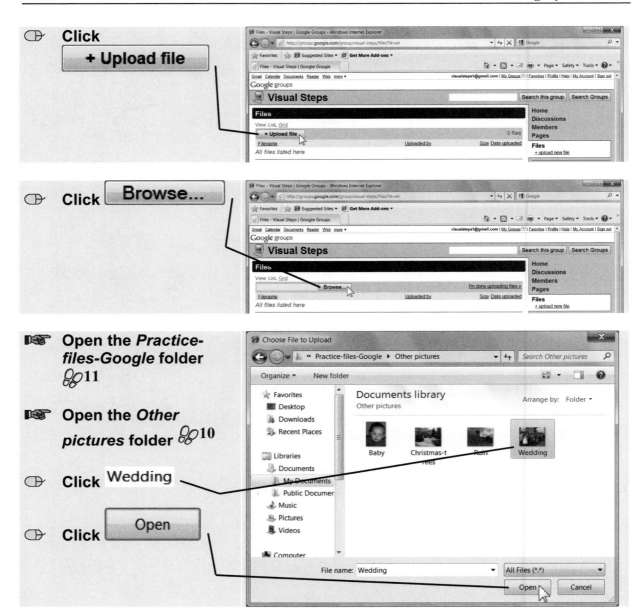

Click **Browse...**

☞ Open the *Practice-files-Google* folder 11

☞ Open the *Other pictures* folder 10

Click Wedding

Click Open

✖ HELP! I cannot find the practice files.

Have you not yet downloaded the practice files? In *Appendix C Download Practice Files* you can read how to do this.

Uploading the file may take a while, depending on its size. After the file is uploaded, you will see:

Click <u>Wedding.jpg</u>

You now see the picture in a new window:

You (or one of the other members) can print this picture or save it to your computer by right-clicking the image.

Close the window &&3

You have now learned how to use the main functions of *Google Groups*. For a club, or other organization, a discussion group can be a great way to spread information quickly to its members, in addition to its regularly published newsletters or magazines.

In the right-hand side of the window:

Click <u>Sign out</u>

5.7 Installing Google Talk

Google Talk is a program used for chatting or calling other people. You can chat or call anyone who has access to the Internet, no matter where they live.

☞ **Browse to www.google.com/talk** 👣**²**

First, you will need to download and install *Google Talk*:

Click
Download Google Talk

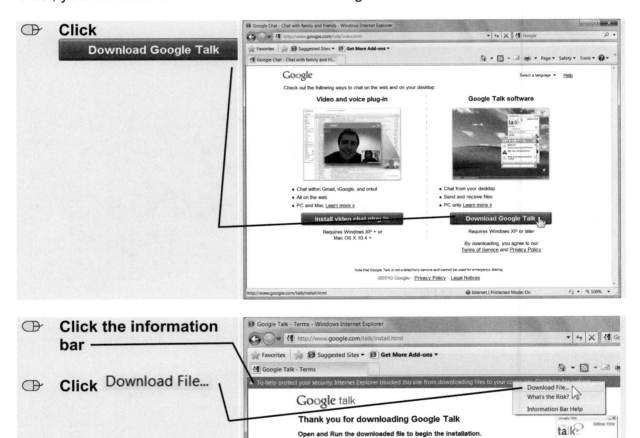

Click the information bar

Click Download File...

In the next two windows:

Click  Run

To agree to the license terms:

▢ **Click** [I Agree]

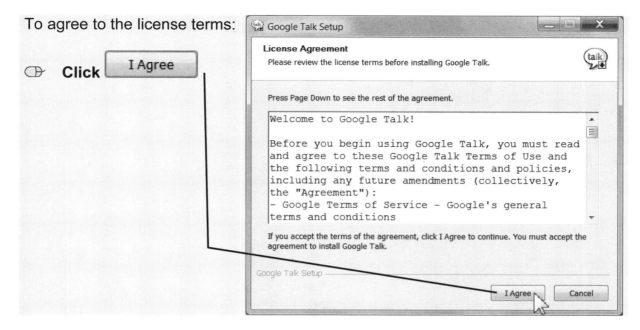

Now the program will be installed:

When the installation is finished, you will see this window:

▢ **Click** [Finish]

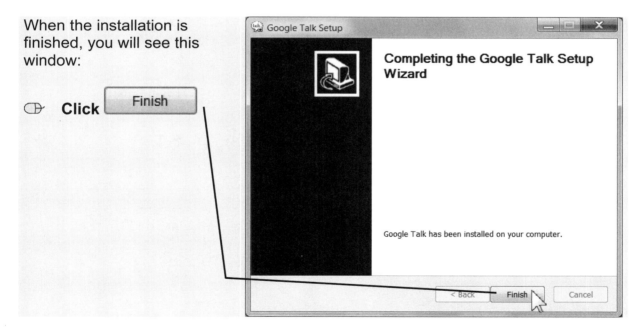

Type your *Gmail* user name and password

Click
Sign In

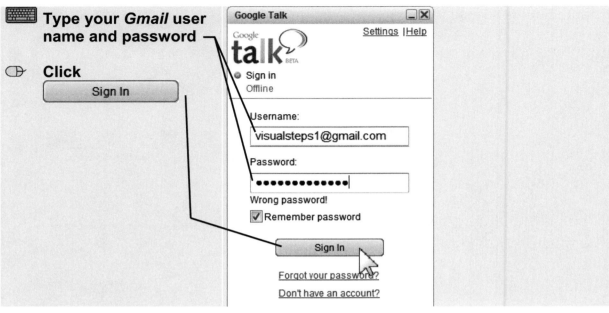

You will see the *Google Talk* window.

Before you start, you will need to adjust the settings:

Click Settings

Uncheck the box ☑ next to
Start automatically when starting

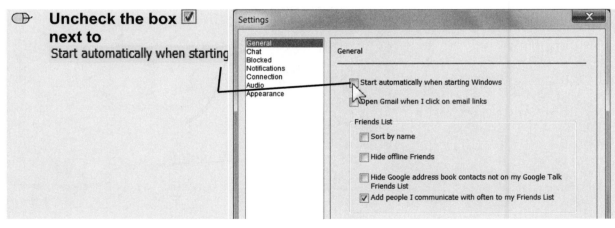

In the left-hand side of the window:

⊕ **Click** Chat

Usually it is not necessary to save your chat history:

⊕ **Click the radio button** ⊙ **next to**
Don't save chat history in my Gr

⊕ **Click** OK

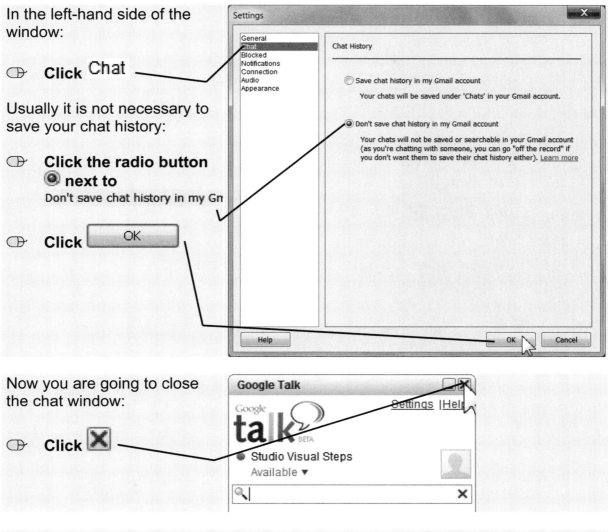

Now you are going to close the chat window:

⊕ **Click** ✖

☞ **Close** *Internet Explorer* ⚹³

5.8 Chatting with Google Talk

With *Google Talk* you can send short messages, comparable to the SMS messages you send with your cell phone. Carrying on a conversation like this is called *chatting*.

On your desktop:

☞ **Double-click** Google Talk

HELP! I do not see Google Talk on the desktop.

If you do not see *Google Talk* on your desktop:

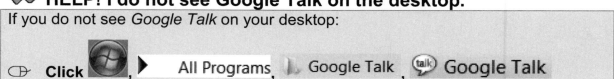

☞ **Click** ⊞ , ▶ All Programs , Google Talk , Google Talk

You now see the *Google Talk* window. From time to time, you may see an alert from *Google Gmail* or *Google Calendar*, indicating messages received or new appointments. They will appear in the bottom right-hand corner of the screen:

These alert messages will disappear on their own after a few seconds.

Before you can chat with someone, he or she must be added to your contact list. You can add a contact like this:

In the bottom part of the window:

☞ **Click** +Add

Type the e-mail address of the person you want to add

You can enter more than one e-mail address at a time by typing a comma between the addresses.

Click

> Next >>

💡 **Tip**

Add Gmail contacts

You can add *Gmail* contacts by clicking the

> Choose from my contacts...

button.

Click

> Finish

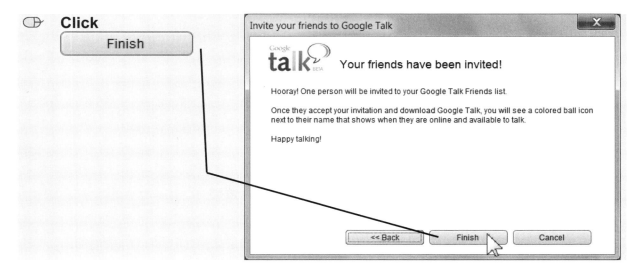

If this contact has already installed *Google Talk*, you can start chatting right away. Otherwise, the contact will receive an invitation by e-mail along with a link to the information page regarding *Google Talk* and how to install the program.

The contact will receive a
message. He or she can
accept the invitation by
clicking **yes** :

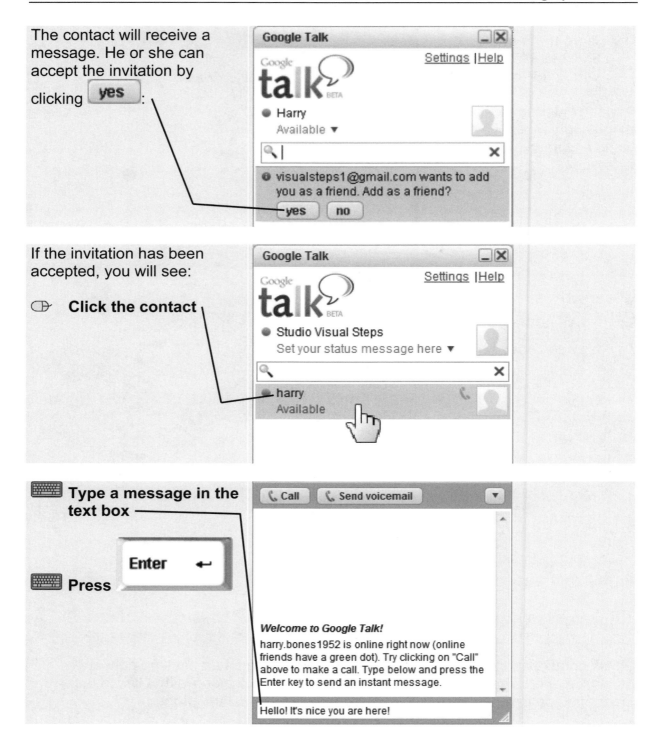

If the invitation has been
accepted, you will see:

☞ **Click the contact**

⌨ **Type a message in the text box**

⌨ **Press** **Enter ↵**

You now see the message appear in the chat window. You will find the answer there as well:

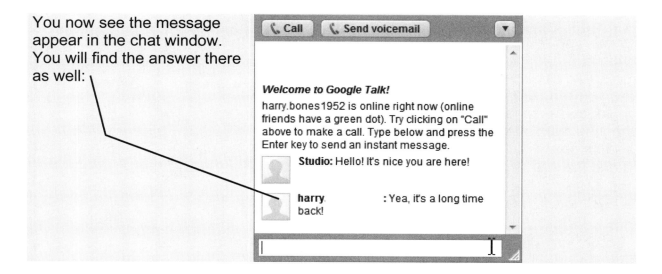

5.9 Making a Phone Call with Google Talk

With *Google Talk* you can use the Internet to make free phone calls. The person you are calling must be online at the same time in order to do this.

To make a phone call, you will need a microphone and speakers. To achieve optimum quality it is recommended that you use a *headset* (a headphone with a built-in microphone). You do not need to use a phone number. The connection is made through the Internet. It does require however a *Gmail* email address.

Click [Call]

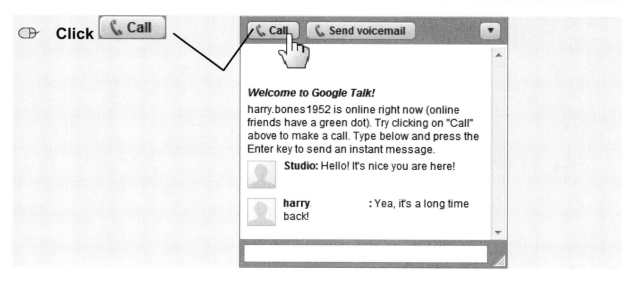

If the other person accepts the call, you will see this window:

Now you can carry on a regular conversation, by using the microphone and headphone of your computer. To end the call:

☞ **Click** [📞 **End Call**]

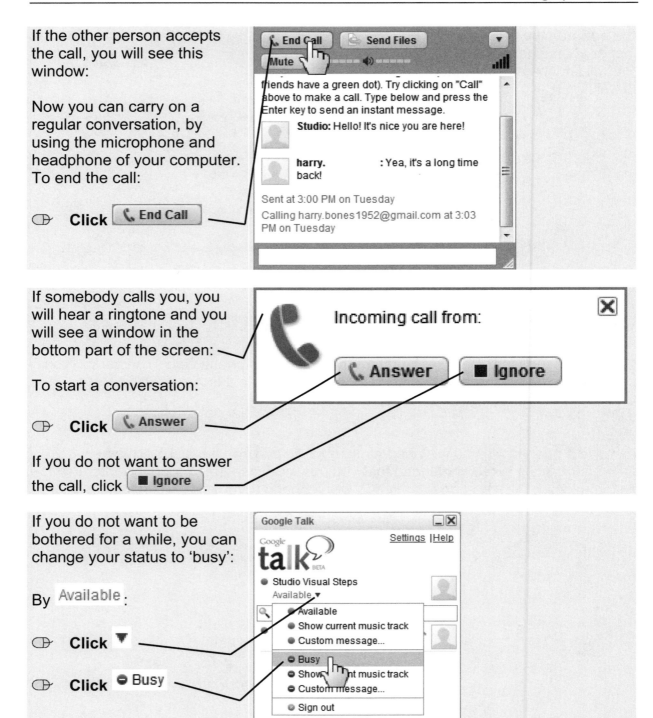

If somebody calls you, you will hear a ringtone and you will see a window in the bottom part of the screen:

To start a conversation:

☞ **Click** [📞 **Answer**]

If you do not want to answer the call, click [■ **Ignore**].

If you do not want to be bothered for a while, you can change your status to 'busy':

By [Available] :

☞ **Click** ▼

☞ **Click** [⊖ **Busy**]

If you are available again:

By `Busy`:

⊕ **Click** ▼

⊕ **Click** ● `Available`

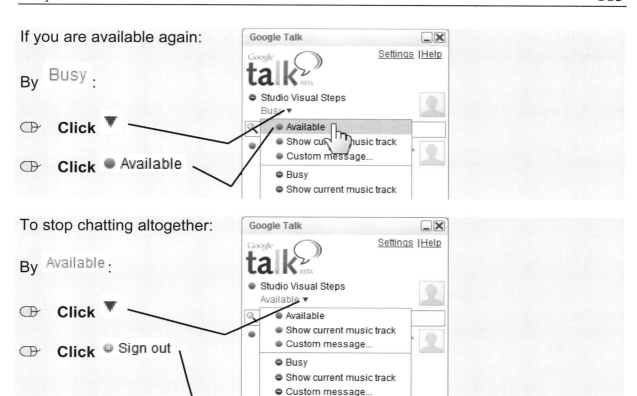

To stop chatting altogether:

By `Available`:

⊕ **Click** ▼

⊕ **Click** ● `Sign out`

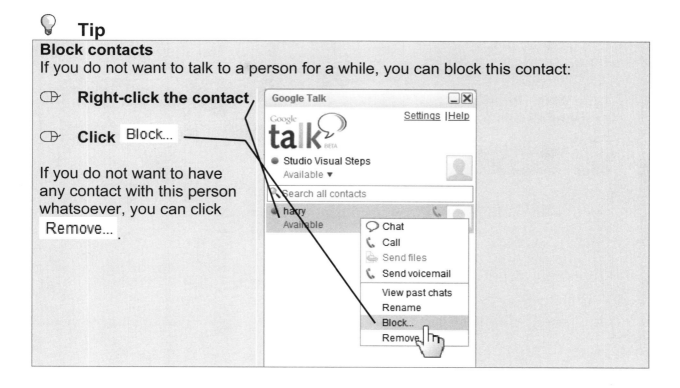

💡 Tip

Block contacts
If you do not want to talk to a person for a while, you can block this contact:

⊕ **Right-click the contact**

⊕ **Click** `Block...`

If you do not want to have any contact with this person whatsoever, you can click `Remove...`.

After you have signed out, people can no longer reach you via *Google Talk*, but you will still be able to send and receive messages with *Gmail*.

☞ **Click** ✖

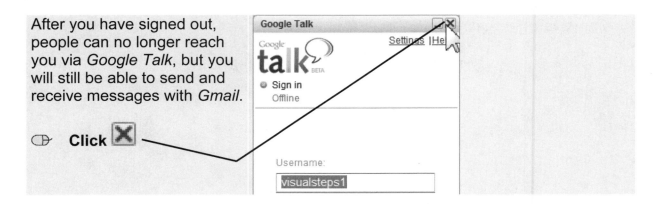

5.10 Creating a Blog

A blog is a type of website that is comparable to a diary, but then on the Internet. The word blog comes from the words website and log (logbook). A blog is also sometimes called a *weblog*. Somebody who keeps a blog is called a *blogger*. The *Google* program for creating and maintaining a blog is also called *Blogger*. This is how you install *Blogger*:

☞ **Open *Internet Explorer*** ✇¹

☞ **Browse to www.blogger.com** ✇²

In the top right-hand side of the window, sign in:

⌨ **Type your *Gmail* user name and password**

☞ **Click** **SIGN IN**

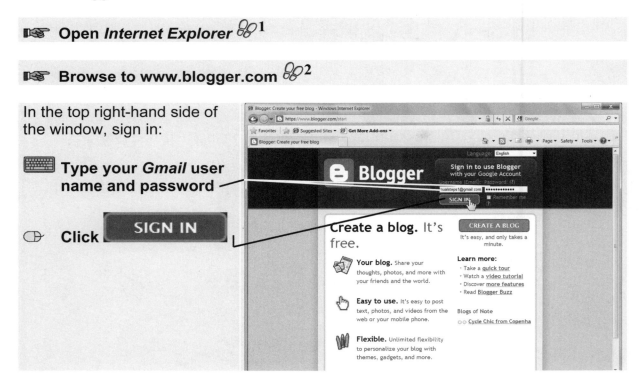

By Display name :

⌨ **Type the name you want to display in your messages**

🖰 **Check the box ☑ next to**
I accept the Terms of Servic

🖰 **Click**

CONTINUE

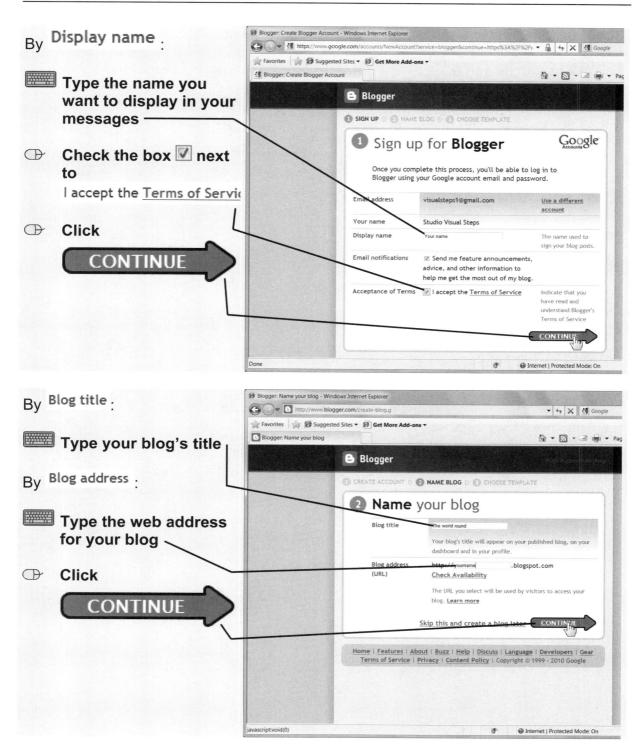

By Blog title :

⌨ **Type your blog's title**

By Blog address :

⌨ **Type the web address for your blog**

🖰 **Click**

CONTINUE

The name you just entered is now checked for availability. You cannot use an existing name. Also, punctuation marks are not allowed. If the name is not accepted, you will see an error message and you will need to choose a different name:

If your name has been accepted, you can skip this step. If the name is not available:

⌨ **Type a different name**

At the bottom of the window:

☞ **Click**

CONTINUE

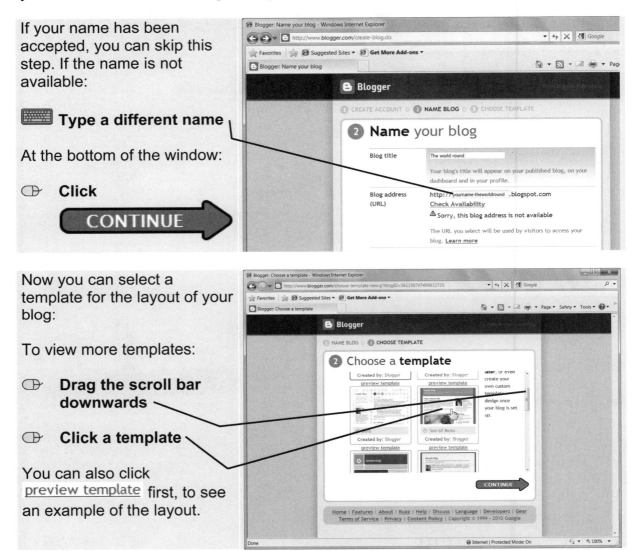

Now you can select a template for the layout of your blog:

To view more templates:

☞ **Drag the scroll bar downwards**

☞ **Click a template**

You can also click preview template first, to see an example of the layout.

☞ **If necessary, drag the scroll bar downwards**

☞ **Click**

CONTINUE

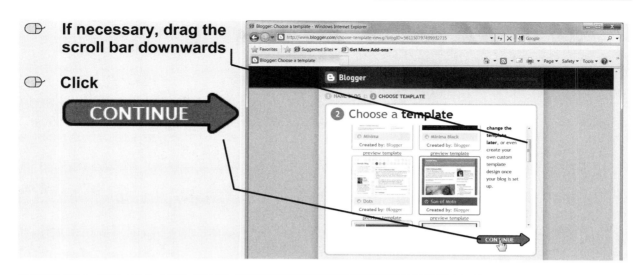

Now you can actually start editing your blog:

☞ **Click**

START BLOGGING

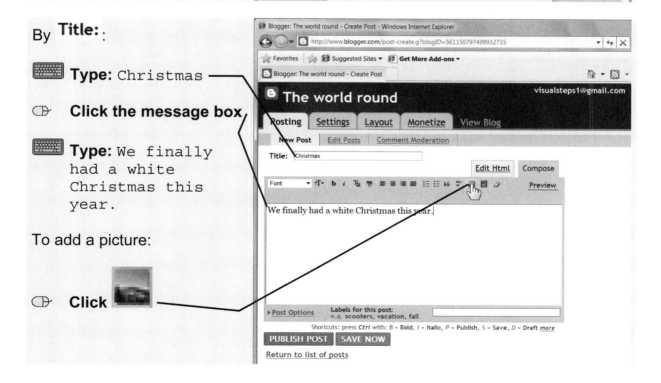

By **Title:** .

⌨ **Type:** Christmas

☞ **Click the message box**

⌨ **Type:** We finally had a white Christmas this year.

To add a picture:

☞ **Click**

👉 **Click** Browse...

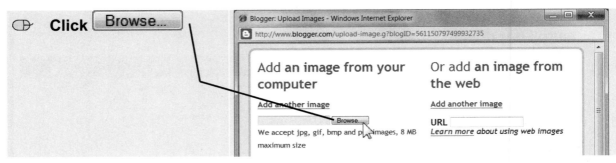

👉 **Open the *Practice-files-Google* folder** 👣11

👉 **Open the *Other pictures* folder** 👣10

👉 **Click the *Christmas-trees* photo**

👉 **Click** Open

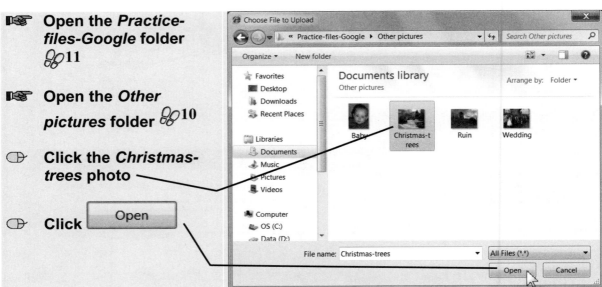

To center the picture on the page:

👉 **Click the radio button** ⦿ **by** Center

👉 **Check the box** ☑ **next to** I accept the Terms of Service

👉 **Click** UPLOAD IMAGE

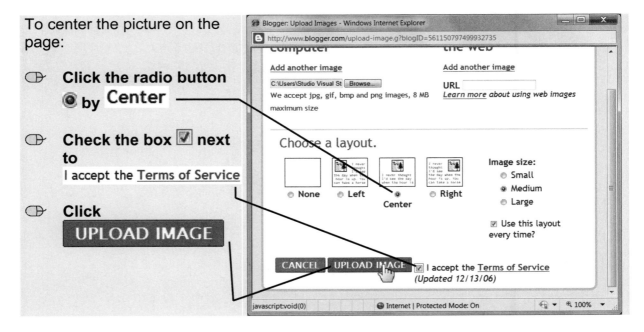

Uploading the image may take a while, depending on its size. In the meantime you will see this window:

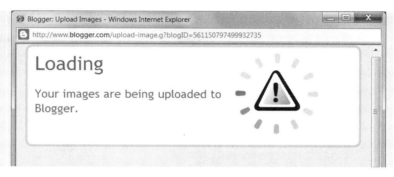

After the image is uploaded, you will see:

⊕ **Click** DONE

The image has been inserted above the text. If you want to move the image and place it under the text:

⊕ **Drag the scroll bar downwards, until you can see the text message**

⊕ **Place the mouse pointer on the image**

The pointer will turn into ✥ :

⊕ **Drag the image under the text**

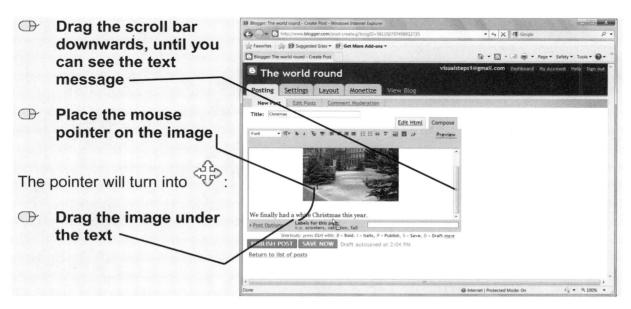

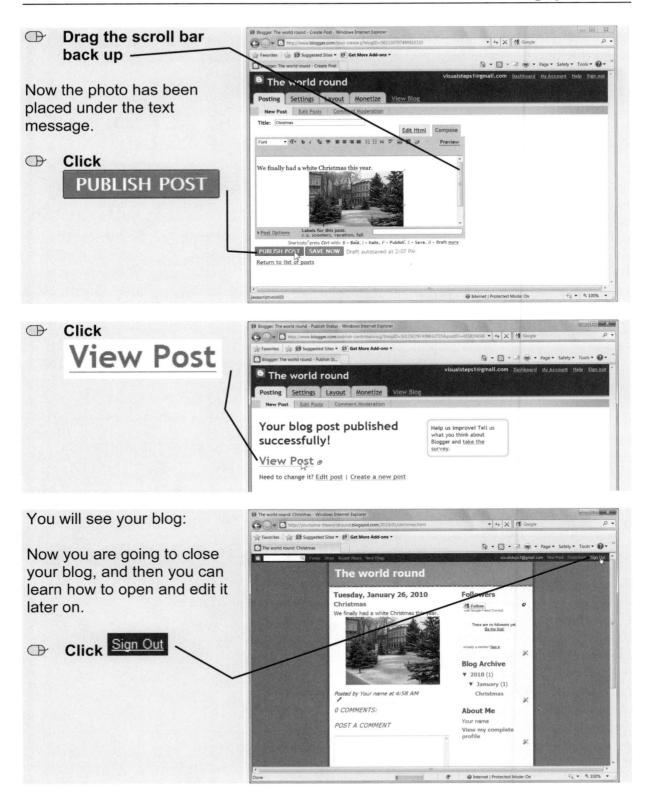

☞ **Drag the scroll bar back up**

Now the photo has been placed under the text message.

☞ **Click**
PUBLISH POST

☞ **Click**
View Post

You will see your blog:

Now you are going to close your blog, and then you can learn how to open and edit it later on.

☞ **Click** Sign Out

5.11 Update Your Blog

Usually a blog is updated regularly, for instance once a week, or once a day. In this way you are creating a kind of diary, or travel journal. But you will need to open the blog first. The blog's web address is identical to the blog's name, followed by blogspot.com. In the example in this book the blog is called yourname-the worldround.blogspot.com.

☞ **Open your blog**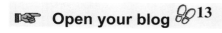

 Please note:

Do not type www at the beginning of the web address.

You now see your blog:

You can only edit your blog, if you are signed in. You can go ahead now and sign in:

👉 **Click** Sign In

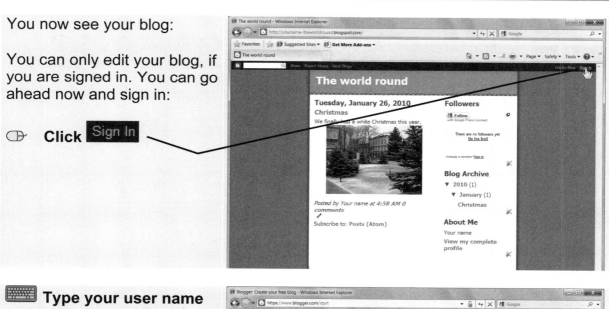

⌨ **Type your user name and password**

👉 **Click**

SIGN IN

You now see the *Dashboard*: This is where you manage your blog.

To edit a message, click **Edit Posts**:

To add (post) a new message to your blog:

☞ **Click** NEW POST

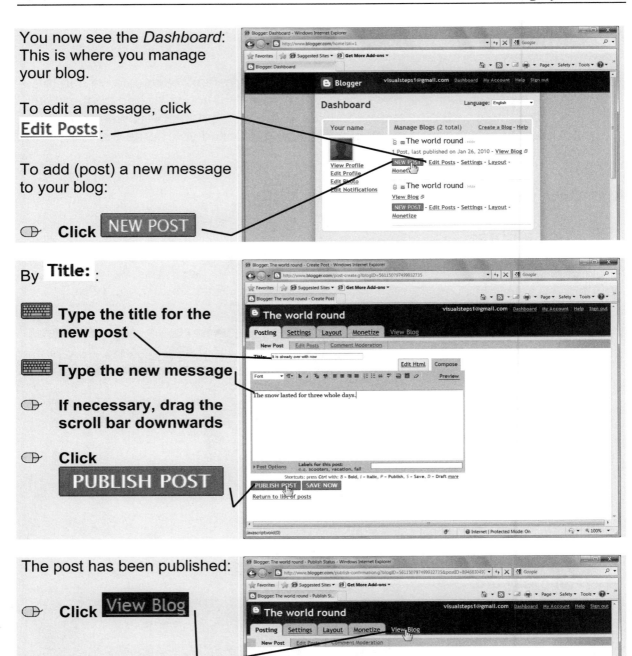

By **Title:**:

⌨ **Type the title for the new post**

⌨ **Type the new message**

☞ **If necessary, drag the scroll bar downwards**

☞ **Click**
   PUBLISH POST

The post has been published:

☞ **Click** View Blog

Your blog post published successfully!

You now see both posts:

You will also find all the posts in the *blog archive*:

 Click Sign Out

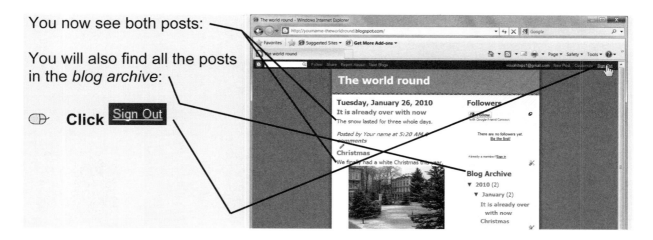

5.12 Viewing a Blog

To visit a blog, you will need to know its web address. The blog's owner can send this address to you by e-mail, or you might find the address on a website, in a magazine or newspaper. Now you are going to view your blog as a regular visitor. The web address is identical to your blog's name, followed by blogspot.com. In the example in this book the blog is called yourname-the worldround.blogspot.com

☞ **Open your blog** ✍13

⮕ **Please note:**

Do not type www at the beginning of the web address.

You now see your blog. The blog cannot be edited because you are not signed in. The New Post and Customize buttons are only visible when you are signed in:

However, some blogs do allow comments to the posts.

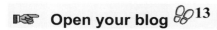 **Click**
It is already over with now

⌨ Type a comment

To post a comment, you will need to sign in first:

By **Comment as:** .

☞ **Click** ▼

☞ **Click** Google Account

☞ **Click**
Post Comment

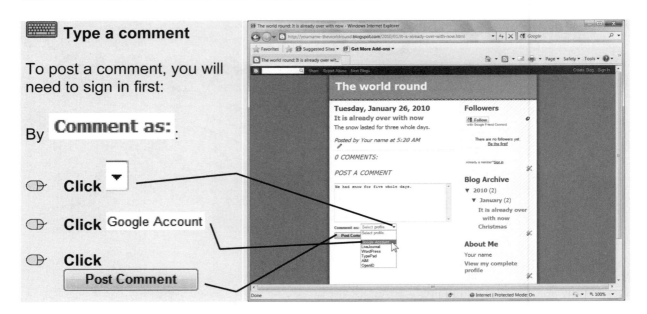

🔖 Please note:

People who do not have a *Google* account, or one of the other accounts that are displayed in the list, will be able to view the blog but cannot post a comment.

☞ Sign in to your *Google* account 👣⁹

You now see the post, and an example of a comment:

Because you have signed in with your own account, you will also see the New Post hyperlink, as well as the other links you can use to manage your blog:

If you have signed in with a different account, you will not see these links.

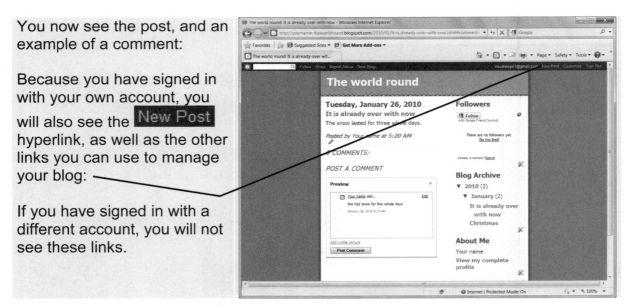

☞ **Drag the scroll bar downwards**

☞ **Click** Post Comment

Now the comment will be sent to the blog.

☞ **Click** Home

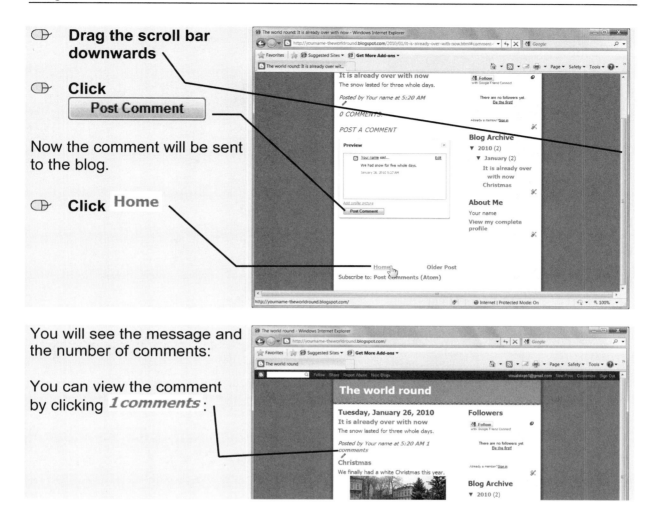

You will see the message and the number of comments:

You can view the comment by clicking *1 comments* :

5.13 Restricted Access

By default, anyone can view your blog and post comments. If you want to restrict the access to your blog and prevent people from posting inappropriate comments, you can adjust the settings:

In the top right-hand corner of the window:

☞ **Click** Customize

Click the **Settings** tab

Click **Permissions**

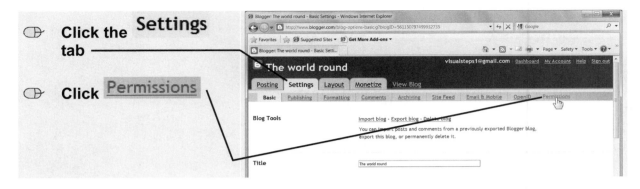

Tip

Delete a blog

On the **Settings** tab you can also delete your old blog:

Click **Delete blog**

You are the author of this blog, as well as the administrator. If necessary, you can add other authors with **ADD AUTHORS**:

You can invite friends to view your blog, and restrict the access to others:

Click the radio button ⦿ next to **Only people I choose**

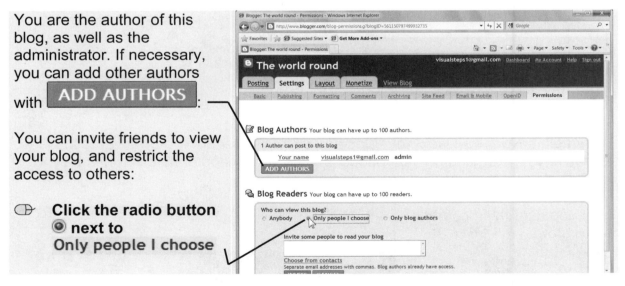

Type the e-mail address

As a test, you can type your own e-mail address first. If you want to enter multiple addresses, you can do so by typing a comma between the various e-mail addresses.

To select *Gmail* contacts, you click **Choose from contacts**.

⊕ **Click** **INVITE**

Now the invitation has been sent.

You will see the people you have invited. You can invite more people by clicking **ADD READERS**:

☞ **Close** *Internet Explorer* ⍩³

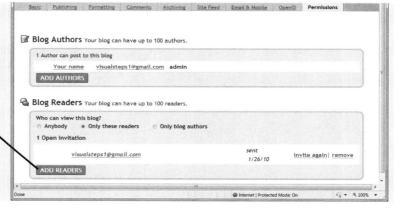

If you have invited yourself, you will receive a message in your e-mail program:

☞ **Open the message**

To visit the blog:

⊕ **Click the hyperlink**

Before you can access the
blog, you need to sign in:

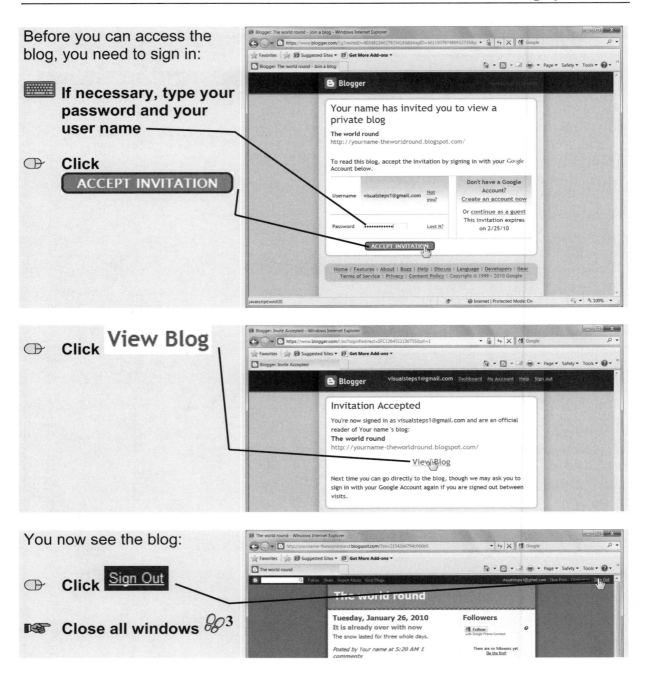

⌨ **If necessary, type your
password and your
user name**

🖰 **Click**

ACCEPT INVITATION

🖰 **Click View Blog**

You now see the blog:

🖰 **Click Sign Out**

☞ **Close all windows** 👣³

In this chapter you have learned how to create and edit a blog. Updating a blog does
not necessarily require a lot of work and it is great fun to keep your blog up-to-date.

5.14 Background Information

Dictionary	
Blogger	Somebody who keeps a blog.
Chat	Carrying on a conversation with someone by typing short messages to each other over the Internet, in real-time. These messages are also called *express messages*.
Dashboard	Summary page which displays the main functions and services of a program. For example, a blog program.
Discussion group	Location on the Internet, where a public or private group can post messages, exchange information, or download files.
Download	Copying a file from another computer, or from the Internet, to your own computer.
Moderator	A person given special privileges on the Internet, to lead discussions and remove inappropriate comments.
Publish	Posting a message on the Internet.
Talk	A communication program from *Google*, used for chatting or making phone calls by means of the Internet.
Upload	Copying a file from your own computer to the Internet, or to another computer.
Weblog, blog	A blog is a website that is best described as an Internet diary. The word 'blog' comes from the words website and log (logbook). A blog is also called a *weblog*.

Source: Google Help, Windows Help and Support, Wikipedia

5.15 Tips

 Tip

Public groups
Besides the private discussion groups, such as the one you have created in this chapter, there also public groups. If you want to discuss a specific topic, or if you want to ask a question, try visiting one of the existing discussion groups.

☞ **Click a subject**

Or:

⌨ **Type a keyword**

☞ **Click**
   Search for a group

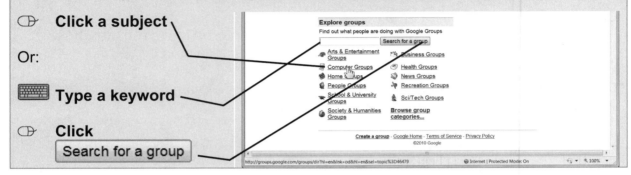

 Tip

Unsubscribe to a discussion group
If you no longer want to be a member of the group, you will need to unsubscribe:

☞ **Click**
   Edit my membership

☞ **Click**
   Unsubscribe

6. Editing and Publishing Texts

If you rarely need to use a text editor and advanced text processing options are not needed than *Google Docs* can be a great tool. The functions of the *Google Docs* program are very suitable for simple text editing, but for professional use the program might not be adequate enough.

The program is not very exceptional with regard to its text editing features, but the online processing of data is special. Just like many other *Google* programs, *Google Docs* processes and stores your data online, and you can use the program wherever you have access to the Internet. Your document is created on the Internet, and saved to a *Google* server. One of the great advantages is that you can use any computer to view and edit your documents. You can also share documents with others, which can come in handy when working in a group related project.

In this chapter the text editing functions will be discussed only briefly. The emphasis will be on the online processing of data.

In this chapter you will learn how to:

- create and save a document;
- create and use folders;
- upload documents from your computer;
- view and save public documents;
- share your own documents with others;
- export documents to your computer;
- translate text, documents, and web pages.

 Please note:

You will need a *Google* account to perform the operations in this chapter. If you do not have one yet, read *Appendix A Creating a Google Account* first and learn how to create an account.

 Please note:

To perform the operations in this book a basic knowledge of text editing programs is required. For instance, *Microsoft Word*, *Microsoft WordPad* or the text editing options available in your e-mail program.

Please note:

This chapter contains screen shots from the *Google Docs* and *Google Translate* programs. Because these programs are subject to regular changes, the screen shots in this chapter may differ from your own screen. This should not affect the operation of the programs.

 Please note:

To perform the operations in this chapter, you will need to download the corresponding practice files to your computer's hard disk. You can read how to do this in *Appendix C Download Practice Files* at the end of this book.

6.1 Text Editing with Google Docs

Unlike other well-known text editing programs, such as *Microsoft Word*, *Google Docs* does not require installation first. All the work is done online. This goes for the program as well as for the documents. To use *Google Docs*, you will need to sign in with your *Google* account:

☞ **Open** *Internet Explorer* ¹

☞ **Browse to www.google.com/options** ²

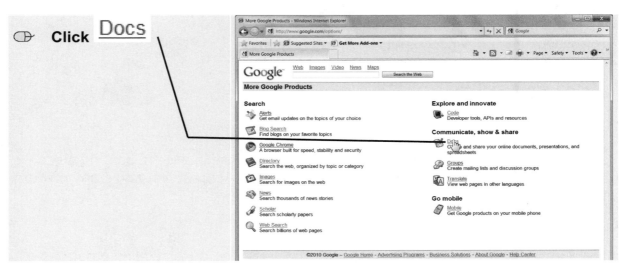

In the right-hand side of the window:

By Email:

⌨ **Type your *Google* account user name**

By Password:

⌨ **Type your password**

☞ **Click** Sign in

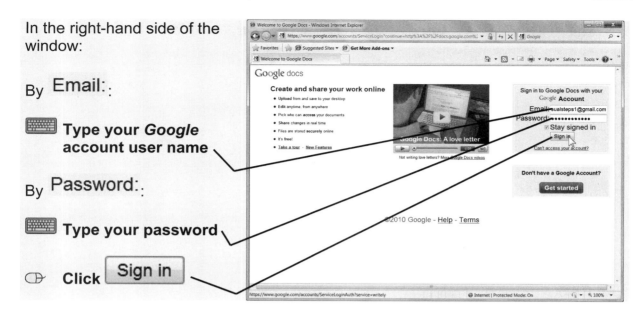

You might see a welcome message first:

☞ **If necessary, click** Close

You now see the *Google Docs* window. To create a new document:

☞ **Click** Create new ▾

☞ **Click** ▤ Document

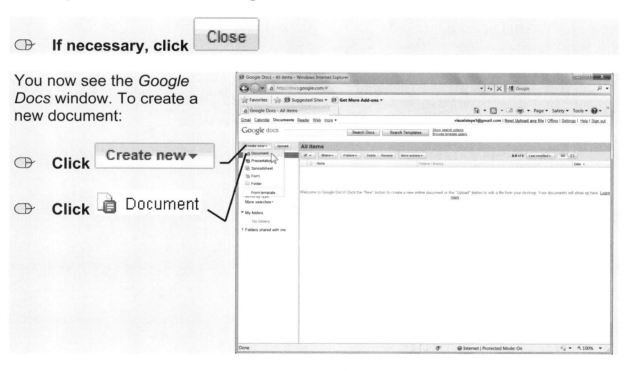

Now an empty document will be opened in a new window. Most of the text editor icons are similar to those found in other well-known text editors and also in *Gmail*.

An important difference is that the document margins are not displayed by default. Here is how to display them:

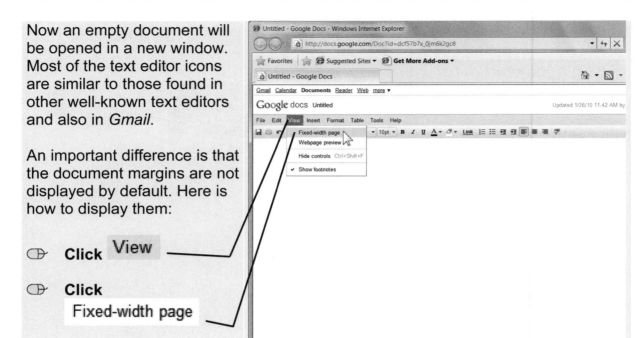

⊕ **Click** View

⊕ **Click**
    Fixed-width page

Now you see the borders of the document:

⌨ **Type a short text, start with:** Member Meeting

☞ **Try out some of the text editing options**

In the top right-hand corner of the window:

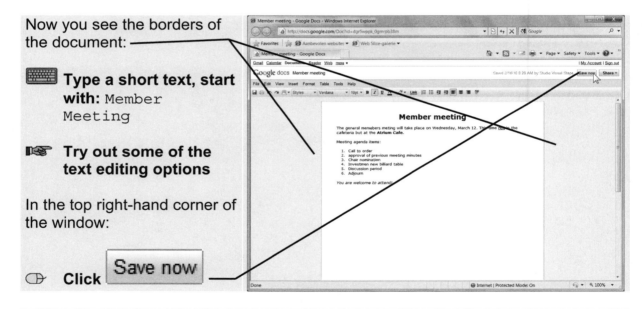

⊕ **Click** Save now

☞ **Close the window** ⏣³

💡 Tip

Change margins
The default margin is one inch for all sides. To select different margins, you need to change the print settings:

☞ **Click** File

☞ **Click** Print settings...

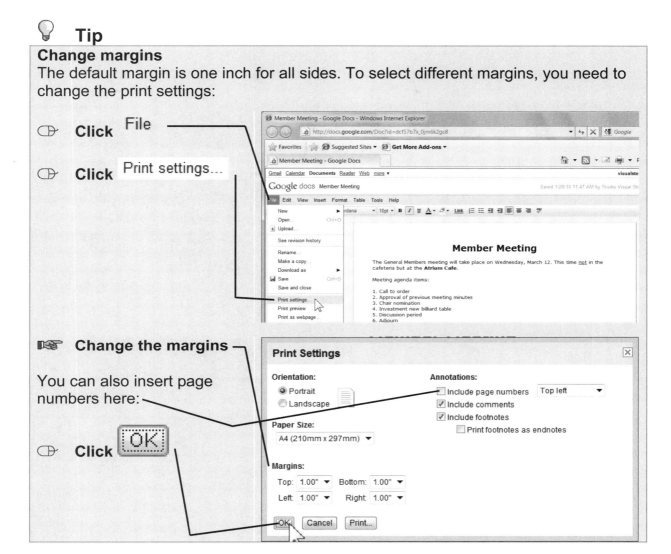

☞ **Change the margins**

You can also insert page numbers here:

☞ **Click** OK

You will see the contents page:

The document is named after the first line of the text. To change this name:

☞ **Check the box** ☑ **next to** Member Meeting

☞ **Click** Rename

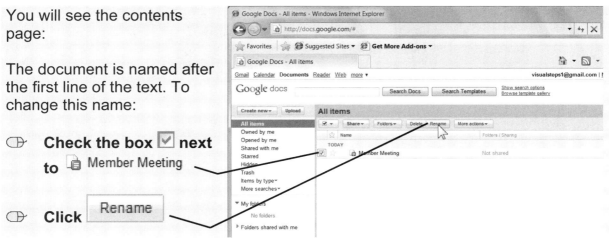

➥ Please note:

Your documents will be stored on an Internet server. That is why it may take a while before your document is displayed on the contents page. If necessary, you can click ⟲ to refresh the page.

Type: Invitation

Press Enter ↵

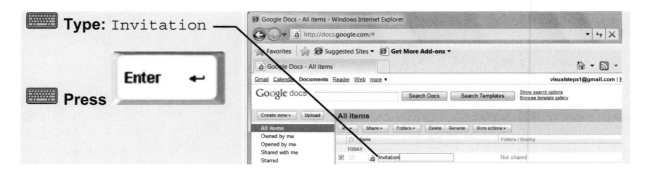

You can create folders to organize your documents:

Click Create new ▾

Click 📁 Folder

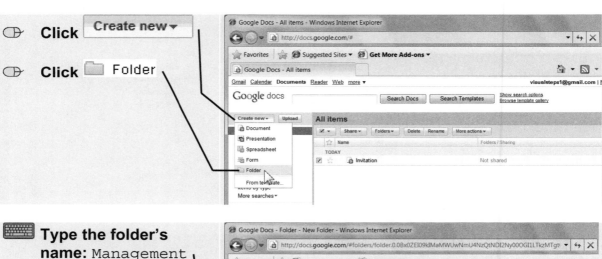

Type the folder's name: Management

Click Save

First you will see a new, empty folder:

☞ **Click** Owned by me

You will see your document:

☞ **Drag** 📄 Invitation **to** 📁 Management

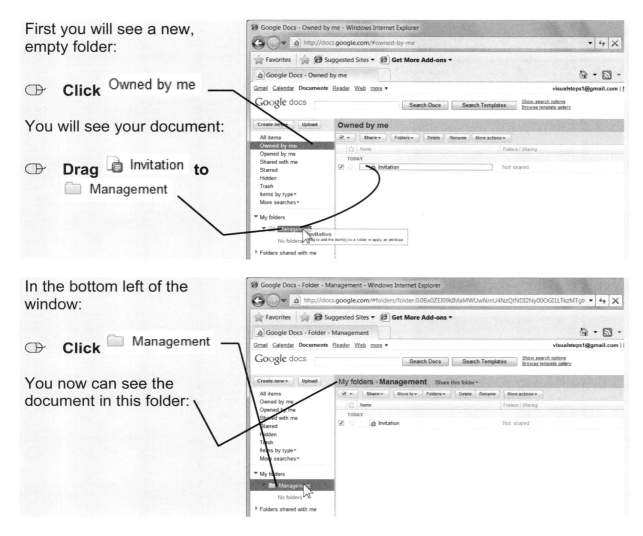

In the bottom left of the window:

☞ **Click** 📁 Management

You now can see the document in this folder:

Just as in *Gmail*, the folder merely contains a link to the document. The original document is stored in *All items*.

💡 Tip

Mark important documents with a star
If a document is important, or still has to be dealt with, you can mark it with a star:

In the document line:

⊕ **Click** ⭐ **or** ☆

The star will turn into ☆.
In the Starred folder you can find all the starred documents. You can remove the star by clicking ☆.

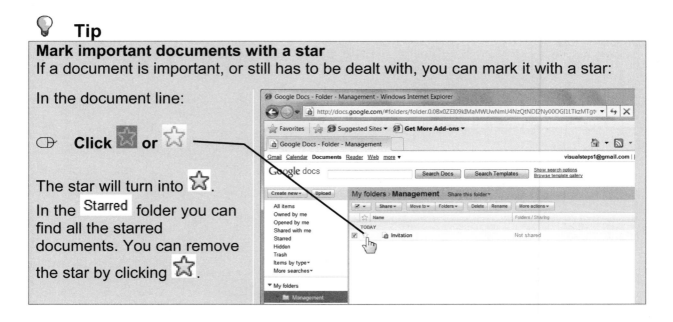

6.2 Uploading Documents

You can also upload documents from your computer to *Google Docs*, and edit them online:

⊕ **Click** Upload

⊕ **Click**
Select files to upload

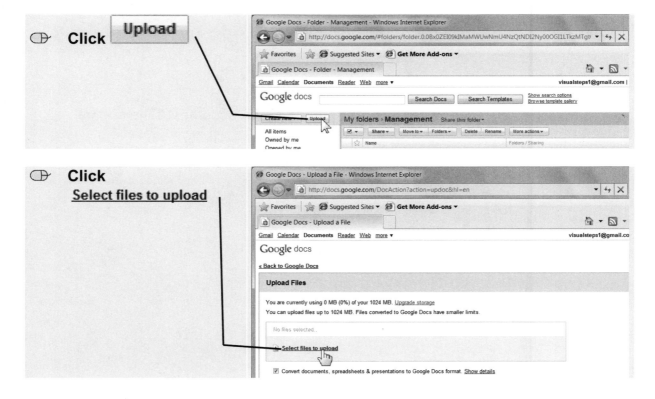

Open the *Practice-files-Google* folder 🐾11

Click exercise

Click Open

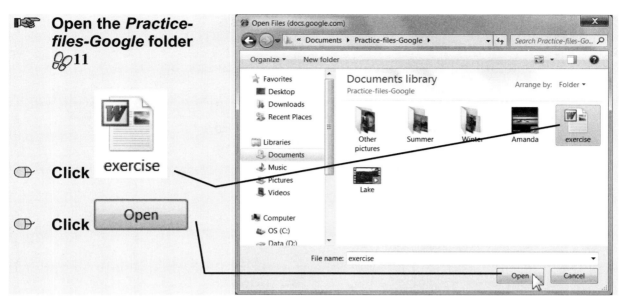

If you want to upload more files, click ⬆ Select more files :

Click Start upload

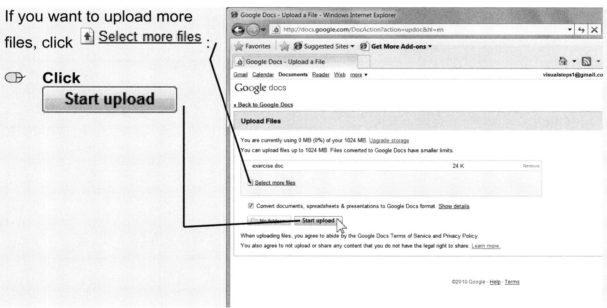

💡 Tip

Save a document directly to a folder

You can save an uploaded document directly to a specific folder:

☞ **Click** 📁 No folder ▾

☞ **Click the folder in which you want to store the document**

☞ **Click** Start upload

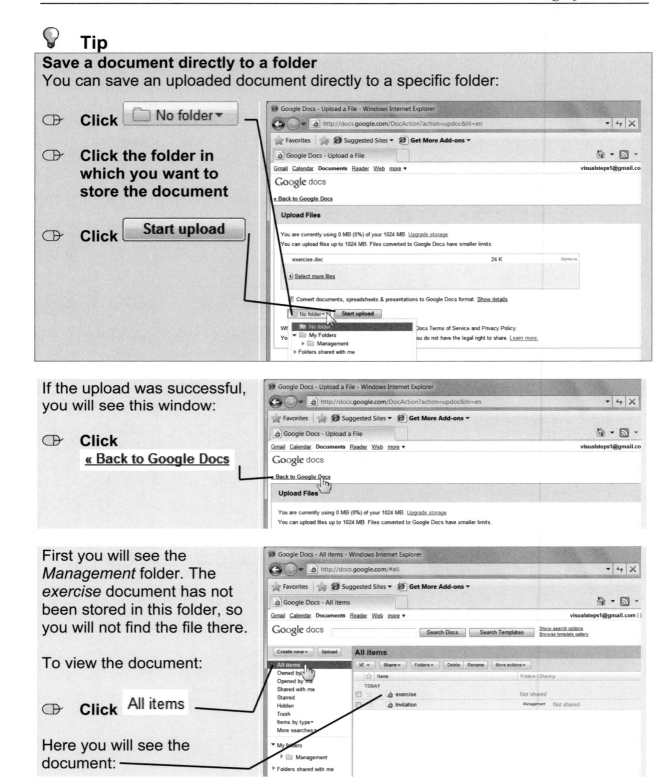

If the upload was successful, you will see this window:

☞ **Click** « Back to Google Docs

First you will see the *Management* folder. The *exercise* document has not been stored in this folder, so you will not find the file there.

To view the document:

☞ **Click** All items

Here you will see the document: ——

6.3 Public Documents

An important advantage of online documents is the possibility to edit them with a group of people. You can allow others to access your document, and access other people's documents yourself. This way, you can create a paper or a report together.

Of course, you can only access those documents for which you have been granted permission or public documents. For each document you create yourself, you can decide if it can be edited or just viewed (read-only). You can open a public document by surfing to the web address of that particular document. That address may be sent to you by e-mail. The practice document contains an example of such a web address:

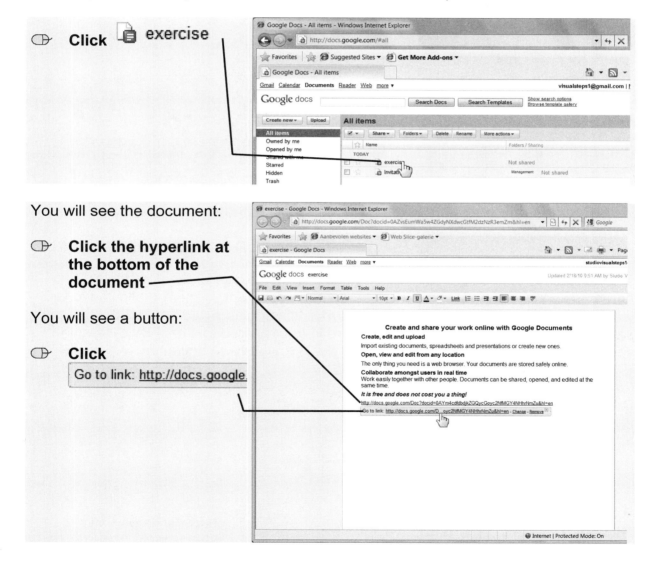

Click 📄 **exercise**

You will see the document:

Click the hyperlink at the bottom of the document

You will see a button:

Click

Go to link: http://docs.google.

Now the document has been opened in a new window:

This document has been protected and is read-only. You will not see any of the text editing icons. But you can however, copy this document and edit the copied document:

⊕ **Click** File

⊕ **Click** Make a copy...

⊕ **Click** OK

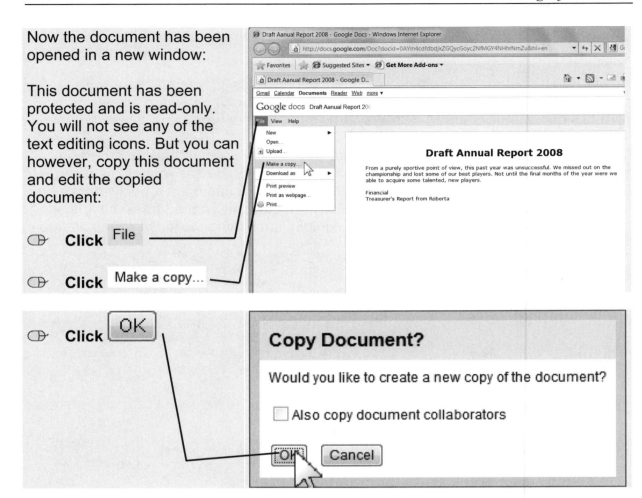

The access rights of the document (assigned by the creator of the document) determine whether or not you can edit a shared document. If you are allowed to edit the document, you will be able to use all text editing options and you will be able to save the edited document, so others can read your altered text. In the next section you will learn how to assign these access rights to your own documents.

You will see a copy of the document, which you are now allowed to edit. You are going to rename this document:

⊕ **Click** File

⊕ **Click** Rename...

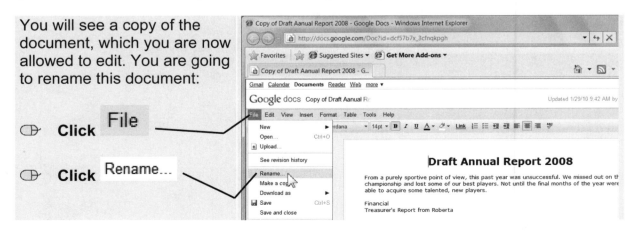

Type a new name:
Revised annual
report

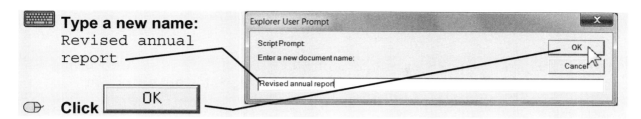

Click OK

HELP! My screen looks different.

Depending on the security settings of your web browser, you may not see a script window, but a warning message:

Click the warning message

Click
Temporarily Allow Scripted Wind

Repeat the previous step

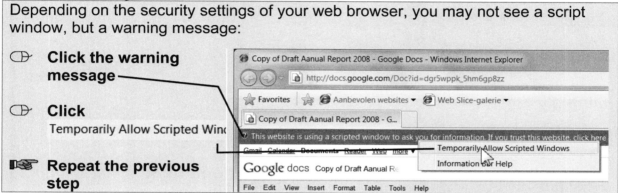

You now see the new name:

If necessary, click
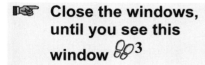

Close the windows, until you see this window 𝒫𝒫³

6.4 Sharing Documents

In most cases, you will probably only want to share a document with a few colleagues or acquaintances. This is how you set up access privileges to your document:

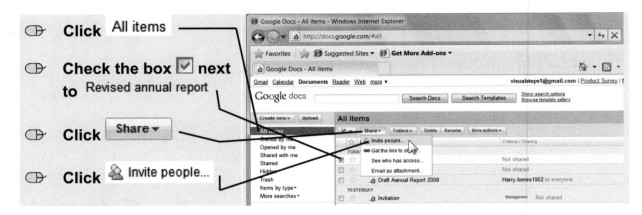

HELP! I cannot see the Revised annual report document.

If you do not see Revised annual report:

☞ Click

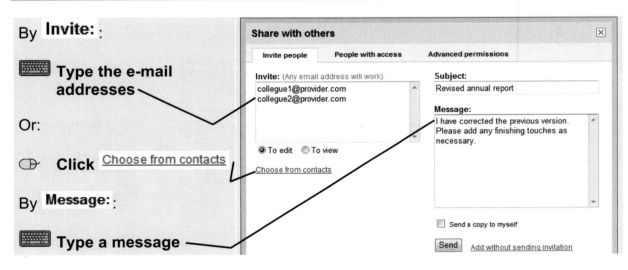

Check the box ☑ next to Send a copy to myself

Click Send

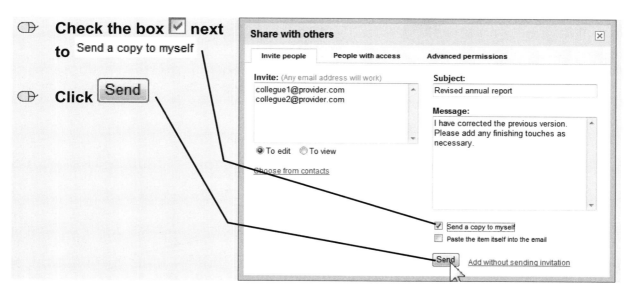

You will see an overview of all the invites:

Click Save & Close

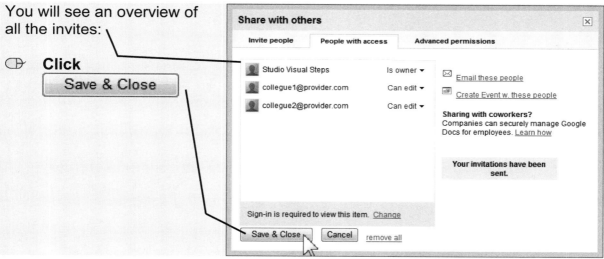

💡 Tip

Individual access rights

All of these colleagues are now able to edit your document. If that is not what you want, you can set the access rights separately for each person:

Next to the e-mail address:

☞ **Click** Can edit ▾

☞ **Click the desired access level for this address**

You can also determine whether a person should sign in first:

☞ **Click** Change

In the next window:

☞ **Click the desired option**

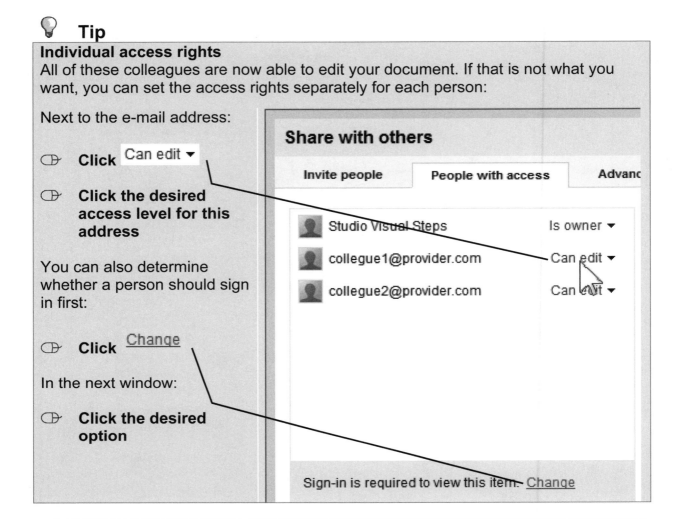

Share with others

| Invite people | People with access | Advanc |

Studio Visual Steps   Is owner ▾

collegue1@provider.com   Can edit ▾

collegue2@provider.com   Can edit ▾

Sign-in is required to view this item. Change

All persons listed under *People with access* will receive an invitation by e-mail. This is what it looks like:

By clicking the hyperlink the document will be opened.

6.5 Exporting Documents to Your Computer

All the documents are saved online. If you want to save a document on your own computer, you will need to export it:

First, you select the document:

☞ **Uncheck the box** ☑ **next to**
  Revised annual report

☞ **Check the box** ☑ **next to** exercise

☞ **Click** More actions ▾

☞ **Click** Export...

☞ **Select the desired file format, for example PDF**

At the bottom of the window:

☞ **Click** Download

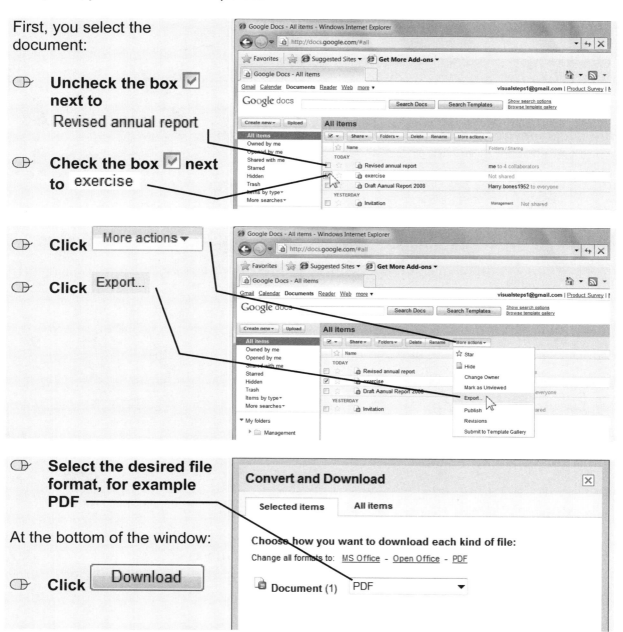

Click Save

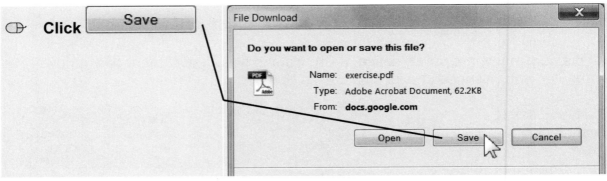

If you want, you can change the document's name or select a different folder for storage.

Click Save

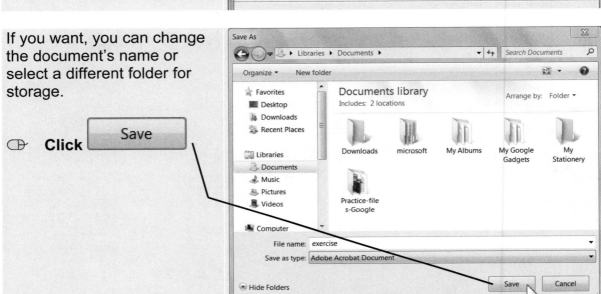

Now the document will be downloaded. When the downloading process is finished:

Click Close

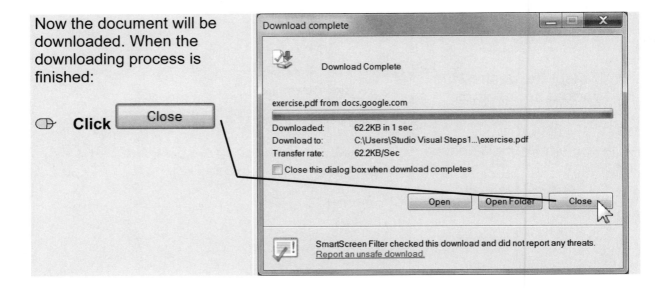

The document has been stored to your hard disk.

You will not see this in your window.

 Tip

Document properties
For each document, you can tell who the owner is and whether the document is shared:

You are the owner of Revised annual report , and you share this document with others: ———

The exercise document is not shared, that is why you are the owner: ——

The Invitation document is stored in the Management folder and is not shared: ——

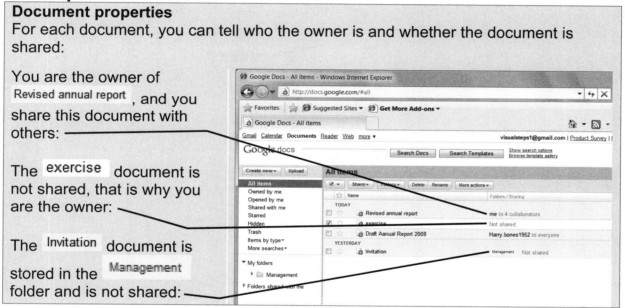

6.6 Translations

For a long time, people have desired a program that would be able to translate texts automatically. But a language is not a logical thing and words often have multiple meanings, which makes automatic translation difficult. *Google Translate* allows you to translate text from and to a large number of languages.

 Please note:

When we were putting this book together, the final version of *Google Translate* was not yet available. That is why we have used the beta edition (this is the most recent test edition). This means the screens and operations in this book may look somewhat different from what you see on your own computer.

Please note:

Even *Google Translate* will make mistakes. The translated text generated by this program should be treated as a draft version. You will still need to make final corrections to the text yourself.

☞ **Click** <u>more</u>

☞ **Click** Translate

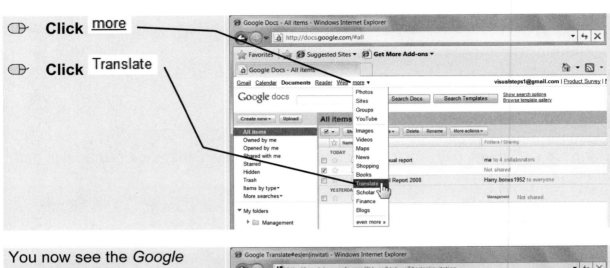

You now see the *Google Translate* window:

⌨ **Type:** invitation

By default, the text will be translated from Spanish to English. If you want to translate from English to Spanish:

☞ **Click** ⟳

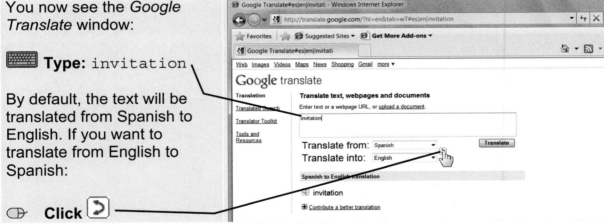

Now, *Google Translate* will translate the text from English to Spanish:

☞ **Click** Translate

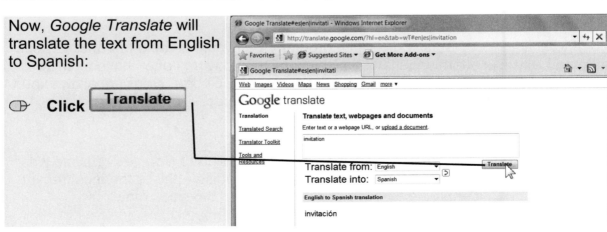

You will see the translation:

You will see some alternatives as well:

The correct translation will depend on the meaning of the text.

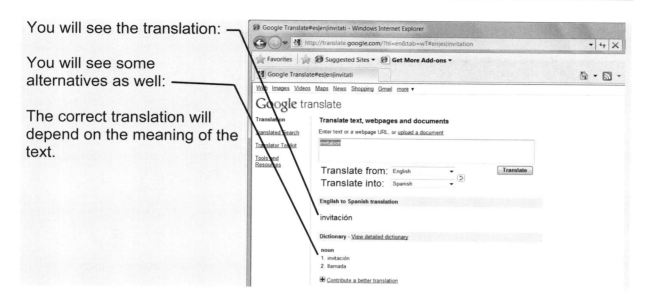

You can translate more than a single word. You can do a full web page or document that is stored on your computer. You can also switch to a different language:

⌨ **Type:**
www.visualsteps.com

By Spanish.

🖱 **Click** ▼

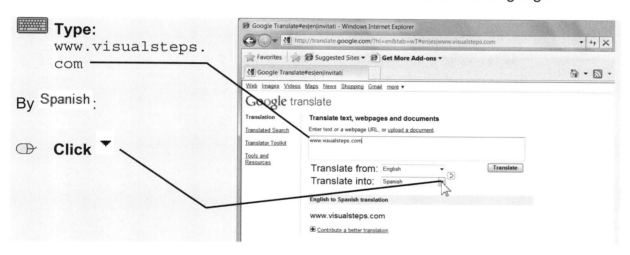

Click German

Click **Translate**

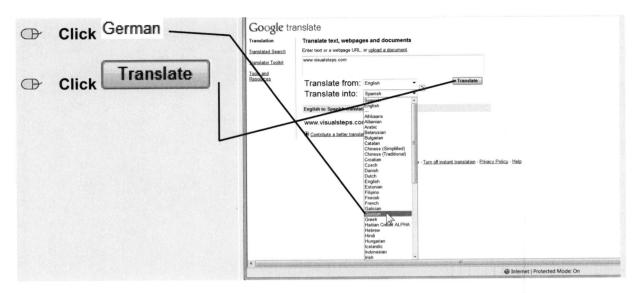

Now you will see the translation of the web page:

If you know how to read German, you will see that the translation contains a few errors.

Click

HELP! The text has not been fully translated.

A logo or banner is very often an image. Text in an image cannot not be translated.

To translate a document you have saved:

👆 **Click** upload a document.

Click Browse...

👉 **Open the *Practice-files-Google* folder** 📶11

Click exercise

Click Open

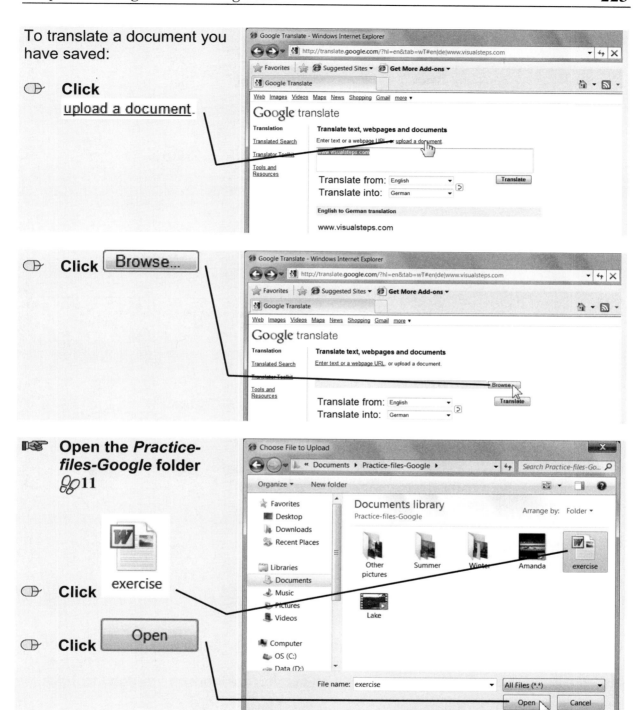

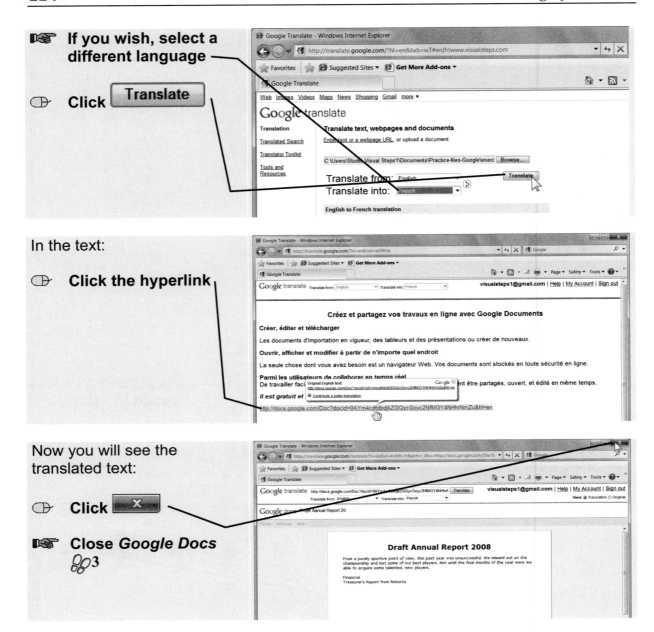

☞ **If you wish, select a different language**

🖰 **Click** **Translate**

In the text:

🖰 **Click the hyperlink**

Now you will see the translated text:

🖰 **Click** **X**

☞ **Close** *Google Docs* %3

While we were writing this book, this option was not fully functional. In this example you will see that the text has not been translated. It is possible that these functions do work correctly on your computer, by the time you are working through this book.

Translating with the help of a translation program is far from flawless. But such a program can provide you with a rough outline of the translation, and afterwards you can improve the translation manually. Often, this will save you time and you will not need to look up all the words you do not know.

6.7 Background Information

Dictionary	
Download	Copying a file from another computer, or from the Internet, to your own computer.
Export	Downloading a file from a program to your computer, in a different file format. You can access and edit the file offline.
Online/offline	If you are connected to the Internet, you are online. If you are not connected, you are offline.
Public documents	Documents that can be viewed and sometimes altered by everybody else. You can access such a document by clicking a hyperlink in an e-mail message, or on a web page.
Publishing	Placing a document on the Internet and making it accessible to other users.
Share document	Allowing others access to your documents. Access rights can be assigned when a document is created. They can be limited, for instance, read-only, or editing privileges may be allowed. A document may be viewed or shared with specific persons, or it may be public.
Upload	Copying a file from your own computer to another computer or to the Internet.

Source: Google Help, Windows Help and Support, Wikipedia

6.8 Tips

💡 Tip

Revision history
This revision history option allows you to quickly detect any alterations in a document. These may be your own alterations, or those of other people, in case the document is shared.

☞ **Check the box ☑ next to the document**

☞ **Click** More actions ▾

☞ **Click** Revisions

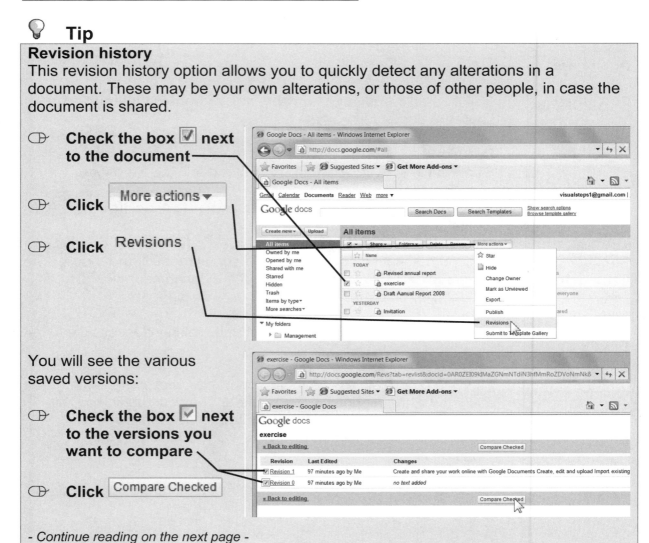

You will see the various saved versions:

☞ **Check the box ☑ next to the versions you want to compare**

☞ **Click** Compare Checked

- Continue reading on the next page -

The differences will be underlined in blue.

The background color is the color of the author who is indicated by **Authors:** Me . If other persons have edited the document as well, you will see various different colors.

Click

« Back to Revision History

☞ **Close the window** 🐾³

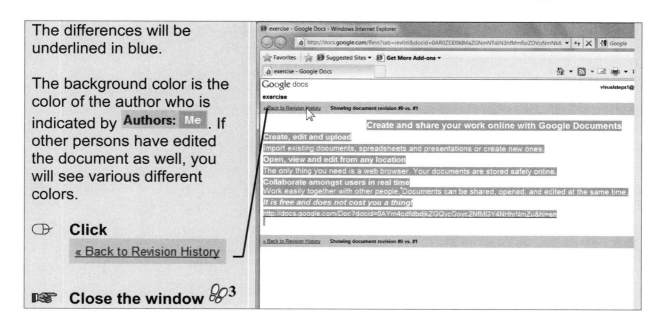

Tip

Write a Knol

Knol is a *Google* application or project which at the time of this writing was still in the beta stage. *Knol* is a sort of encyclopedia that includes user-written articles on a range of different topics. Anyone can add an article or comment on someone else's article. Compared to the Internet encyclopedia *Wikipedia*, *Knol* looks more like a forum. If you possess interesting information, expertise or want to share your views on a specific topic, you can publish your article in *Knol*.

If you want to know more about *Google Knol*:

☞ **Browse to knol.google.com** 🐾**1, 2**

Here you can read more about the purpose and possibilities of this project. You will also see the most popular categories and recent articles.

☞ **If necessary, drag the scroll bar downwards**

☞ **Click a *Knol***

Now you will see a *Knol*:

You can edit this *Knol* by clicking $\boxed{\textbf{Edit this knol}}$, or write a new *Knol* yourself with $\boxed{\textbf{Write a knol}}$.

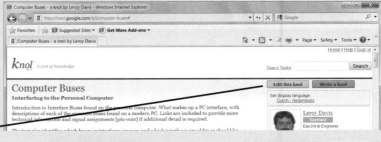

To write a *Knol* you need to sign in with your *Google* account.

To find out more about this feature:

☞ **Click** $\underline{\text{Learn More}}$

7. Publishing Web Pages and Videos on the Internet

There are several different ways of publishing information on the Internet. You have already learned a bit about this subject in the chapters covering discussion groups and *Blogger*. In this chapter you will learn how to upload video clips to *YouTube* and how to create your own website with *Google Sites*.

The nice thing about having your own website is that you are completely free to determine what the site will look like and what to publish on the site. Applications such as *Blogger* and *YouTube* are designed for specific goals and their layout is suited to their use. With *Google Sites* however you can publish your videos or travel journals on the Internet and determine yourself what the windows will look like. Furthermore, you can use *Google Sites* to create an attractive website on any possible subject, for instance a site about your family or hobbies.

One of the most popular websites these days is the *YouTube* website. You could consider *YouTube* as your own personal Internet TV set. *YouTube* is a very large website that contains digital videos on every conceivable subject. *YouTube* is special because its users supply the videos themselves. The content of the clips is very diverse. It ranges from holiday videos to video clips in which somebody sings a song or recites a poem. But you can also find fragments of TV shows and movies. For your information, it is illegal to upload copyright protected TV shows or movies.

Anyone can view videos on the *YouTube* website. By registering, you will gain access to the *YouTube* community. You will then be allowed to upload your own (home) videos to *YouTube*. Your friends or anyone else who is interested will then be able to view your videos.

In this chapter you will learn how to:

- create a website;
- arrange the layout of your web page, add text and images;
- add an index to a page;
- create hyperlinks;
- add *Google* functions to a website;
- play videos with *YouTube*;
- sign up for *YouTube*;
- upload a video;
- add friends to *YouTube*;
- remove your video.

Please note:

The content and layout of the *YouTube* website changes daily. The screen shots in this book may differ from what you see on your own screen. This should not affect the operations covered in this chapter. Any major changes to the *YouTube* functions will be noted on the website that goes with this book.

 Please note:

To perform the operations in this chapter, you will need to download the corresponding practice files to your computer's hard disk. You can read how to do this in *Appendix C Download Practice Files* at the end of this book.

7.1 Create a Website with Google Sites

Creating a new website with *Google Sites* is quick and easy. You will not have to apply for a domain name first so you can start right away:

☞ **Open *Internet Explorer*** ✌¹

☞ **Browse to www.google.com/sites** ✌²

☞ **Sign in to your *Google* account** ✌⁹

⊕ **Click** | Sign in |

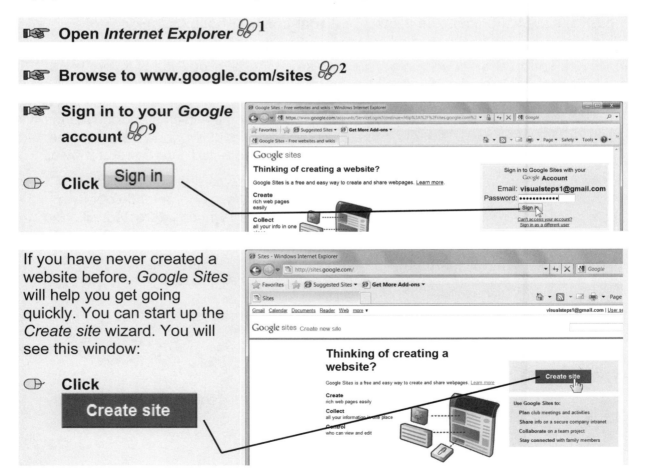

If you have never created a website before, *Google Sites* will help you get going quickly. You can start up the *Create site* wizard. You will see this window:

⊕ **Click** | Create site |

By **Name** your Site: .

⌨ **Type the name of your site** ⸻

Now you will see your site's web address: ⸺

By **Choose a theme** :

☞ **Click** ⊞ ⸻

🐦 **Please note:**

A web address consists exclusively of letters and digits. All other symbols are excluded. The name of your website cannot be identical to an existing website or a *Gmail* user name (except your own user name).

For now, you are going to create a public website. In the *Tips* at the end of this chapter you can learn how to restrict access to your website.

Here you see various themes that can be used for the layout of your site. To see more:

☞ **Drag the scroll bar downwards** ⸺

☞ **Click the desired theme** ⸺

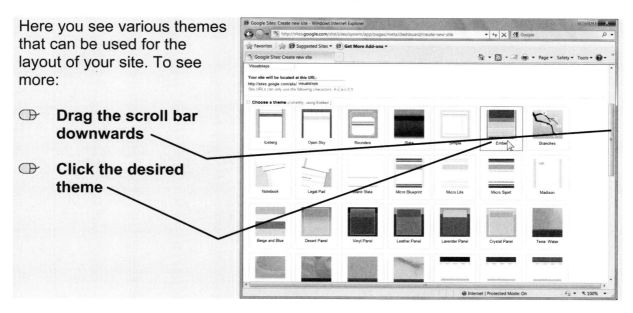

☞ **Drag the scroll bar downwards further**

⌨ **Type the code**

Please note: you will see a different code on your screen.

☞ **Click**

Create site

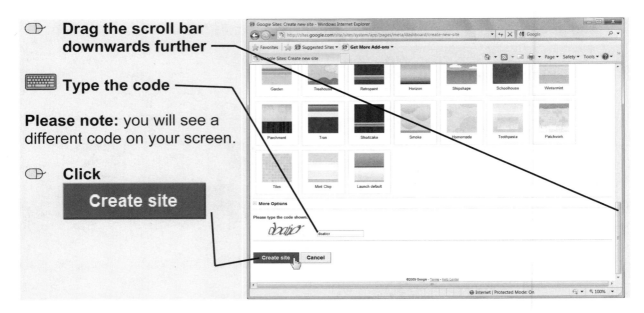

7.2 Creating Web Pages

If the name is available, you will see the home page for this website. You can now insert additional text and images if desired:

☞ **Click** ✎ **Edit page**

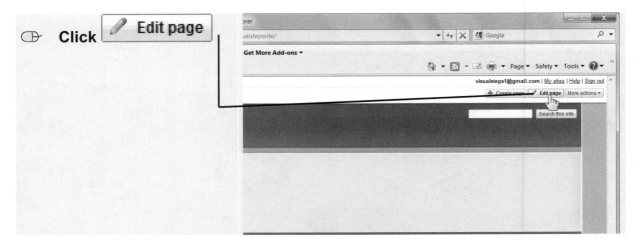

Type: This website shows pictures of my recent vacation.

You can edit and format the text by clicking the text editing icons shown above the website.

To change the title:

☞ **Double-click** Home

Type: Welcome

To insert an image:

☞ **Click** Insert

☞ **Click** Image

☞ **Click** Browse...

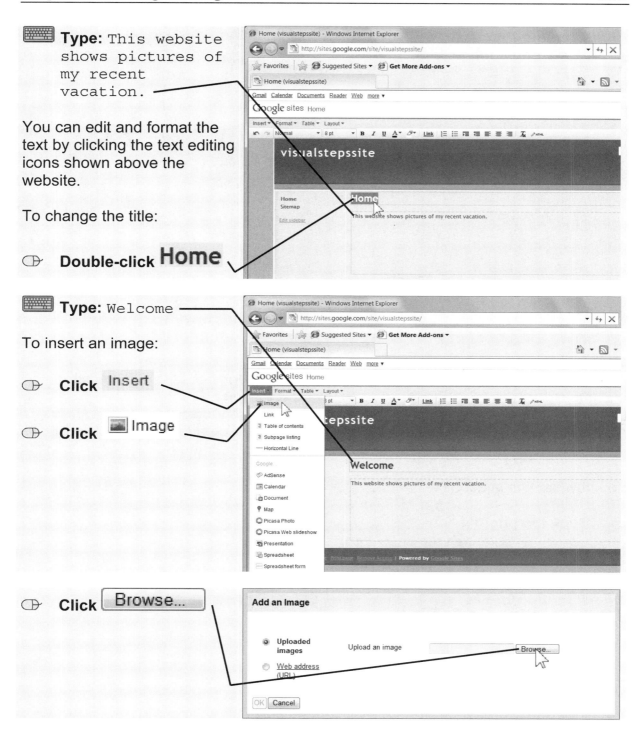

☞ **Open the *Practice-files-Google* folder** 👣11

☞ **Open the *Summer* folder** 👣10

👉 **Click the *City* photo**

👉 **Click** [Open]

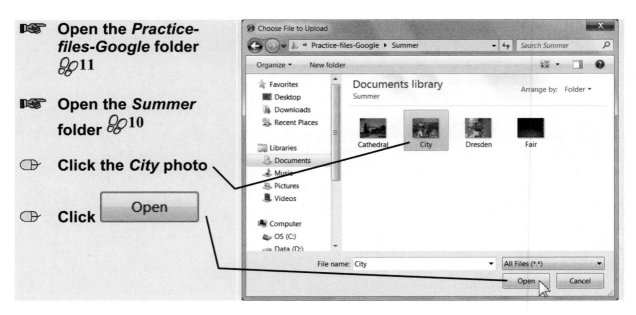

💡 Tip

Limit the file size of your images
It is best to use smaller image files for your website. Your website will load faster and the images will take up less space on your web server.
Large photo files can be reduced by using a photo editing program. For example, *Picasa* lets you export a photo file in various formats and image qualities. Usually, the minimum file size is good enough for publishing to the Internet.

You now see the image:

👉 **Click the photo**

👉 **Click** [OK]

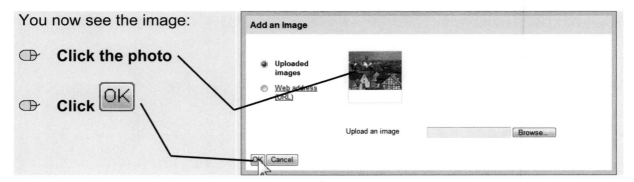

Now the photo will be displayed. If the photo is very large, you can make it smaller:

☞ **Click **

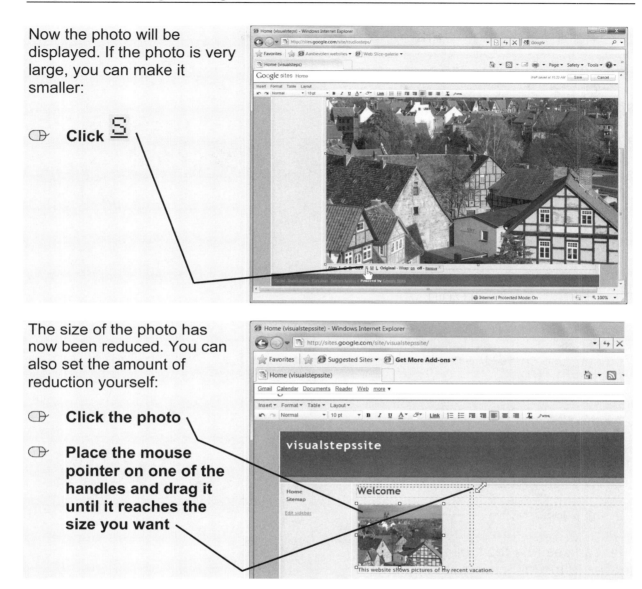

The size of the photo has now been reduced. You can also set the amount of reduction yourself:

☞ **Click the photo**

☞ **Place the mouse pointer on one of the handles and drag it until it reaches the size you want**

➥ Please note:

If you are going to set the image size yourself, you need to remember that the height and width aspect ratio must be preserved. Otherwise the picture will be distorted. Therefore, it is best to drag the handles located in any corner of the picture.

The text now stands underneath the photo. If you would rather have the text positioned on the right-hand side of the photo:

☞ **Click the photo**

A toolbar now appears underneath the photo.

By Wrap::

☞ **Click on**

You can also center the photo or move it to the right.

☞ **Click the photo again**

In the toolbar by Align::

☞ **Click R**

You can see that the toolbar moves to the left, center or right each time you set the alignment of the photo.

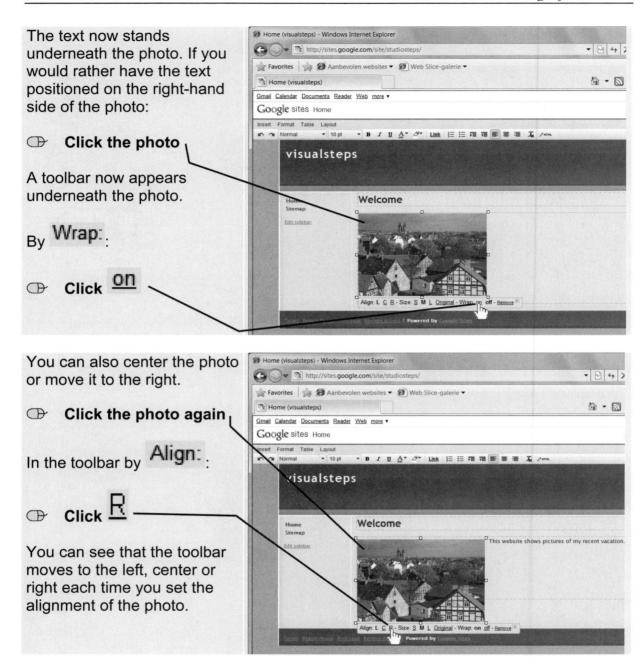

Now you see the text positioned on the left side of the photo:

Before you can view the adjustments you made, you must save the webpage first.

In the top right-hand corner of the window:

Click **Save**

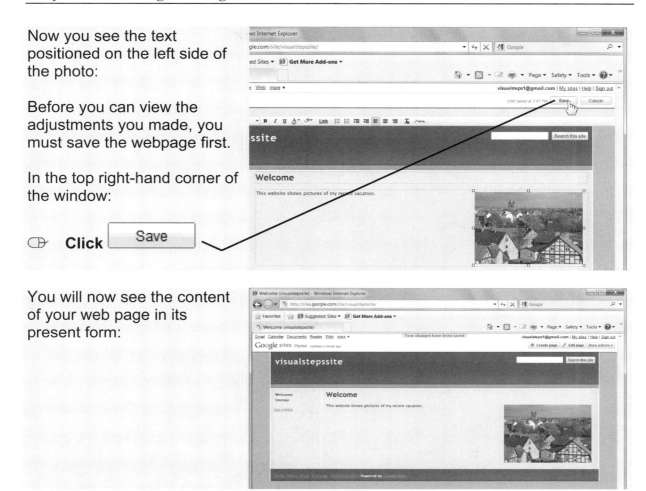

You will now see the content of your web page in its present form:

7.3 Adding New Pages

If you want to keep your website well organized, it is best to create multiple pages. This is how you add a new page to your website:

In the top right-hand side of the window:

Click **Create page**

The default web page will be selected:

By **Name:** :

⌨ **Type:** Summer vacation

☞ **Click the radio button ⦿ next to** Put page under **Welcome**

☞ **Click** Create Page

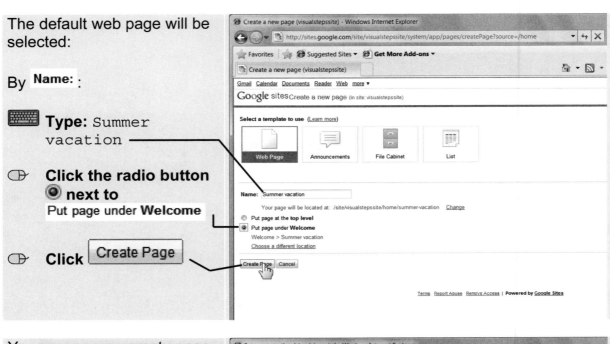

You now see an empty page. You are going to add a *header*:

☞ **Click** Format

☞ **Click** Minor heading (H4)

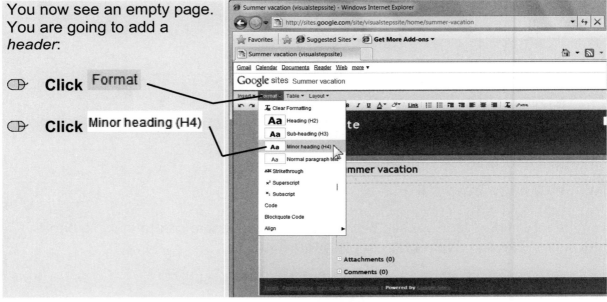

Type: 2008

Press Enter ←

Type: Our first destination was the city of Stolberg.

The header will automatically be printed in bold letters. The following lines are printed in the regular font.

Press Enter ← three times

Press ↑

Now insert a horizontal line:

👆 **Click** Insert

👆 **Click** — Horizontal Line

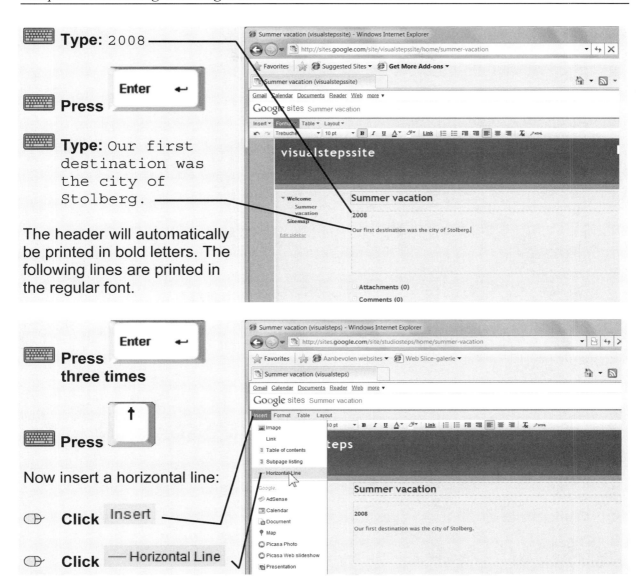

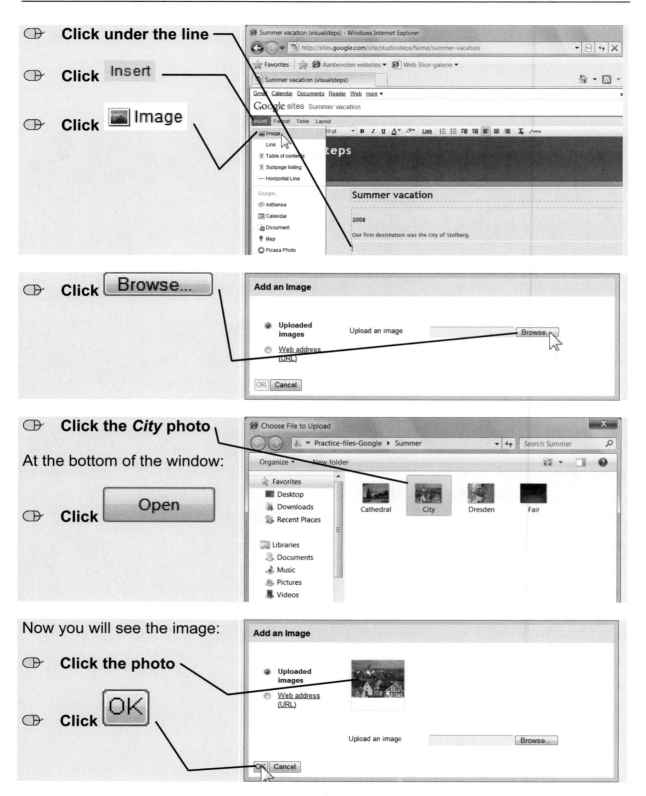

Click under the line

Click Insert

Click 🖼 Image

Click Browse...

Click the *City* photo

At the bottom of the window:

Click Open

Now you will see the image:

Click the photo

Click OK

You can see that the photo in its original form is too large for the webpage.

☞ **Click the photo**

By Size: :

☞ **Click M**

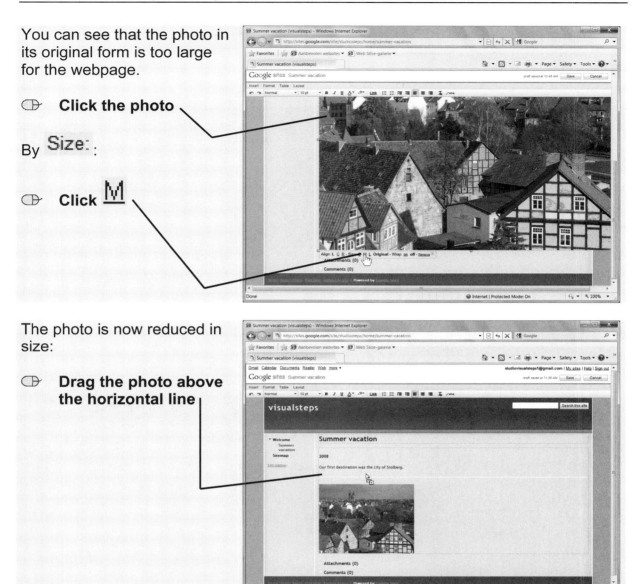

The photo is now reduced in size:

☞ **Drag the photo above the horizontal line**

👆 **Click under the horizontal line**

⌨ **Press twice**

Enter ⏎

👆 **Click** Format

👆 **Click** Minor heading (H4)

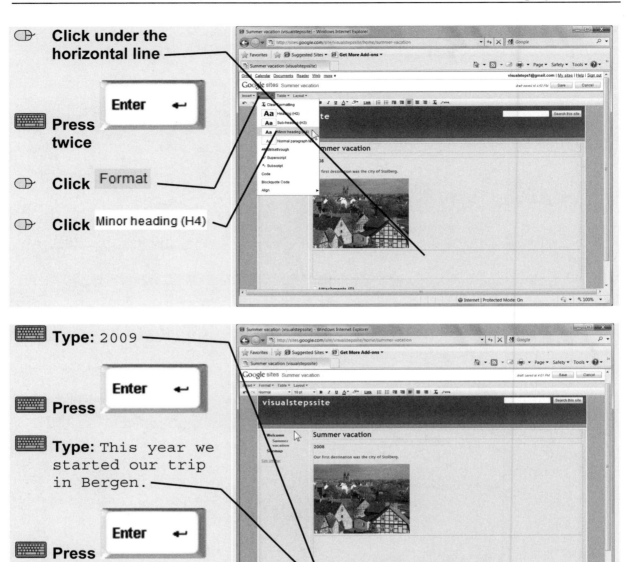

⌨ **Type:** 2009

⌨ **Press** Enter ⏎

⌨ **Type:** This year we started our trip in Bergen.

⌨ **Press** Enter ⏎

7.4 Creating a Table of Contents

The text headers will automatically be marked as a *hyperlink* and will be included in the index. You can add the table of contents to the top of the page. First, you will need to edit the layout:

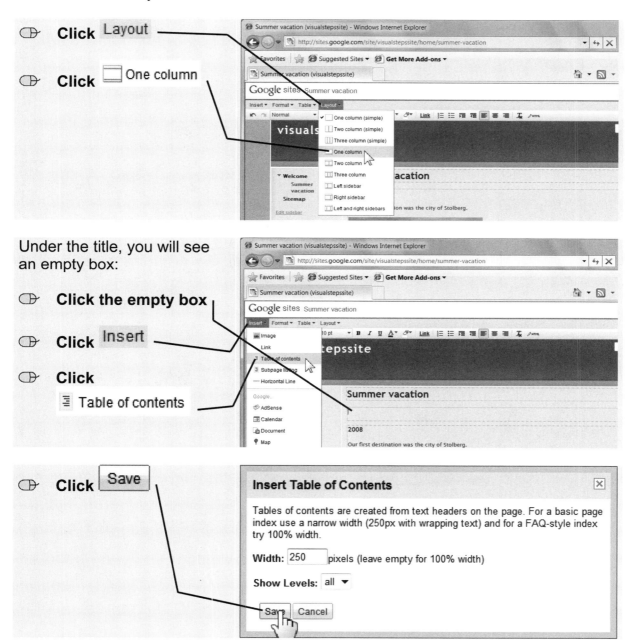

☞ **Click** Layout

☞ **Click** ☐ One column

Under the title, you will see an empty box:

☞ **Click the empty box**

☞ **Click** Insert

☞ **Click**

　　▥ Table of contents

☞ **Click** Save

Insert Table of Contents　　⊠

Tables of contents are created from text headers on the page. For a basic page index use a narrow width (250px with wrapping text) and for a FAQ-style index try 100% width.

Width: 250　　pixels (leave empty for 100% width)

Show Levels: all ▼

Save　Cancel

Now you see a rectangular box that will contain the table of contents. ———

You can enlarge, reduce, or move this box, in the same way you adjust images.

☞ **Click** Save

Now you see the table of contents:

☞ **Click** 2 2009

You will see the description for 2009:

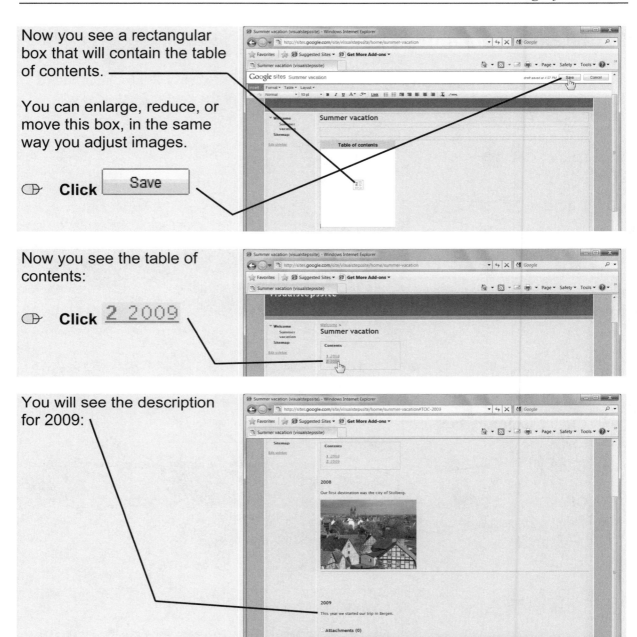

7.5 Adding Google Functions

In addition to regular text and images, you can also add various *Google* functions to your website. For instance, you can add a map from *Google Maps*:

 Please note:

The map you are going to add to your website is interactive. A visitor can enlarge the map, zoom in and out and many other things. This would not be possible if you were to add the map to your website as a regular image.

☞ **Drag the scroll bar up**

In the top right of the window:

☞ **Click** ✚ **Create page**

Now the default web page has been selected:

By **Name:**:

⌨ **Type:** Map Bergen

☞ **Click the radio button** ⦿ **next to**
    Put page under **Summer va**

☞ **Click** Create Page

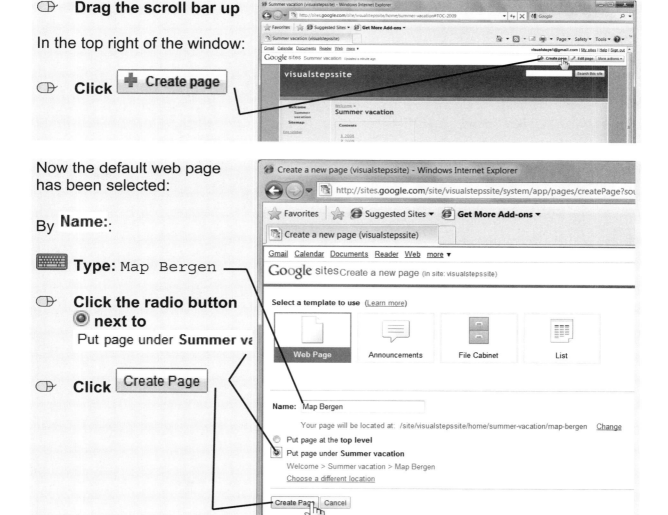

Click Insert

Click ♥ Map

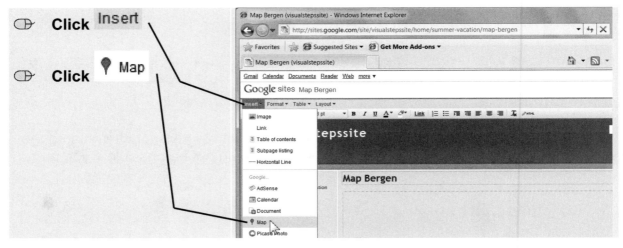

In the search box:

Type: Bergen Netherlands

Click Search

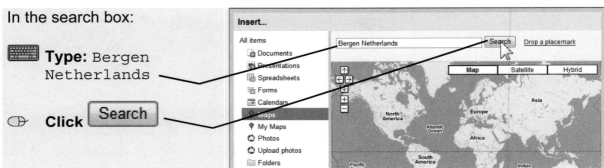

To close the information window:

Click ✕

You will be able to zoom in or out or move around in the map just like you learned to do in *Chapter 2 Exploring the World*.

Click Select

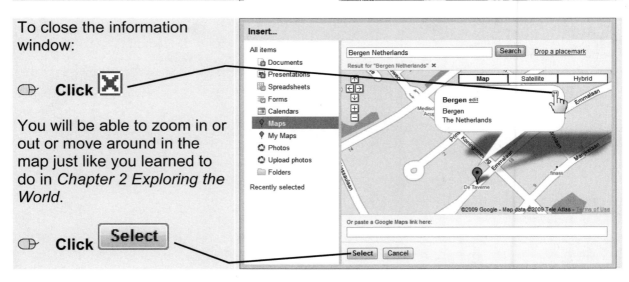

Click Save

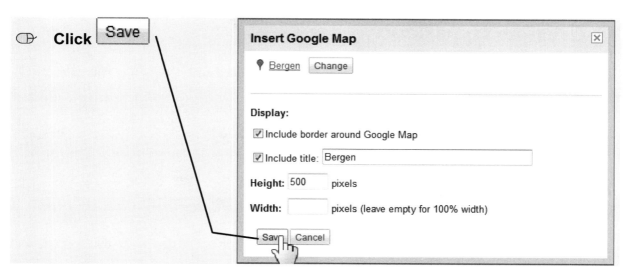

In the top right of the window:

Click Save

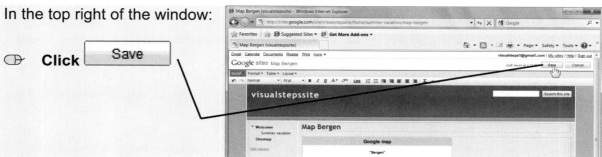

Now you see the map:

Click
Summer vacation

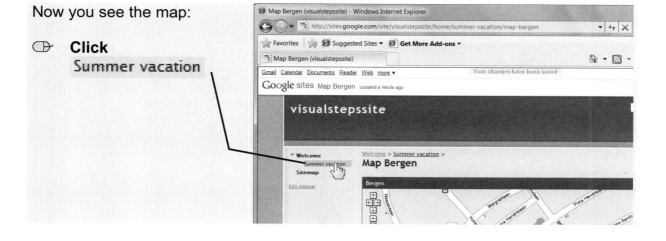

7.6 Creating Hyperlinks

Since you have added the map to the *Summer vacation* page, the page will now contain a link to the map (at the bottom of the page). You can add an extra hyperlink to your map by using a word or sentence. To create a link from *Bergen* to the map:

In the top right of the window:

Click Edit page

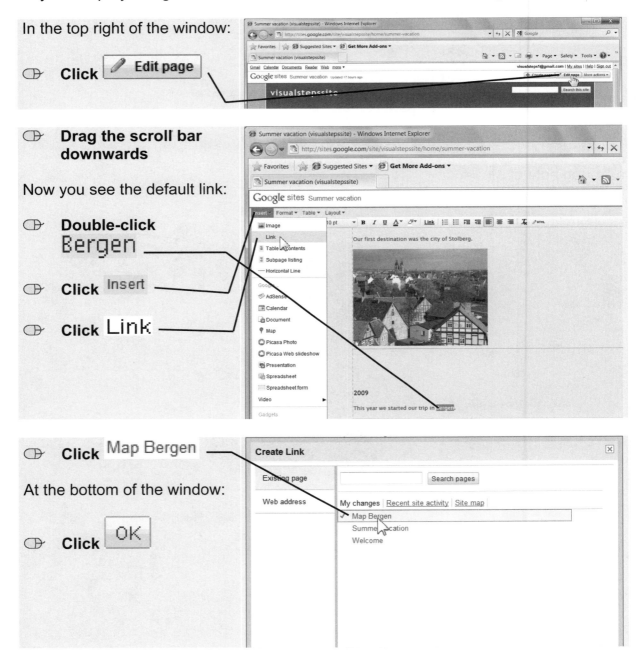

Drag the scroll bar downwards

Now you see the default link:

Double-click Bergen

Click Insert

Click Link

Click Map Bergen

At the bottom of the window:

Click OK

Now Bergen has become a link: ——

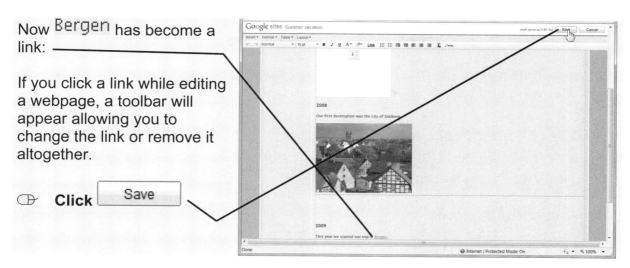

If you click a link while editing a webpage, a toolbar will appear allowing you to change the link or remove it altogether.

☞ **Click** | Save |

💡 Tip

Attachments and comments
The owner can add comments and attachments to a webpage. Visitors will be able to view the comments and download the attached files. In this way you can add larger images or other documents such as PDF files to your website. Visitors who are interested can download these files.

Comments and attachments can only be added or removed by the owner of the website. As the owner of the website, you can remove an attachment when editing the webpage by clicking the *Delete* link next to the title of the attachment.

☞ **Drag the scroll bar up**

☞ **Click** Sign out

☞ **Close all windows** 𝒪𝒪3

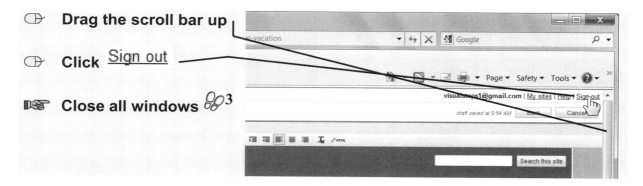

You can update your website by signing in to the *google.sites.com* webpage (you do not need to type the 'www'). Other people can view your website by surfing to the *sites.google.com/site/sitename* web page. Instead of *sitename* they will need to type your website's name. In this chapter we have used the address: *sites.google.com/site/visualstepssite*. Since these web addresses are rather long and not easy to remember, it is best to inform your friends or family about your new site by sending them an e-mail message with a link to the website. This link can easily be clicked to open your website.

7.7 Playing Videos with YouTube

You might not know it, but *YouTube* is also a *Google* program. If you want to use *YouTube*, you need to visit the website:

☞ **Open** *Internet Explorer* ✍¹

☞ **Browse to www.youtube.com** ✍²

You now see the *YouTube* website:

Search for videos: ——

Current videos: ——

Please note: because new videos are added on a daily basis, you will see different videos on your screen.

There are various ways to find and play videos on *YouTube*. On the *YouTube* home page you will find several videos that you can play right away. Among these are the most popular videos, or videos that are rated highly by users:

👆 **If necessary, drag the scroll bar downwards**

By 🔲 **Featured Videos** .

👆 **Click a video** ——

Please note: you will see a different video.

You will see that the selected video will start playing right away, in the video screen:

☞ **Click** ⏸

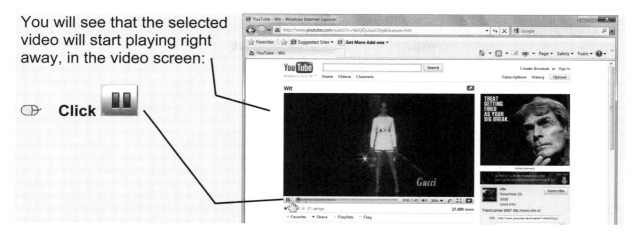

The videos on *YouTube* are stored in a format that is often used on the Internet. They are *streaming* videos. This means they start playing while they are downloaded to your computer. In other words, you do not need to wait until the video is fully downloaded. You can start watching the video right away.

Many *YouTube* videos are created in such a way that the downloading process is faster than playing the video. But high quality videos take up more bandwidth and the time it takes to download them will be longer. This is also the case if you have a slower Internet connection. In that case the video will be played one bit at a time. You will have to wait until the video is fully downloaded, before you can watch the entire video. The video player will show you the download process:

The faded portion of the red bar at the bottom of the player indicates the amount of video that has already been downloaded:

That bright portion of the red bar indicates the part of the video that has already been played:

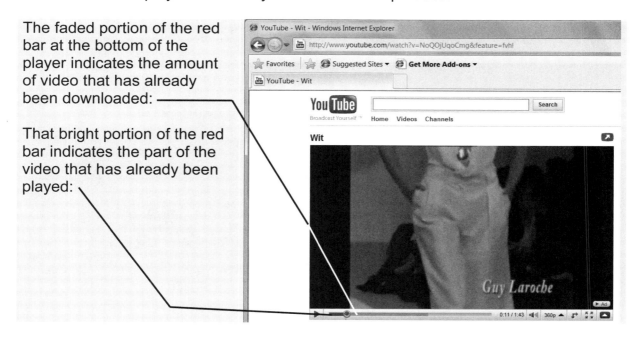

The *YouTube* video player is very easy to use. Just wait until the complete video has been downloaded and played. Then if you want to replay the video:

Click

Now the video will be played again:

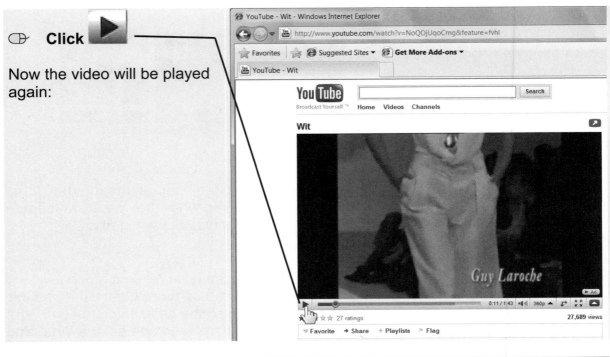

To pause:

Click

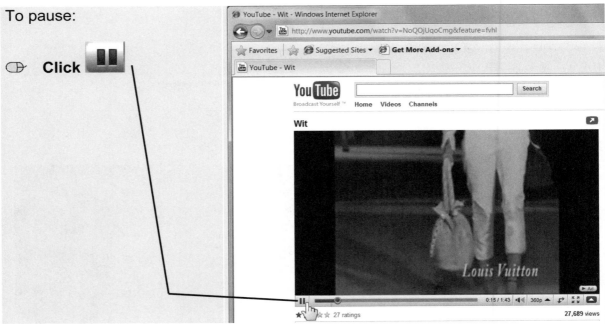

By dragging the slider to
the left or right, you can
quickly view a different part of
the video:

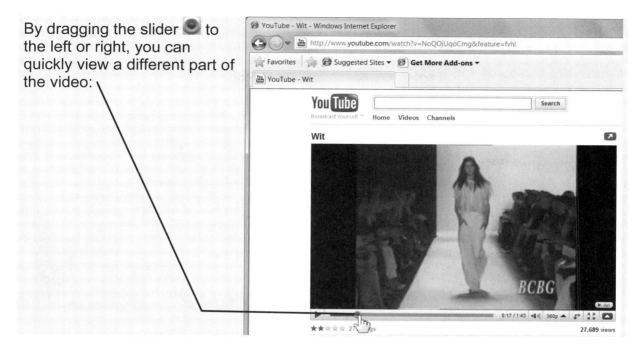

In the bottom right section of the video player you will see:

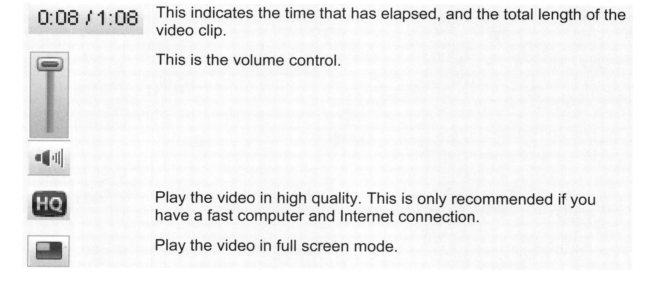

0:08 / 1:08 — This indicates the time that has elapsed, and the total length of the video clip.

This is the volume control.

HQ — Play the video in high quality. This is only recommended if you have a fast computer and Internet connection.

Play the video in full screen mode.

7.8 Searching for Videos on YouTube

If you want to search for a video by title or subject, you can use *YouTube*'s search engine:

In the search box:

Type: new york

You can also click one of the items shown in the list under the box, if that is what you are looking for:

☞ **Click** Search

You will see a summary of the videos that were found by searching for the keyword 'New York':

Please note: the videos you see on your screen will be different than the ones shown in this example.

Click the corresponding link to watch a video:

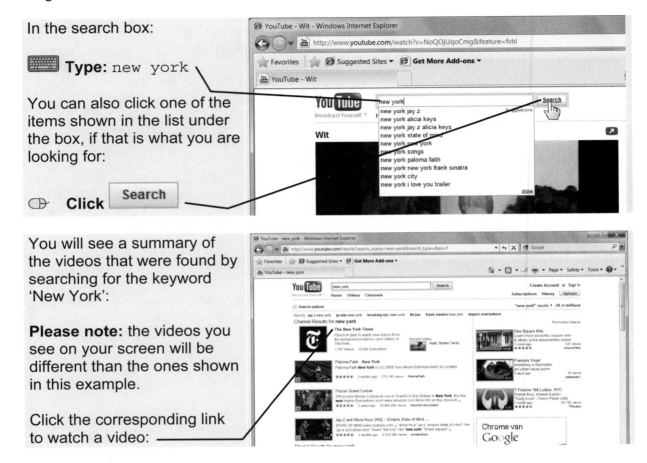

7.9 Sign Up for YouTube

The registration is free and you will gain access to various extra features. For instance, you can rate the videos, and upload videos to *YouTube* yourself. This is how you sign up:

In the top right-hand corner of the window:

☞ **Click**
Create Account

By Username: :

⌨ **Type a user name**

In *YouTube* you can only use letters and digits. So you cannot always use your *Google* user name.

☞ **Click** Check Availability

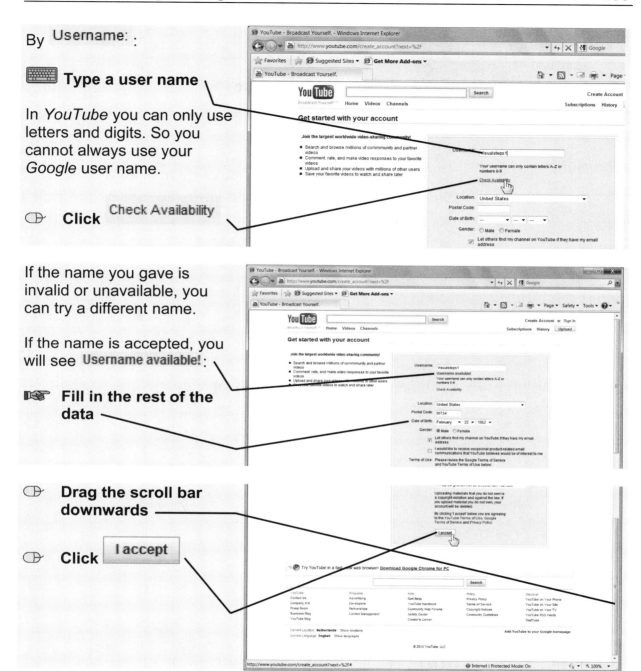

If the name you gave is invalid or unavailable, you can try a different name.

If the name is accepted, you will see Username available! :

☞ **Fill in the rest of the data**

☞ **Drag the scroll bar downwards**

☞ **Click** I accept

☞ **Sign in to your** *Google* **account** 🦶⁹

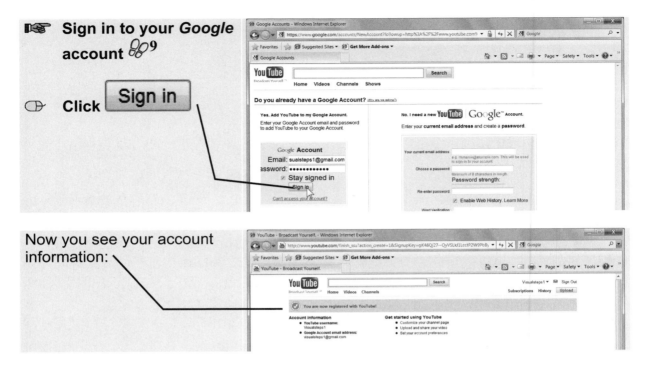

☞ **Click** Sign in

Now you see your account information:

Once you are registered, you are allotted a certain amount of free web space on *YouTube*. Here you can upload, edit, and remove your videos. This web space is called *My Videos*.

💡 **Tip**

Sign in faster
The next time you open the *YouTube* website (after you have registered). You can go directly to your web space by signing in. Just click the Sign In button located in the top right of the window.

7.10 Uploading a Video to YouTube

Now that you have signed up, you will be able to upload videos to *YouTube*. To practice this, you can use the video file from the practice files.

In the top right of the window:

☞ **Click** Upload

Click
Upload Video

Open the *Practice-files-Google* folder ✂11

Click *Lake*

Click **Open**

Now the practice video will be uploaded:

The time this will take depends on the speed of your Internet connection.

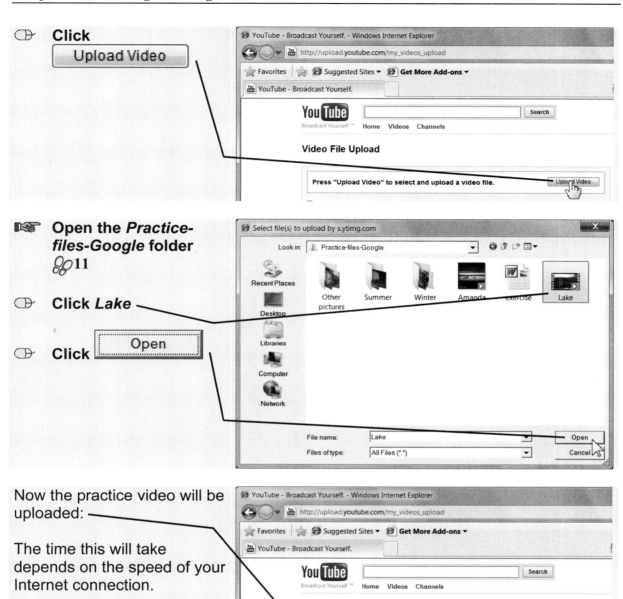

Once you have uploaded the video, you can enter additional information about the clip:

By **Description**.

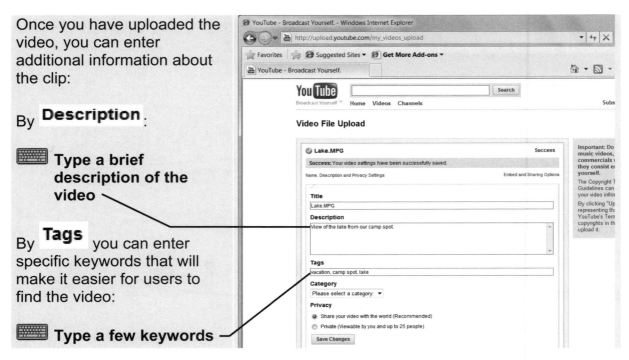

Type a brief description of the video

By **Tags** you can enter specific keywords that will make it easier for users to find the video:

Type a few keywords

By Please select a category:.

Click ▼

Click Travel & Events

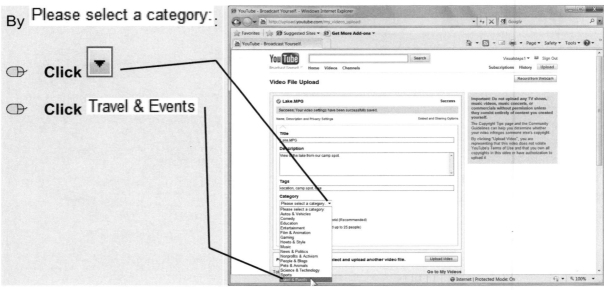

☞ **Drag the scroll bar downwards**

If you do not want to share your video with everyone else:

☞ **Click the radio button ◉ next to**
Private (Viewable by you and up to

☞ **Click**

Save Changes

☞ **Drag the scroll bar up**

☞ **Click**
Go to My Videos

Now you see your own web space on *YouTube*:

Here is the video you just uploaded:

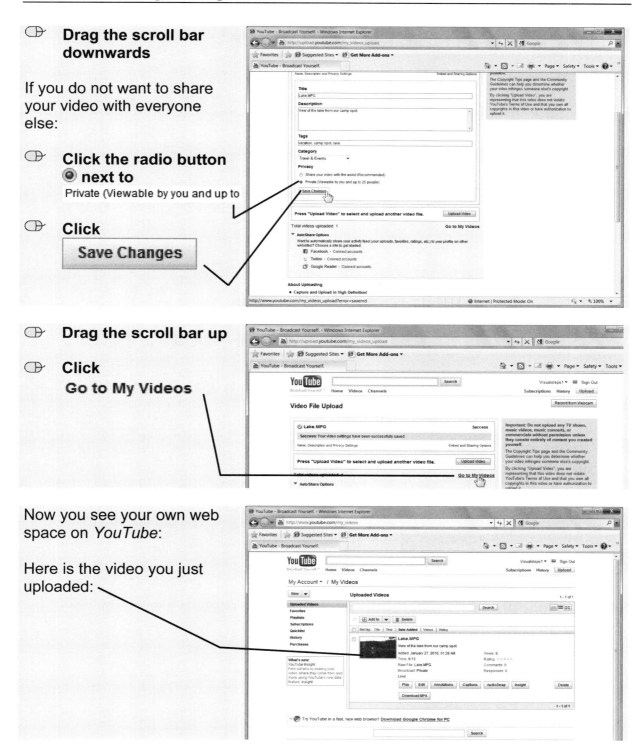

7.11 Adding YouTube Friends

You have not shared your video with the rest of the world. Your *YouTube* friends are the only people who are allowed to view your video. This is how you add friends who will be allowed to view the video:

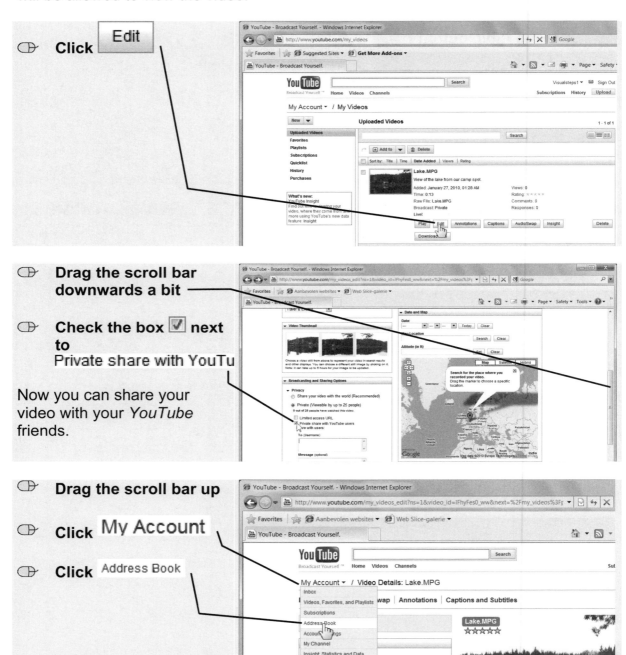

Click **Edit**

Drag the scroll bar downwards a bit

Check the box ☑ next to
Private share with YouTu

Now you can share your video with your *YouTube* friends.

Drag the scroll bar up

Click **My Account**

Click **Address Book**

Click **New**

Click Contact...

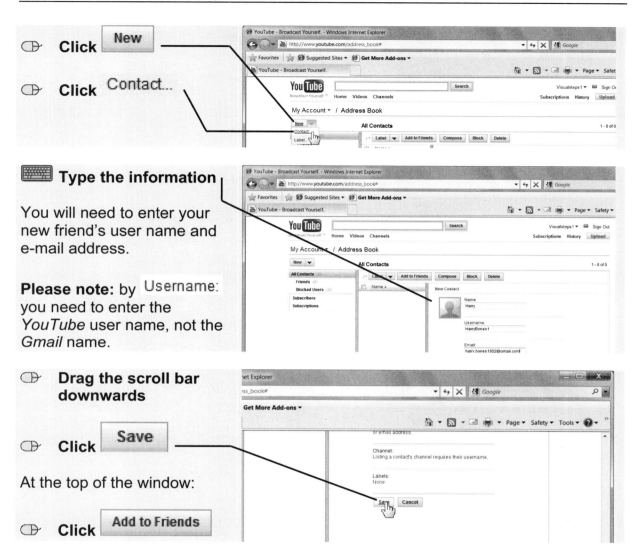

⌨ **Type the information**

You will need to enter your new friend's user name and e-mail address.

Please note: by Username: you need to enter the *YouTube* user name, not the *Gmail* name.

Drag the scroll bar downwards

Click **Save**

At the top of the window:

Click **Add to Friends**

The friend will be invited and will receive an e-mail message. At the e-mail message:

Click Inbox

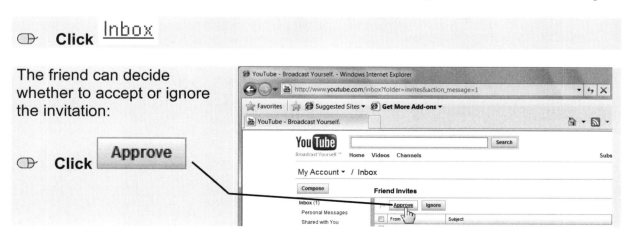

The friend can decide whether to accept or ignore the invitation:

Click **Approve**

If the friend has accepted the invitation, you can add this person to your friends:

⊕ **Drag the scroll bar up**

⊕ **Click**

Add to Friends

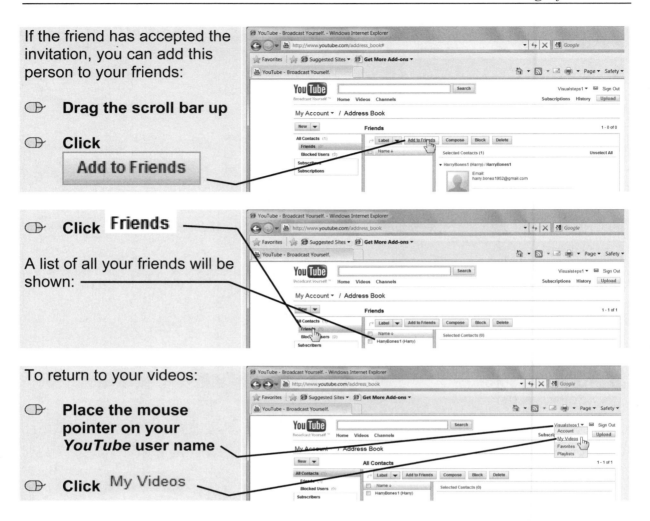

⊕ **Click** **Friends**

A list of all your friends will be shown:

To return to your videos:

⊕ **Place the mouse pointer on your** *YouTube* **user name**

⊕ **Click** My Videos

7.12 Playing or Removing Your Video

You can play your own videos in the *My Videos* window:

You will see your video. To play it:

⊕ **Click** Play

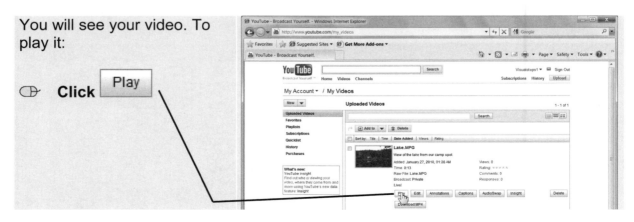

When you have finished:

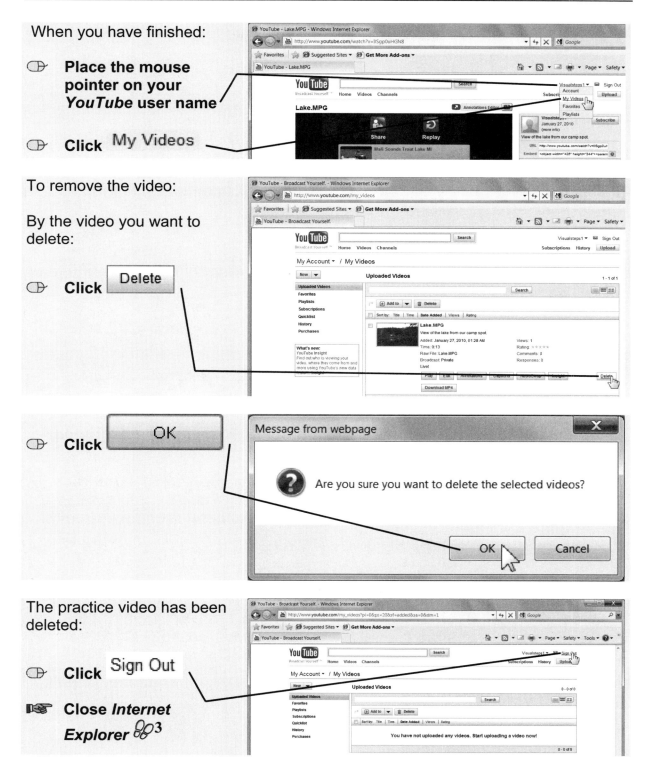

☞ **Place the mouse pointer on your *YouTube* user name**

☞ **Click** My Videos

To remove the video:

By the video you want to delete:

☞ **Click** Delete

☞ **Click** OK

The practice video has been deleted:

☞ **Click** Sign Out

☞ **Close *Internet Explorer* ✔️³**

You have learned how to watch videos on *YouTube*, and how to upload and delete a video. You can now get started with your own videos.

7.13 Background Information

Dictionary

Copyright	Copyright means that it is forbidden to copy and publish content (in this case videos) without the author's permission.
Download	Copying a file or program from an Internet computer to your computer's hard disk.
Named anchors	Another name for a hyperlink.
Publish	Post new content (images, videos, text) to the Internet.
Streaming video	A video that starts playing before it is completely downloaded.
Theme	A collection of matching visual elements (colors, fonts, images), used for the layout of a webpage.
Upload	Copying a file from your computer to an Internet computer.
Video player	Software which allows you to play videos.
Website	A website is a collection of pages that are linked together and available on the Internet.
Wizard	A component of a computer program that helps the user carry out a certain task. The user will receive step-by-step assistance and will be informed of the task's progress.

Source: Google Help, Windows Help and Support, Wikipedia

Video file formats
You can upload various video formats to *YouTube*: WMV, AVI, MPG (MPEG) and MOV. *YouTube* itself suggests the following formats for best quality:
- MPEG4 (Divx, Xvid);
- 320 x 240 resolution.

For audio:
- MP3-audio;
- Thirty frames per second.

Keep in mind that high quality files are larger, which means that uploading and downloading the file (for playback) will take longer.

7.14 Tips

💡 **Tip**

Sharing the website
A site can be shared with specific users, or with the rest of the world. *Google Sites* allows different access levels. This is how you set up the access rights:

While editing the site:

☞ **Click** More actions ▼

☞ **Click** Share this site

To restrict access:

☞ **Uncheck the box ☑ next to** Anyone in the world may view this site

☞ **Click the radio button ⊙ next to status of your visitors**

⌨ **Type the e-mail addresses**

Or, if you want to choose your contacts:

☞ **Click** Choose from contacts

☞ **Click** Invite these people

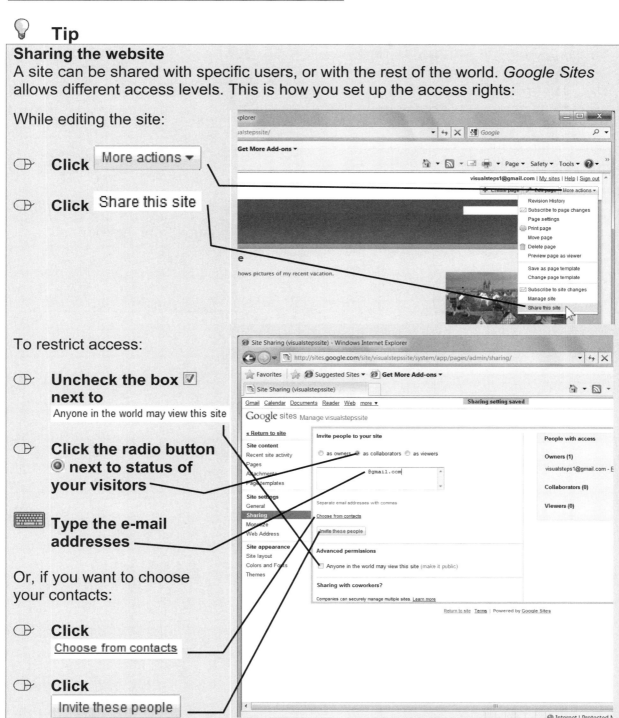

- Continue reading on the next page -

Here is an explanation of the various access levels offered by *Google Sites*:

- *Owners*, they are allowed to:
  • invite other owners, collaborators, or viewers;
  • change the theme and layout of a site;
  • change the name of the site;
  • delete the site;
  • do anything a collaborator can do.

- *Collaborators*, they are allowed to:
  • create, edit, and delete pages;
  • move pages;
  • add attachments;
  • add comments;
  • add pages to the navigation sidebar, and remove pages from this sidebar;
  • sign up for changes made to the site or its pages.

- *Viewers*, they are only allowed to:
  • view pages.

8. Picasa Photo Editing and Web Albums

In the old days, you simply threw away your badly exposed or blemished photos. Nowadays you can use photo editing programs, such as *Picasa* to correct your photos. The *Picasa* program is a *Google* program that has quickly become very popular. Not only is the program free, it also offers a wide variety of photo editing options and features an easy-to-use interface. In most cases you will be able to enhance your photo in such a way that you can use it for a multitude of purposes.

In this chapter, you will also learn about the different ways to save your enhanced photos. If you want to make sure your original photos remain intact, it is important that you use the correct method for storing the files.

Once you have perfected your photos, you will want to share them with others. The web album is a great tool for this. You can collect your photos and copy them to an Internet web album and you can decide who is allowed to view these photos.

In this chapter you will learn how to:

- download and install *Picasa*;
- import your photos into the *library*;
- view and organize photos;
- edit photos;
- touch up blemished photos;
- save, export, and restore photos;
- correct red eyes and apply special effects;
- upload photos to a web album;
- share your web album with others.

 Tip

Do more with Picasa
In this chapter you will read about *Picasa's* main features, and you will learn how to create a web album. In the book **Picasa for Seniors** however you will learn much more about the extensive options and functions of this program. You can find more information on this book at **www.visualsteps.com/picasa**

Please note:

This chapter contains various screen shots of the *Picasa* program. Because this program is subject to regular changes, the screen shots may differ from your own screen. This should not affect the operations covered in this chapter.

 Please note:

To perform the operations in this chapter, you will need to download the corresponding practice files to your computer's hard disk. You can read how to do this in *Appendix C Download Practice Files* at the end of this book.

8.1 Downloading and Installing Picasa

First, you will need to download *Picasa*, before you can install the program. This is how you download the program:

☞ **Open** *Internet Explorer* 𝒪𝒪¹

☞ **Browse to www.google.com/picasa** 𝒪𝒪²

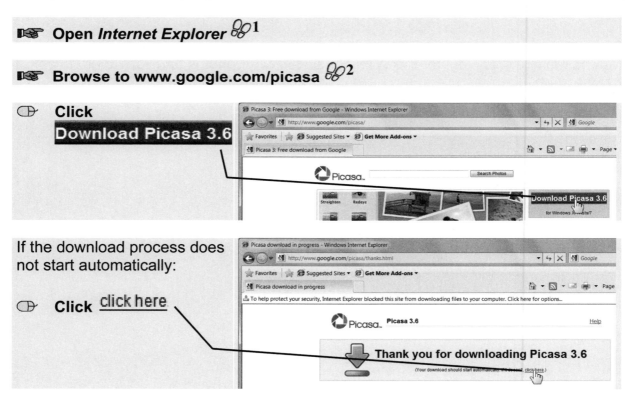

In the next window:

Picasa will be downloaded:

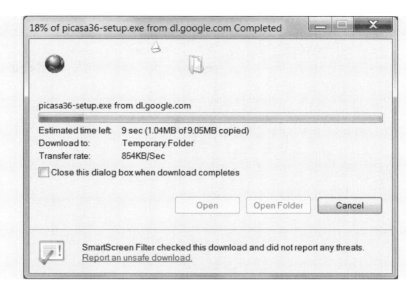

In the next window:

 **Click** Run

In *Windows Vista* and *Windows 7* your screen will now turn dark and you will need to give permission to continue:

Click Continue **or** Yes

If you accept the license terms:

Click I Agree

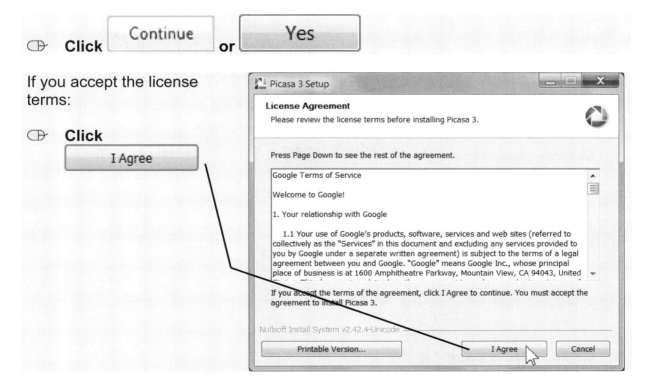

⊕ **Click**

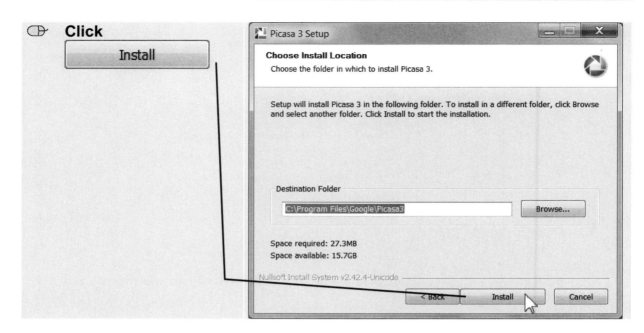

Picasa will be installed:

You will see the *Picasa 3
Setup* window:

⊕ **Uncheck the boxes** ☑
   next to
   Set Google as my default search eng

   Send anonymous usage stats to

   and Run Picasa 3

⊕ **Click** Finish

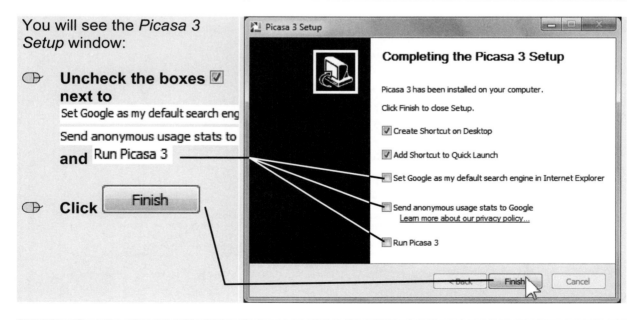

☞ **Close** *Internet Explorer* ✂³

8.2 Import Your Photos in Picasa

The first time you open *Picasa*, the program will search your computer for images. On your desktop you will see a new shortcut to *Picasa*. Click the icon to open the program:

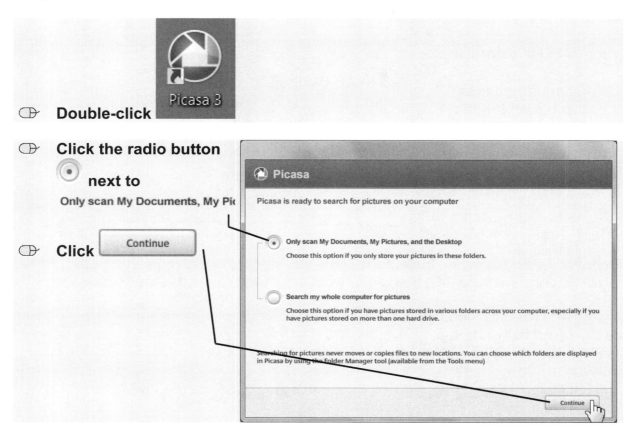

☞ **Double-click**

☞ **Click the radio button**

◉ **next to**

Only scan My Documents, My Pi

☞ **Click** Continue

➥ Please note:

If you have not saved all of your photos in the (*My*) *Documents* or (*My*) *Pictures* folders, you can search your entire computer for pictures with the Search my whole computer for pictures option. However, in that case, *Picasa* will also include other types of images in its *library*, such as buttons and icons. Your computer might contain hundreds of these images. That is why it is recommended to select the Only scan My Documents, My Pictures, and the Desktop option and add other photo folders to *Picasa* later on.

The *Picasa* program includes a photo viewer. When you start up *Picasa* for the first time, you can set this viewer as your default viewer:

The default viewer option is enabled:

All file formats are selected:

If your screen looks different:

☞ **Check the boxes ☑ next to all the file formats**

☞ **Click**

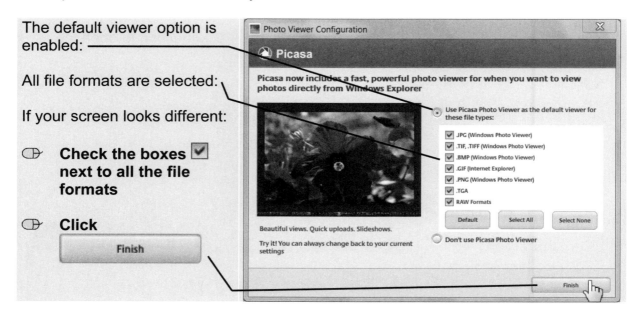

Picasa will start searching for images in the selected folders on your computer's hard drive. Folders which contain images or videos will be displayed in the *Picasa library*.

The photos that are found will be displayed in the startup window, the *library*.

The folder list:

The thumbnail overview:

The *Photo Tray*:

Please note: your screen may look different.

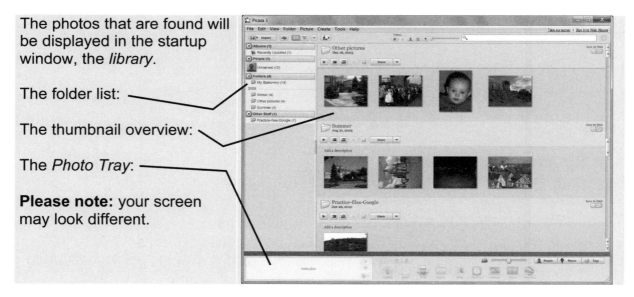

Elements of the library window

- The folder list contains folders and albums. A folder is a location on your computer's hard drive, used to store files. Photo files are stored to folders. A *Picasa* album is a virtual collection of photos. Virtual means that the album does not really exist as a physical folder. *Picasa* uses albums to display the photos you have selected together in one overview. In fact, an album just contains links to the photos on your hard drive, and not the actual photos. This means the actual photos will not be moved to the album, but will merely be displayed as part of the album. Folders and albums are sorted by the creation date of the first photo in the folder or album.

- The thumbnail view displays miniature images of all the photos *Picasa* has found in a folder or an album. You will see the name of the folder or album, and the date of the first picture.

- In the *Photo Tray* you can execute operations for one single photo, or for multiple photos. For example, printing, moving, or sending the photos by e-mail.

Please note:

In the folder list you will only see the name of the folders where the photos are actually stored. If the photos are stored in a subfolder, the name of the last folder will be displayed. You cannot see in which folder the subfolder is stored.

Tip

Changing the order

By default, the folders are displayed by creation date. If you would like to sort them differently, you can change the sorting type:

In the top left of the window:

☞ **Click**

☞ **Click the desired sorting order**

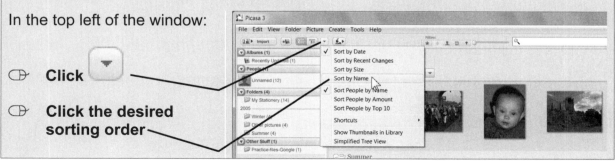

8.3 Viewing and Managing Photos

You can use the thumbnail view to search for photos, and view them. To view your pictures:

👉 **Click the *Other pictures* folder**

👉 **Double-click**

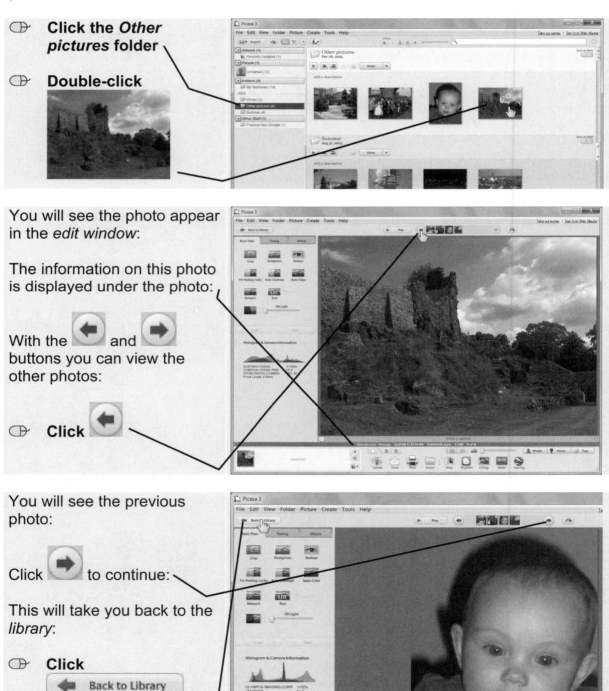

You will see the photo appear in the *edit window*:

The information on this photo is displayed under the photo:

With the ⬅ and ➡ buttons you can view the other photos:

👉 **Click ⬅**

You will see the previous photo:

Click ➡ to continue:

This will take you back to the *library*:

👉 **Click ⬅ Back to Library**

When *Picasa* is scanning your hard drive for images, the program will retain the classification of the folders in the same structure you see in *Windows Explorer*. You can change this classification in *Picasa*. If you want to arrange your photos differently in *Picasa*, this is how you do it:

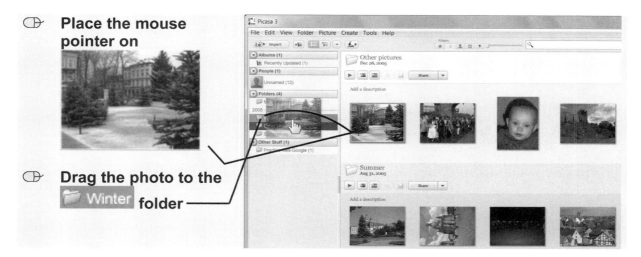

☞ **Place the mouse pointer on**

☞ **Drag the photo to the Winter folder**

Now you will see the *Confirm Move* window. To confirm the move:

☞ **Click** Move Files

To view the photo in a different folder, click this folder in the folder list:

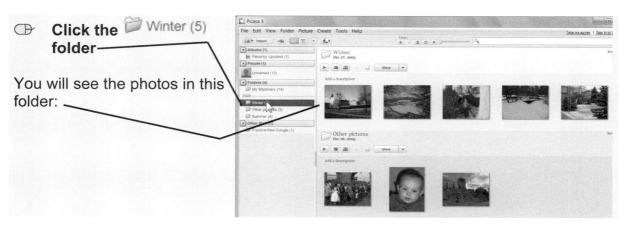

☞ **Click the Winter (5) folder**

You will see the photos in this folder:

Tip

Albums

If you move a photo in *Picasa*, it will also be moved on your computer's hard drive. If you do not want that to happen, or if you want to organize your *Picasa* photos in a different way, you can use albums. In an album you can incorporate links to photos in various folders, without the actual photos being moved. To create an album:

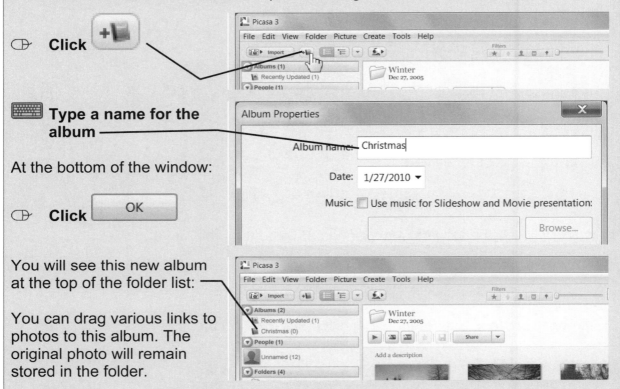

Click

Type a name for the album

At the bottom of the window:

Click OK

You will see this new album at the top of the folder list:

You can drag various links to photos to this album. The original photo will remain stored in the folder.

Albums are especially useful if you want to collect all the photos on a single subject from different folders.

You can delete pictures in the same way as you delete *Windows* items:

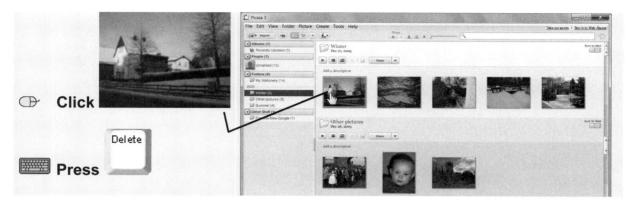

 Click

 Press

To confirm the deletion:

 **Click** Delete Image

Please note:

If you delete a photo from *Picasa*, this photo will also be removed from your hard disk. If you have accidentally deleted the wrong photo, you can restore it via the *Windows Recycling Bin*.

💡 Tip

Browsing with scroll bars
In the thumbnail view, the operation of the scroll bar is a little different from the standard *Windows* action.

To scroll through the folders:

Click ⏶ **or** ⏷

To scroll through the photos:

Click ⏶ **or** ⏷

Or:

Drag the scroll bar up or down

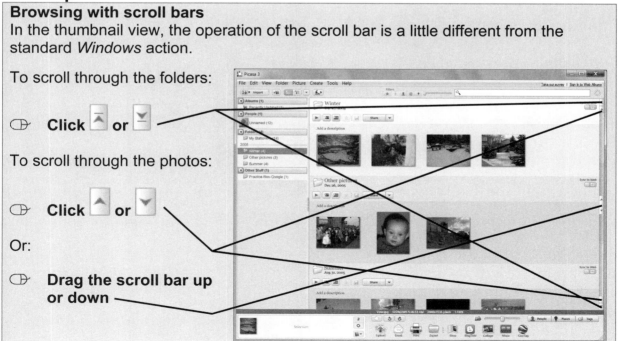

8.4 Editing Photos

Nowadays you can use *Picasa* to correct a photo that is badly expose or blemished, whereas in the past you may have simply discarded such a picture. In many cases the correction will be so successful that you can print the photo in a regular way, or use it in a slide show.

☞ **Open the *Summer* folder** 👣 8

⊕ **Double-click**

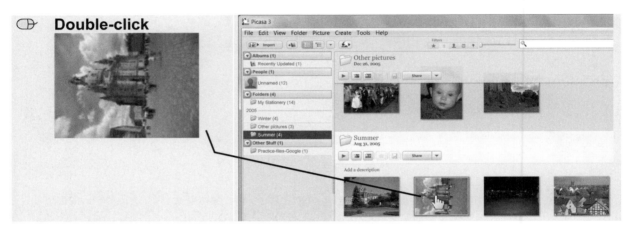

To rotate the photo:

⊕ **Click** 🔄

Enhancing a photo involves a number of steps. To accomplish improvements quickly, you may want to try *Picasa's* automatic correcting option first:

☞ **Click**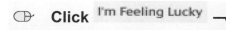

This will correct the exposure, as well as the sharpness and colors of the picture.

💡 **Tip**

Manual correction of photos

With  the photo will be corrected automatically. If this does not produce the desired result, you can try to enhance the photo manually:

☞ **Click the** **tab**

Here you can correct the exposure and color settings yourself.

The photo has become sharper and clearer. If you do not like the result, click

| Undo I'm Feeling Lucky |

Now you are going to straighten the church:

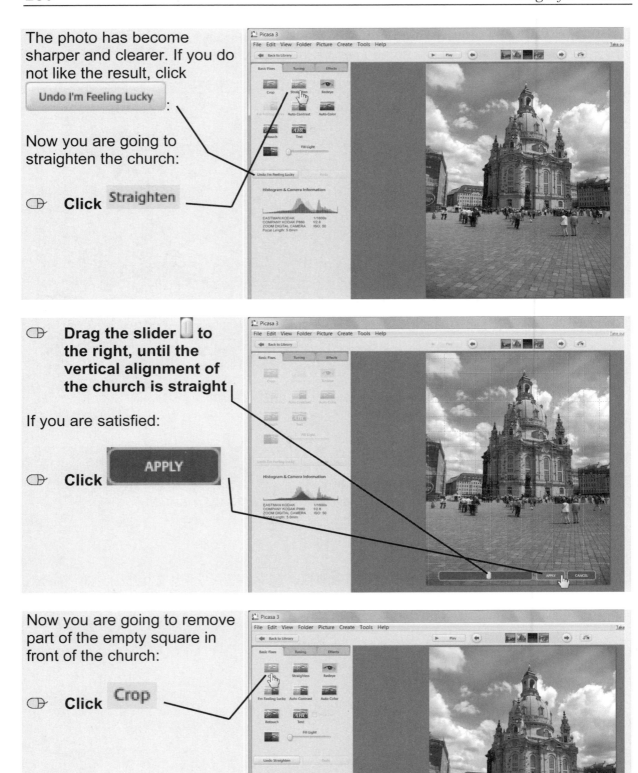

⊕ **Click** Straighten

⊕ **Drag the slider ▯ to the right, until the vertical alignment of the church is straight**

If you are satisfied:

⊕ **Click** APPLY

Now you are going to remove part of the empty square in front of the church:

⊕ **Click** Crop

To prevent problems while printing the photo, or using it in slide shows, you will need to maintain the current height/width ratio (this is called aspect ratio):

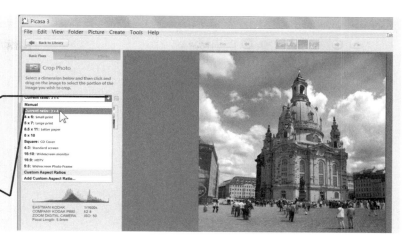

☞ **Click** ▼

☞ **Click** Current ratio: 3 x 4

Now you are going to select a new corner and drag the photo from there:

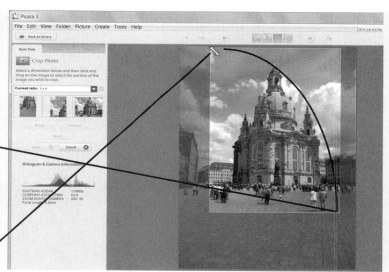

☞ **Place the mouse pointer somewhere to the bottom right-hand side of the photo**

☞ **Drag the mouse up diagonally, until the church is placed within the selection area**

If you are satisfied with the result:

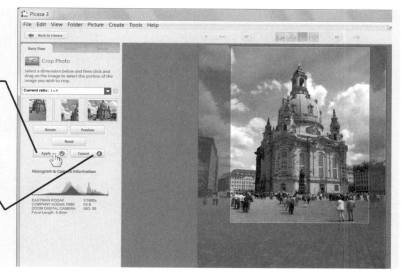

☞ **Click** Apply ✓

If you want to select the area once more:

☞ **Click** Cancel ✗

If you see spots or other smudges on the photo, you can *retouch* the photo. First, you will need to enlarge the photo:

In the bottom right of the window:

☞ **Drag the slider ⬜ at the bottom right to 100%**

In the thumbnail you will see **Zoomed to 100%** :

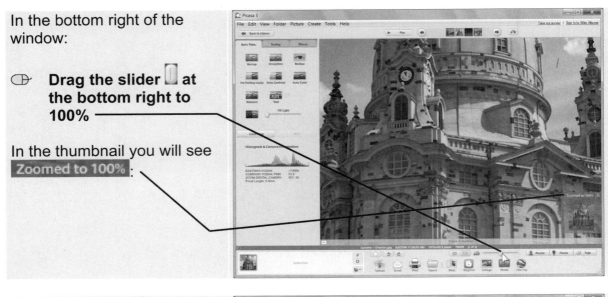

☞ **Place the mouse pointer on the photo**

The pointer will turn into 🖐 :

☞ **Drag the photo until you see the scratch mark to the right of the cathedral tower**

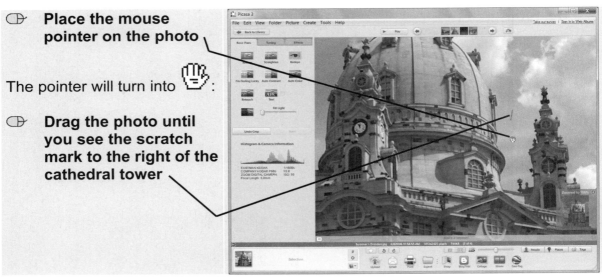

☞ **Click Retouch**

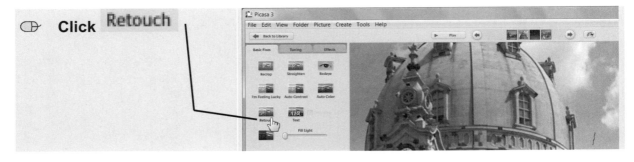

Now the mouse pointer will turn into a small circle. To enlarge the circle:

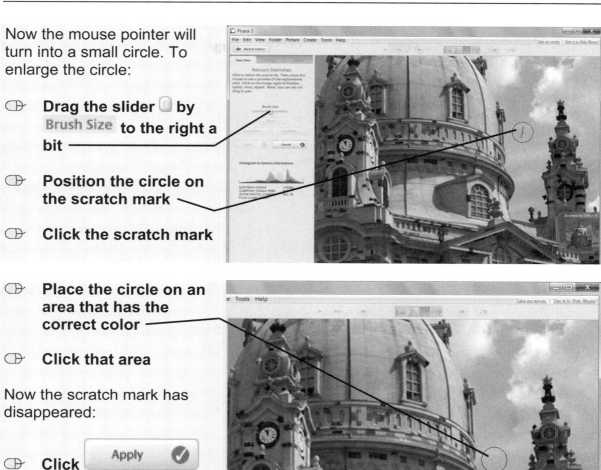

☞ **Drag the slider ⬭ by Brush Size to the right a bit** ——————

☞ **Position the circle on the scratch mark**

☞ **Click the scratch mark**

☞ **Place the circle on an area that has the correct color** ——

☞ **Click that area**

Now the scratch mark has disappeared:

☞ **Click** [Apply ✓]

If you want to try this again:

☞ **Click** [Cancel ✗]

 Tip

Undoing changes

You can undo each edit, step-by-step, by clicking [Undo Retouches]. The button will show you which operation will be undone.

8.5 Saving and Restoring Photos

Saving a photo in *Picasa* is different from other programs, because the original photo will always be saved as well. This is why you will always be able to restore the original version, if necessary, even after you have saved an altered version.

Click **File**

Click **Save**

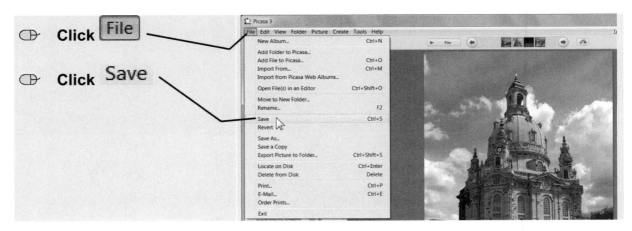

 HELP! I cannot select the Save option.

You can only save photos that have been edited in *Picasa*.

You now see the *Save* menu:

Click **Save**

Since *Picasa* always makes a copy of your original photo, you will be able to restore it if necessary. For this, you have two options:

Click **File**

Click **Revert**

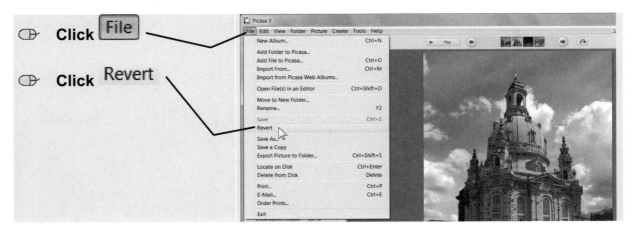

You will see the *Revert* window:

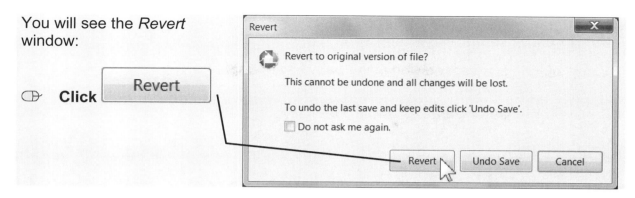

☞ **Click** [Revert]

Now you can see the original photo with the church still skewed to the right and the unfortunate scratch.

☞ **Return to the *library***

Select [Undo Save] if you want to keep the changes you have made. In *Picasa* you can always go back and undo all the edits one by one, if you change your mind later. Or you can use this version of the photo and make new corrections.

Select [Revert] if you want to undo all the changes and return to the original photo.

Please note:

These functions will only work in *Picasa*. If you have subsequently edited the photo in another program, reverting back to the original photo will not work.

8.6 Red Eyes and Special Effects

The use of the flash has resulted in the baby having red eyes. To correct this:

☞ **Open the** *Other pictures* **folder** 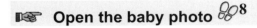[8]

☞ **Open the baby photo** [8]

You can see a red glow in the baby's eyes: ————

⊕ **Click** Redeye

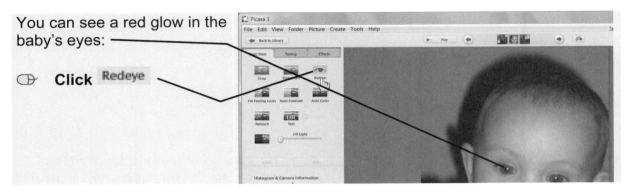

Picasa has recognized and corrected the red eyes: ————

If you are satisfied:

⊕ **Click** Apply ✓

If you want to try this again:

⊕ **Click** Cancel ✗

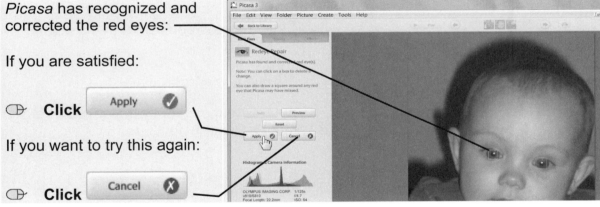

Now the eyes are corrected.

You can also add special effects to the photo:

⊕ **Click the** Effects **tab**

You will see various effects:

⊕ **Click** Sepia

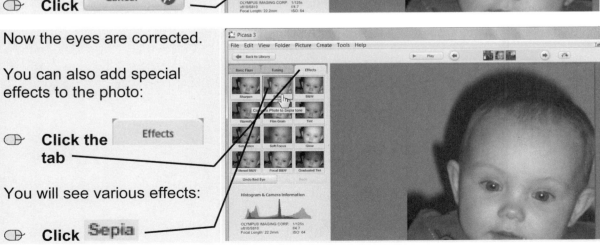

Now the photo has an old-fashioned look:

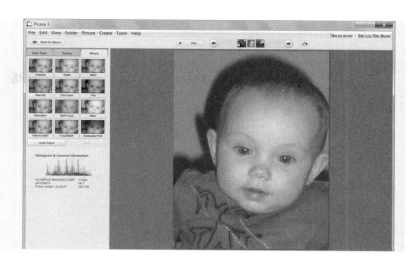

8.7 Exporting Photos

You can use the *Picasa Export* option to save copies of the photos you have edited. Afterwards you can view the photo and use a different program to edit it further, if you want. Normally, the corrections will only be visible in *Picasa*.
You can also use the *Export* option to copy the photo to a different location, and you can select the size and quality for the photo you want to export. Now you are going to try this:

☞ **Click** File

☞ **Click**
   Export Picture to Folder...

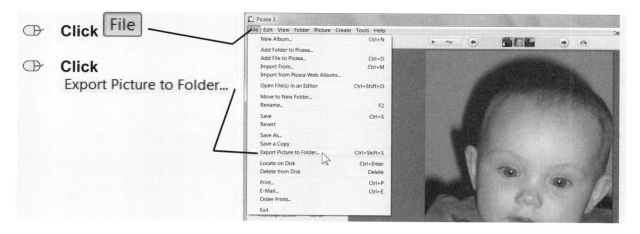

You now see the folder where the copy of the photo will be stored:

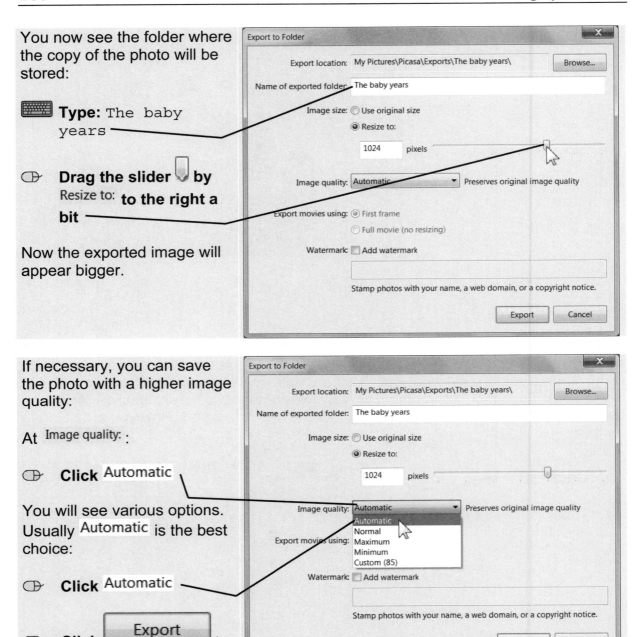

Type: The baby years

Drag the slider by Resize to: **to the right a bit**

Now the exported image will appear bigger.

If necessary, you can save the photo with a higher image quality:

At Image quality: .

Click Automatic

You will see various options. Usually Automatic is the best choice:

Click Automatic

Click Export

You will see a new window
with the exported folder:

⊕ **Click** ❎

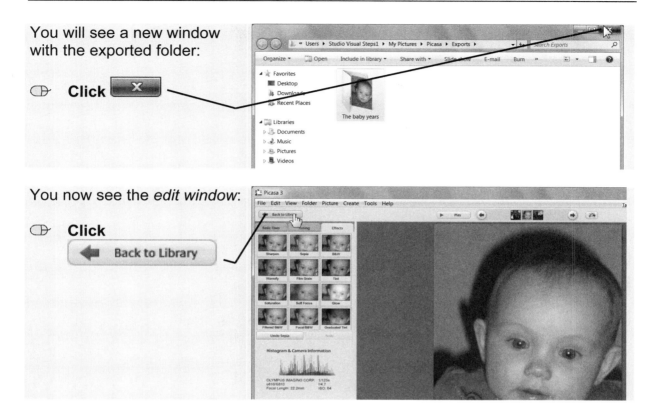

You now see the *edit window*:

⊕ **Click**

◀ **Back to Library**

By default, *Picasa* will create a new folder (*Exports*) for the exported photos. You can
open this folder in the same way as the other image folders.

Here you see the Exports
folder:

If you have many folders, you
can hide them:

By Exports :

⊕ **Click** 🔽

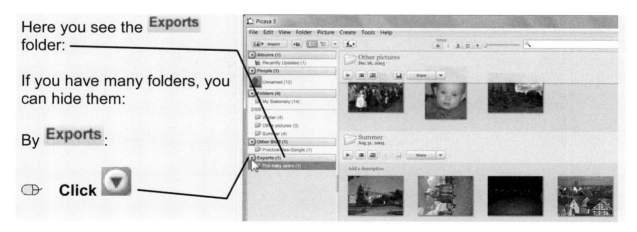

✕ **HELP! I do not see the** Exports **folder.**

☞ **Close** *Picasa* 👣³

☞ **Open** *Picasa* 👣¹⁵

You can see here that the list of exported images is closed:

You can open this list by clicking :

By **Exports**:

☞ **Click**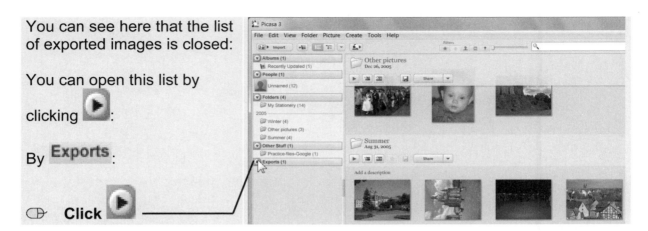

💡 Tip

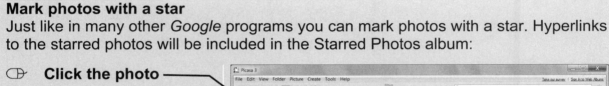

Mark photos with a star
Just like in many other *Google* programs you can mark photos with a star. Hyperlinks to the starred photos will be included in the Starred Photos album:

☞ **Click the photo**

☞ **Click** ⬚

A hyperlink to this photo will be added to the Starred Photos (1) album. You will see a star at the bottom of the photo:

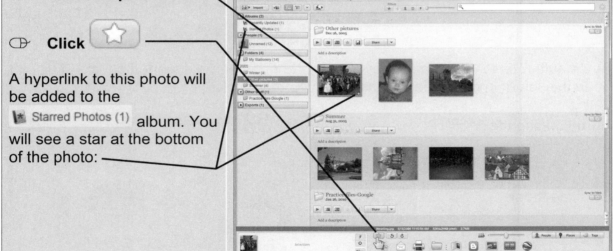

8.8 Uploading Photos to a Web Album

A web album is a location on the Internet where you can put your pictures and share them with others. However, you will need to sign up first. In a web album you can create attractive slide shows including special effects. You can upload the photos you have edited in *Picasa* to any web album on the Internet.

➡️ Please note:

In this section we will only discuss the operations which are necessary to upload your photos to a web album. In the help function of the web album software application you will find more information about other functions and options.

➡️ Please note:

If you want to create a web album you will need to have a *Google* account first. If you do not yet have one, read *Appendix A Creating a Google Account* first and learn how to create an account.

If you do not yet have a web album you will need to create one, before you can start uploading photos:

In the top right-hand corner:

 Click

Sign In to Web Albums

 Type your user name and password

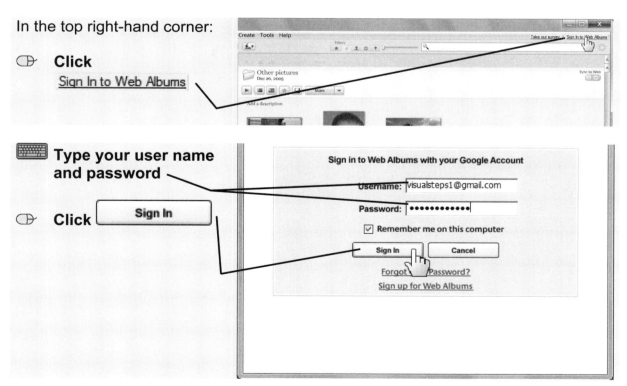

🖰 **Click** Sign In

Tip

Save your web album photos in separate albums
It is recommended to save the photos you want to use for your web album in a separate album. When you upload them, they will be saved on the web in the same album.

Now you are ready to upload photos to this album. To upload photos, you will need to select them first:

☞ **Click the *Summer* folder**

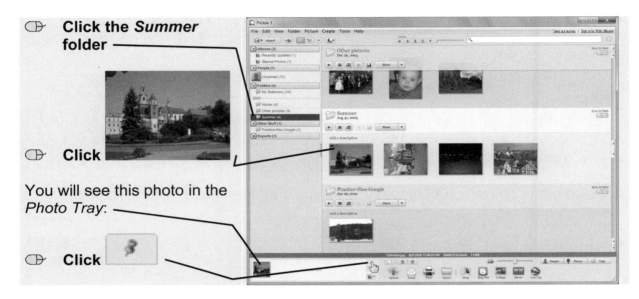

☞ **Click**

You will see this photo in the *Photo Tray*:

☞ **Click**

 Tip

Empty Photo Tray
Does the *Photo Tray* already contain some photos, or do you want to select different

photos? With ⭕ you can remove all the photos from the *Photo Tray* at once.

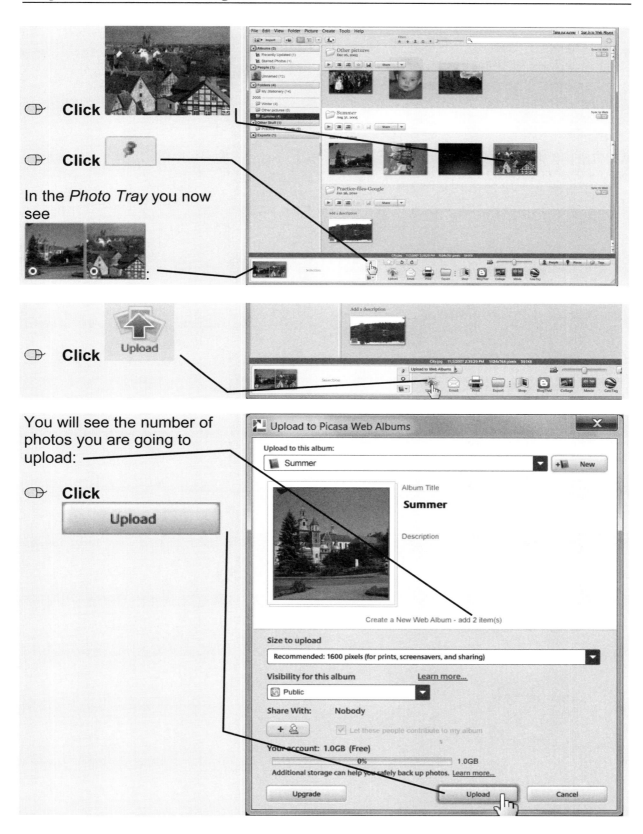

Click

Click

In the *Photo Tray* you now see

Click Upload

You will see the number of photos you are going to upload:

Click Upload

Please note:

By setting the visibility option, you can determine which people are allowed to view your photos. You can choose from *Public*, *Unlisted*, or *Sign-in required to view*. You can read more about this subject in the *Background Information* at the end of this chapter.

During the upload process you will see this window:

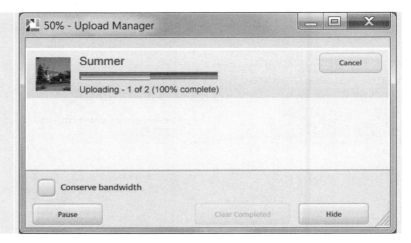

Now you are going to have a look and check if the right photos have been uploaded:

☞ **Click** [**View Online**]

You will see the photos displayed in your web album:

☞ **Click** [**X**]

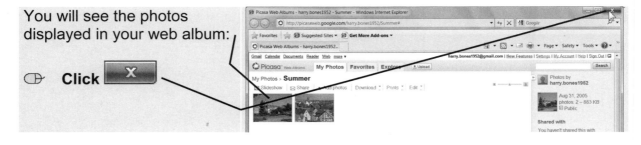

☞ **Click**

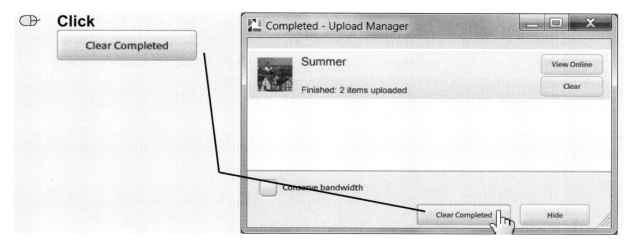

💡 **Tip**

Opening an existing web album

If you have already created a web album and have signed in to your *Google* account, you can open this album right away:

☞ **Click** W̲e̲b̲a̲l̲b̲u̲m̲s̲

8.9 Share a Web Album

If you want other to see your pictures, you can share your album:

In the folder you want to share:

☞ **Click** Share

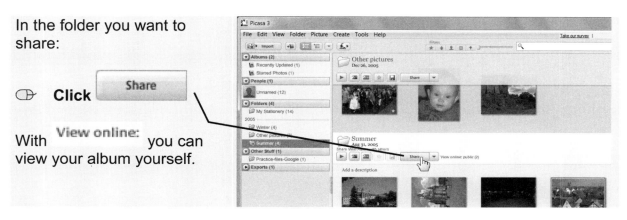

With V̲i̲e̲w̲ o̲n̲l̲i̲n̲e̲: you can view your album yourself.

➥ Please note:

You will see the ⬆ symbol in the images you have uploaded. You will only see this symbol when you are signed in for your web album. After you have signed out you will no longer see this symbol.

Now you are going to send an e-mail and invite the people who are allowed to view your web album:

⌨ **Type the e-mail addresses**

Please note: the addresses should be separated by a semicolon (;).

⌨ **If you want to, type a different subject or message**

☞ **Click**

> **Send**

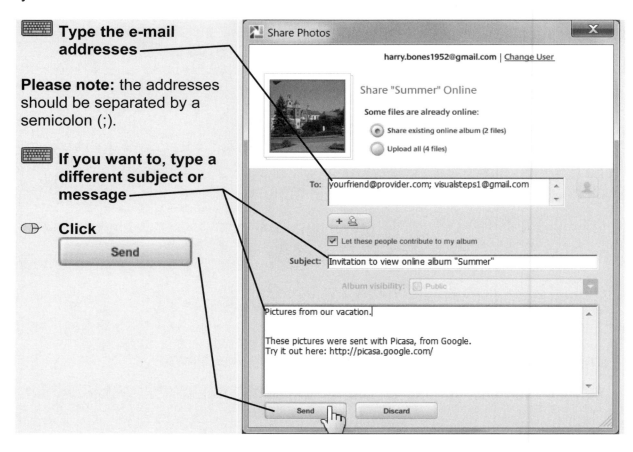

After the message has been uploaded you will see the following window:

☞ **Click**

Clear Completed

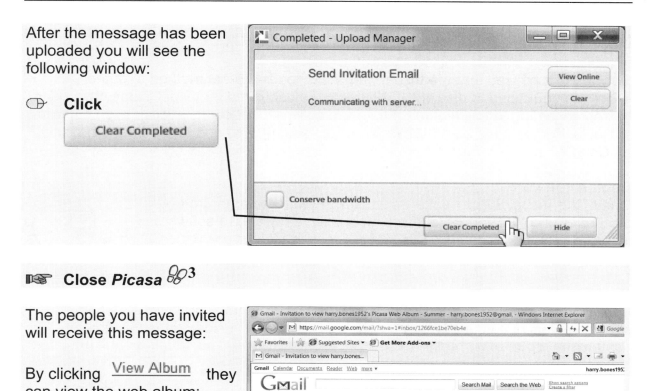

☞ **Close** *Picasa* 🐾³

The people you have invited will receive this message:

By clicking ___View Album___ they can view the web album:

With ___Play slideshow___ the album will be played as a slide show:

In this chapter you have learned how to use some of the most popular features in *Picasa*. The *I'm Feeling Lucky* button will help you achieve a good result quickly without doing too much work. The special effects options can help you create a special photo, but be careful not to overdo it. By putting your photos in a web album you can easily share them with others.

8.10 Visual Steps Website and Newsletter

So you have noticed that the Visual Steps-method is a great method to gather knowledge quickly and efficiently. All the books published by Visual Steps have been written according to this method. There are quite a lot of books available, on different subjects. For instance about *Windows*, photo editing, and about free programs, such as *Google Earth* and *Skype*.

Book + software
One of the Visual Steps books includes a CD with the program that is discussed. The full version of this high quality, easy-to-use software is included. You can recognize this Visual Steps book with enclosed CD by this logo on the book cover:

Website
Use the blue *Catalog* button on the **www.visualsteps.com** website to read an extensive description of all available Visual Steps titles, including the full table of contents and part of a chapter (as a PDF file). In this way you can find out if the book is what you expected.

This instructive website also contains:
• free computer booklets and informative guides (PDF files) on a range of subjects;
• free computer tips, described according to the Visual Steps method;
• a large number of frequently asked questions and their answers;
• information on the free *Computer certificate* you can obtain on the online test website **www.ccforseniors.com**;
• free 'Notify me' e-mail service: receive an e-mail when book of interest are published.

Visual Steps Newsletter
Do you want to keep yourself informed of all Visual Steps publications? Then subscribe (no strings attached) to the free Visual Steps Newsletter, which is sent by e-mail.

This Newsletter is issued once a month and provides you with information on:
• the latest titles, as well as older books;
• special offers and discounts;
• new, free computer booklets and guides.

As a subscriber to the Visual Steps Newsletter you have direct access to the free booklets and guides, at **www.visualsteps.com/info_downloads**

8.11 Background Information

Dictionary

Album	Albums are virtual groups of photos which only exist in *Picasa*. You can combine various photos into a single album, or use the same photo in multiple albums, without taking up extra space on your computer's hard drive. When you delete photos from an album, or delete the album itself, the original photo files still remain stored on your hard drive.
Brightness	The amount of light you see in a photo. When you decrease the brightness, the colors will become indistinct. Increasing the brightness will make the colors seem clearer.
Contrast	The difference in color between adjacent parts of a photo.
Crop	Trimming off parts of the photo that you do not want to display.
Edit window	The window which displays the opened photo file. To the left of this window you will find buttons and tabs for editing this photo.
Export	Saving a photo for use in a different program. You can use the *Export* option to select a different location and change the file format and quality of the copy you want to export.
Folder list	Overview of all the folders and albums on your computer that contain photos. You can find the folder list at the left-hand side of the *library*.
Library	Window which displays the overview of all photos, folders, and albums in *Picasa*.
Photo Tray	In the *Photo Tray* you can execute operations for a single photo or for multiple photos, such as printing, sending them by e-mail or moving them.
Pixel	The smallest element of a digital image, also called a dot.
Red eyes	The red glow in the eye's iris. This may show on flash photos.
Resolution	The sharpness or definition of a photo. The resolution is determined by the amount of pixels of which a photo consists.

- Continue reading on the next page -

Restore	Restoring files from a backup copy to your computer's hard drive.
Sepia	A brownish color which makes a photo appear old-fashioned.
Star	With the *Star* option you can mark favorite photos in your collection.
Thumbnail view	The overview of all miniature photos, on the right-hand side of the *library*.
Web album	Location on the Internet where you can show your photos to other people. Most web album applications require that you signup and create an account. These web albums are often free, but sometimes you need to pay for additional features.
Zoom	Blowing up part of a photo (zooming in) or diminishing a photo (zooming out).

Source: Picasa Help

Album privacy: Visibility options for your album

The *Picasa* web albums allow you to share your photos with anyone else in a simple way. But you can make your albums as private as you like by using the visibility settings. You can adjust these settings during the upload process, and change them whenever you want in the *Picasa* program or in the *Picasa* web albums.

 Public

Set your album's visibility to *Public* if you want your photos to be viewed by anyone who knows the web address (URL) of your public photo gallery. The web address is based on the user name of your *Google* account: http://picasaweb.google.com/username/albumname. By default, your public albums will show up when people are searching for items in public albums.

 Unlisted

Set your visibility to *Unlisted* to restrict the access to your album. All unlisted albums have an authorization key in their web addresses. The key is a combination of letters and numbers that make the album's web address very difficult to guess. People will need the exact web address in order to see your unlisted album.

Sign-in required to view

Select this option to set the highest level of privacy for your album. You specify who has permission to view it, and visitors must sign in to their *Google* account to verify their identity. People who are not listed in the *Shared With* list cannot view the album. In *Picasa Help* you can learn more about adding and removing people from your *Shared With* list.

Source: Picasa Help .

8.12 Tips

 Tip

More information on Google programs
In this book you have been introduced to several *Google* programs. If you want to learn more about these programs, just read the Help function of the program you are interested in.

 Tip

Do more with Picasa

In this chapter you have learned about *Picasa's* main features. In the book **Picasa for Seniors** however you will learn much more about the extensive options and functions of this program.

Learn how to:
- Manage photos
- Improve and retouch photos
- Use facial recognition
- Create collages and web albums
- Make a gift CD
- Create videos and slide shows
- Create a blog

You can find more information on this book at **www.visualsteps.com/picasa**

Appendices

A. Creating a Google Account

Many of *Google's* extra features require that you have a *Google* account. A *Google* account is free. Here is how you create one:

☞ **Open *Internet Explorer*** 👣¹

☞ **Browse to www.google.com** 👣²

Now you will see the *Google* website:

In the top right of the window:

👆 **Click** Sign in

👆 **Click**
Create an account now

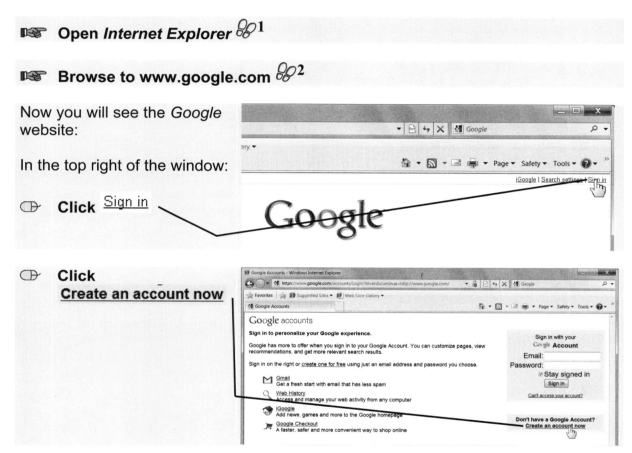

Type your e-mail address

Type a password

Re-type your password

Uncheck the boxes ☑ next to Stay signed in , Enable Web History , and Set Google as my default home

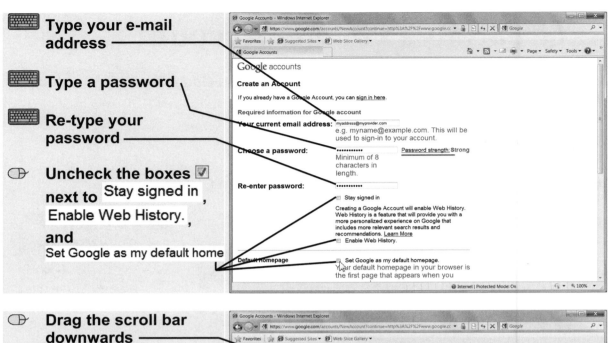

Drag the scroll bar downwards

Type the characters in the picture

Please note: you will see different characters on your screen.

Click I accept. Create my account.

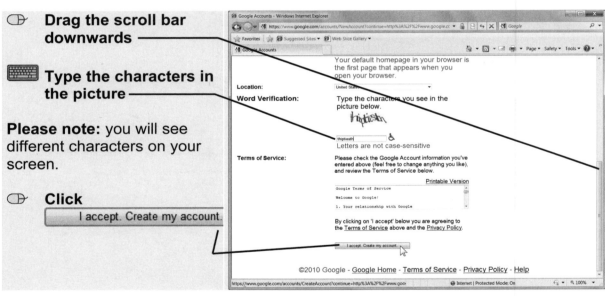

Now you will see this
message:

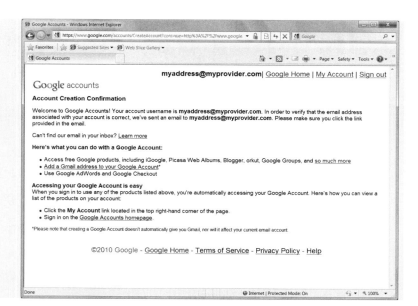

☞ **Open your e-mail program**

☞ **Open the**
✉ **accounts-noreply@google.com ..**
   Google e-mailverificatie

message

☞ **Click the link in the
message** ———

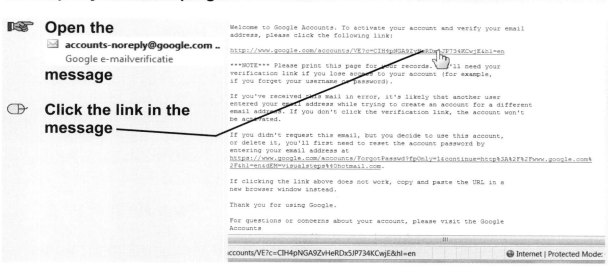

☞ **Close all windows** 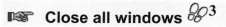**³**

B. How Do I Do That Again?

In this book actions are marked with footsteps: 🐾1
Find the corresponding number in the appendix below to see how to execute a specific operation.

🐾1 **Open *Internet Explorer***
In Windows XP:
- Click **start**

- Click **Internet** Internet Explorer

In Windows Vista and Windows 7:
- Click

- Click ▶ All Programs

- Click Internet Explorer

🐾2 **Visit a website**
- Click the address bar

- Type the web address

- Press **Enter** ↵

🐾3 **Close window or program**
- Click **X**

🐾4 **Open *Google Chrome***
- Double-click Google Chrome

🐾5 **Zoom in or out**
- Click **+** to zoom in
  or **−** to zoom out

Or.
- Drag the slider **−** in the zoom bar

🐾6 **Move satellite photo or map**
- Position the mouse pointer on the map

- Drag the mouse pointer until you can see the right part of the map

🐾7 **Sign in to *Google Calendar***
- By **Email:**, type your *Google* account's user name

- By **Password:**, type your password

- Click **Sign in**

🐾8 **Open photo or folder**
- Click the folder

Or.
- Double-click the photo

9 Sign in to *Google* account
- By Email:, type your user name
- By Password:, type your password

10 Open folder in file list window
- Double-click the folder

11 Open *Practice-files-Google* window
- To the left of the window, click Documents

- Double-click Practice-files-Google

12 Go to the *library*
- Click Back to Library

13 Open blog
- Click the address bar
- Type the blog's web address
- Press Enter ↵

14 Open *Google Chrome Options* window
- Click
- Click Options

15 Open *Picasa*

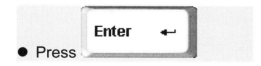

- Double-click

C. Download Practice Files

As you work through this book, you will need to use the practice files to execute certain operations. It is a good idea to download these practice files before you begin. Here is how to do that:

☞ **Open** *Internet Explorer* 👣¹

☞ **Browse to www.visualsteps.com/google** 👣²

Now you will see the website that goes with this book. On the *Practice files* page you can download the files:

☞ **Click** Practice files

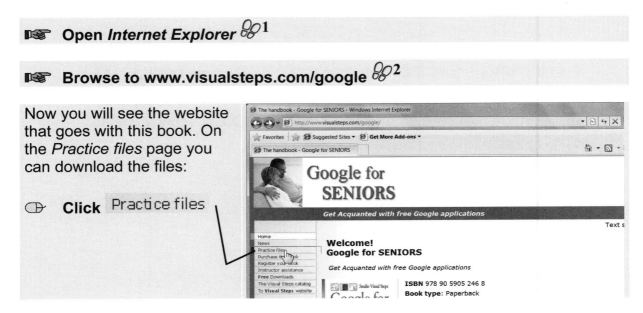

You will see a compressed folder which contains the practice files. Now you are going to copy this folder to the (*My*) *Documents* folder on your computer:

☞ **Right-click**
[Practice-files-Google.zip

☞ **Click** Save Target As...

The *Practice-files-Google* folder is a compressed folder. You are going to save this folder to the (*My*) *Documents* folder.

By Documents :

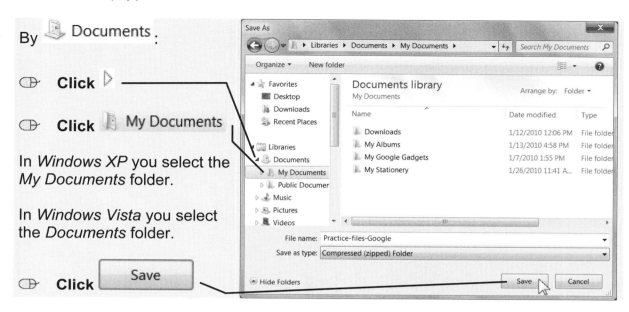

⊕ **Click** ▷

⊕ **Click** 📄 My Documents

In *Windows XP* you select the *My Documents* folder.

In *Windows Vista* you select the *Documents* folder.

⊕ **Click** [Save]

🠖 Please note!

If your computer uses *Windows XP* you will see a different window. But the operations will remain the same as described in this appendix.

☞ **Execute the operations as described above and below**

⊕ **Click** [Save]

When all of the file's contents has been downloaded, you will see this window:

⊕ **Click** [Open Folder]

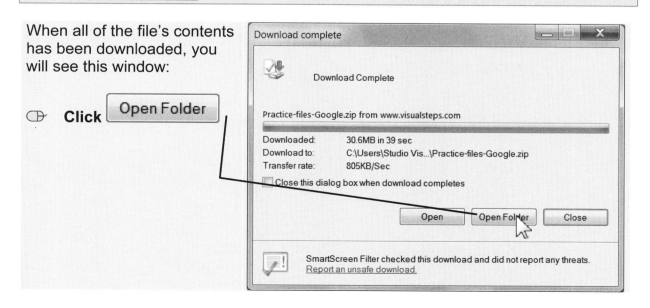

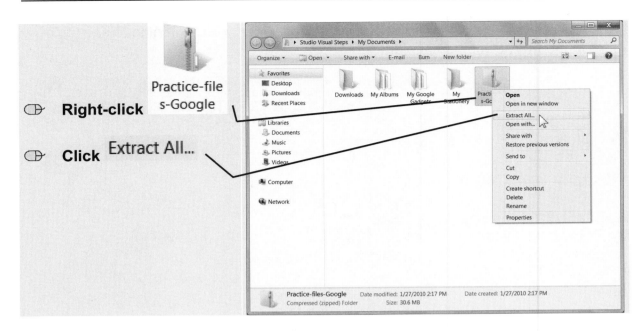

If you are using *Windows XP*, the *Extract files* wizard will now open. In that case, just follow the instructions in the next couple of windows and click [Next >] twice.

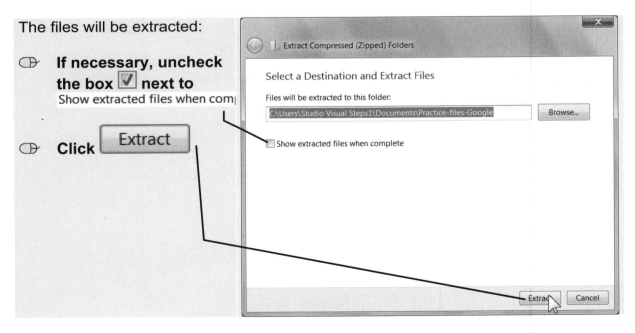

Now the files will be extracted and you will see this window:

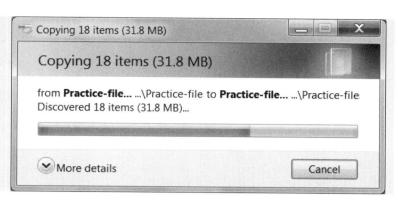

If you are using *Windows XP*, you need to uncheck the box ☑ next to Show extracted files , in the last window of the *Extract files* wizard, click [Finish] .

Now the *Practice-files-Google* folder has been saved to the (*My*) *Documents* folder:

You can delete the compressed folder:

Practice-file
s-Google

☞ **Right-click**

☞ **Click** Delete

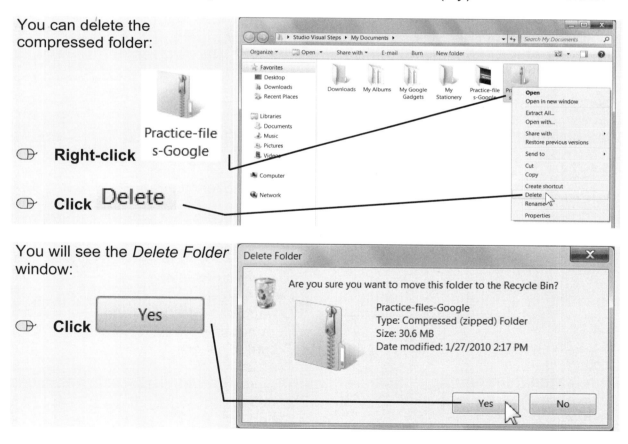

You will see the *Delete Folder* window:

☞ **Click** [Yes]

Now the compressed folder has been deleted:

☞ **Close all windows** 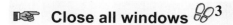³

D. Index

Microsoft Office 2007 for Independent Contractors and Freelancers

Microsoft Office 2007 for Independent Contractors and Freelancers
Practical Office Solutions for the self-employed and freelancer

Author: Studio Visual Steps
ISBN: 978 90 5905 295 6
Book type: Paperback
Nr of pages: 408 pages
Accompanying website:
www.visualsteps.com/office2007freelance

A practical guide for the fast-growing segment of freelancers and independent contractors. Written especially for those who are looking for efficient solutions for everyday tasks such as creating estimates, offers, invoices or budgets and for the easy creation of business cards, brochures, newsletters and company presentations. No time to take a course in business administration? Work instead through this Visual Steps book at home and in your own tempo! Do the chapters that specifically apply to your business. As you follow each step, the results appear directly on your computer screen. In a few short hours you can complete an entire course. You will end up with a series of useful documents that can be directly applied to your business.

Characteristics of this book:
- practical, useful topics
- geared towards the needs of the self-employed, independent contractor or freelancer
- clear instructions that anyone can follow
- handy, ready-made templates available on this website

Topics covered in this book:
- **Excel 2007:** estimates, quotes, invoices, projects, schedules, mileage tracking
- **Word 2007:** letterhead, newsletters and mailing labels
- **Publisher 2007:** business cards, brochures, websites
- **PowerPoint 2007:** company presentations
- **Outlook 2007:** customer, vendor and contact information, organize and archive mail
- **Business Contact Manager 2007:** project administration, manage leads and prospects
- **Windows Vista and XP:** computer maintenance, back-ups and security

Windows Vista and Internet for CHILDREN

Windows Vista and Internet for children
For anyone 9 years old and up

Author: Studio Visual Steps
ISBN: 978 90 5905 056 3
Book type: Paperback
Nr of pages: 208 pages
Accompanying website:
www.studiovisualsteps.com/vista

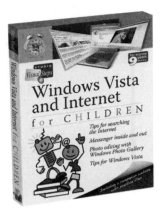

Do your (grand)children chat or mail with friends? Do they know how to use a chat program inside and out? This book will not only show them how to safely use Messenger but lots of other things too. Such as how to best find information on the Internet for their homework assignments. How to make their own e-mail address and do a video chat. How to organize files and folders and how to keep the desktop tidy. And what is really fun, is learning how to use Windows Photo Gallery to edit their own photos.
All of the exercises in this book can be done on their own computer. Everything is clearly explained step by step and each step includes a full color picture. You can get started right away!

In this book children will learn how to:
- mail with Windows Mail and Windows Live Hotmail
- chat with Windows Live Messenger
- do a video chat
- edit photos in Windows Photo Gallery
- search for information on the Internet
- create and open folders
- move, search and delete files
- customize your desktop
- change the color of your windows
- add a gadget to Windows Sidebar

For parents, teachers and caregivers
All Visual Steps books are written following a step by step method. They are designed as self-study guides for individual use. They are also well-suited for use in a group or classroom setting. More information for parent, teachers and caregivers can be found at the companion website for this book: www.studiovisualsteps.com/vista